Happy are the painters, for they shall not be lonely. Light and color, peace and hope will keep them company until the end, or almost to the end, of the day. Painting is a companion with whom one may hope to walk a great part of life's journey."

Sir Winston Churchill

"The man who has found himself in the woods on a bright June day by the side of a running brook amid the hum of insects and the song of birds, the soft air heavy with the perfume of flowers, has realized as pure a dream of beauty as nature is able to provide."

Edward Darley Boit, from "How I Came To Paint"

PREFACE

This book covers a five year time span, and records a few of the events that actually took place during my struggle to carve out a new career for my self at the age of 71. There were times when I wondered if I had taken leave of my senses in basing everything on the expectation that I, as a very latecomer, starting almost from scratch, could earn a living in an occupation so risky as that of the professional fine artist. As you will see, I came close to not making it.

In my case, it meant hanging in there and not becoming unglued by temporary set-backs but, rather, staying focused on the goal and having faith that in time everything would work out for the best—and so it has.

Bill Lewis

FOREWORD

The life journey has many turns—some intended, some not.

As we all travel along this path, we may find ourselves so challenged from the seemingly endless change of direction that it is tempting to allow doubt and worry to depress the will of our once indominable spirits. But when all seems lost and there appears to be no hope in sight, another voice can inspire the weary traveler to continue onward with hope—a voice that says: "Don't worry, keep moving—at least one more step.

Bill Lewis took a step forward with confidence that is an inspiration to us all. Changing careers, letting go of all his possessions, he began a journey toward realising a dream at the age of 71. This industrious and creative man forged ahead even when the challenges he faced seemed insurmountable. His inspiring story is about what can happen when we believe in ourselves and through grit and inspired determination continue toward achieving our goal.

Jeffrey Patnaude
Warrenton, Virginia

TABLE OF CONTENTS

CHAPTER ONE
"The Horse May Learn To Fly"

The Virginia sun was shining brightly through the large bay window of my bedroom. As minutes dragged by, I remained motionless on the side of the bed, staring blankly at the floor.

During a period of about a year and a half I had made an all-out investment in time, energy and money in brokering a proposed $11.5 million public works project, and it had come within a hair's breadth of paying off. Out of 242 nationwide bidders, the field had been narrowed down to only three, with my group being one of the three. Of the three finalists, we were by far the most qualified, and news trickled back that we had made the best presentation to the selection committee. But a phone call from the night before told me that there was obviously a pay-off somewhere along the line, for we didn't get the contract, and the $580,000 commission check that was going to go into my pocket never quite made it. So instead of having enough money to rest easy for a while, I was suddenly faced with the brutal fact that I was 71 years old, had no present source of income and my bank account was getting smaller with each passing day. The problem was overwhelming. What was I going to do? I had no idea.

Slowly, my gaze focused on the piece of furniture directly in front of me, an eighteenth-century American slant-top secretary that had for many years been part of my bedroom trappings. It was a handsome piece, ideal for personal papers and a dozen or so books, all of which were of the pick-up and put-down variety, more suited to bedtime reading than anything else. My eyes came to rest on a small volume that had once been a thank-you gift from a house guest. It contained a collection of inspirational bits and pieces. I felt compelled to go pick up the little book and read whatever message of encouragement it might have to offer.

If, at the time, I had not been in such a morbid and hopeless frame of mind, I might have remembered the humorous story about the guy who, at his wits end and filled with despair, decided he would seek an answer to his problems by turning to the scriptures. So, he closed his eyes, flipped open the Bible, and randomly jabbed his finger to a place on the page. He opened his eyes and read the passage where his finger rested. It said, "And Judas went out and hung himself." So the guy said to himself, "Well, obviously that was a mistake; I'd better try again. For the second time he went through the same procedure: he flipped open the Bible, put his finger on the page, opened his eyes and read: "Go thou and do likewise."

Fortunately, I had far better luck. Riffling the pages to slightly past the middle I read a couple of sentences, and then I came to this:

Calmness in the midst of chaos, serenity in the midst of feverish activity is the secret all commanders must know -- the secret revealed in crises, that the soul that is calm with controlled emotion is performing an act of faith; the easier you play the game of fortitude, the more relaxed you become to each challenge of impatience, the more you control your destiny. A frantic spirit is a stupid one.(*)

Man oh man," I said half aloud. "Does that ever have my name on it. Above all, stay calm. Show some guts. It's not going to be easy and it may take an enormous amount of effort, but I've got to keep my emotions under control."

A lesson from the past came to mind and I suddenly remembered an incident that happened during my stint in the military. The colonel ordered me to lead some men on a potentially dangerous mission into enemy-held territory. As we crawled slowly forward on our bellies, the scene before me had the makings of a trap, and I experienced the odd sensation of the hair on the back of my neck rising, my heart pounding wildly and a strange, empty-heavy feeling in my throat and gut. At the time I felt ashamed for literally being scared out of my wits, but I knew I didn't dare show it and, somehow, I guess I didn't. I accomplished the mission successfully by *acting* like I wasn't afraid. I had to do the same thing now and act like there was nothing to fear. "I'm lucky," I told myself. "This situation is not life threatening, only lifestyle threatening."

What should I do first? I didn't know, but it seemed obvious that I wouldn't solve my problems by sitting all day on the side of the bed. "So get up and get going," I told myself. "Shave, shower, feed the dogs, have breakfast, and act like nothing unusual has happened. And one more thing; don't waste a minute feeling sorry for yourself. Now get up, damn it, and do it!"

Soon after breakfast, and with my three dogs, Dexter, Daisy and Abner fed, it was time, I decided, to do some serious brain-storming. So I loaded an old Sheffield silver gallery tray with a mug and thermos of coffee, several ball point pens, a clipboard holding a legal pad and the cordless phone. With this assortment I headed for the big white lawn chair on the terrace where for hours I would be shaded by a grove of a venerable elms. I was soon seated, clipboard in hand, drinking in the soft beauty of the scene before me, still bathed in the clear light of an early summer morning. High above the tall grass in the little valley where the twin ponds lay, a hungry red-tailed hawk searched out its breakfast, while sleek black Angus cattle grazed the pasture bounded by the same stone fences built centuries before by early settlers. Farther on, all nesting in their rightful place along the range of gently rolling hills were farms, fields and woodlands until at last, silhouetted against the distant sky, stood the Blue Ridge Mountains of Virginia. Peace and plenty came to mind. That's what I somehow need to manifest, I mused, as I sat gazing at the scene.

The nearly two years I had lived on the property had occasioned many happy moments. The first year of my residence I threw an Independence Day party, inviting over 100 friends for food, drinks and fireworks. It was a good party, lasting well into the night. I had arranged for a group of local musicians to serenade us with folk tunes and classical selections. Tables and chairs covered much of the side lawn, where guests were attended by a couple of college students I had hired to grill chicken and hot dogs in the big outdoor stone fireplace and keep the wine and beer glasses filled. After the fireworks display had ended, the star attraction of the evening was Lisa, my friend and former business associate, singing Puccini and Verdi arias from the candlelit front balcony, with cows mooing in the background.

The two-story, five bedroom, white-frame antebellum house I called home was situated near the center of a ten-acre plot on top of a gentle hill in a grove of ancient elms, all of which was enclosed by whitewashed board fences typical of Virginia horse and cattle country. A herd of beef cattle owned by a mean-spirited farmer who rented several hundred acres of grazing land adjacent to the property was supposedly prevented from entering my domain not only by the fences, but by one cattle guard at the driveway entrance and another at the exit. But in spite of these intended constraints, the cows seemed convinced that the grass was indeed much greener beyond the white boards. Occasionally, one or two would break through onto my side of the fence, giving me cause for apprehension any time the hundred or so head of cattle chose to congregate too close to the house. But while I was away on an overnight, this bovine mob broke through a section of the fence.

Upon my return I found the entire herd in the yard, gorging themselves on every shrub and flower in sight, with the end results of their gluttonous spree dumped bountifully over nearly every square foot of ground. There were far too many of these meadow muffins to clean up, so for a long time one needed to step gingerly when walking about outside the house. I thereafter quite sensibly, I felt, referred to Spring Hill Farm, my otherwise quite dignified home, as Cowpie Manor.

Now, sitting on the terrace of Cowpie Manor, pen in hand, staring at the blank piece of paper on the clipboard. I very slowly wrote: "This life is only a test. I repeat, it's only a test. Like the guy on the radio says, 'If it were the real thing we'd all be told where to go and what to do.'" I wish I knew who deserves credit for this comic bit of philosophy, for it suddenly came to mind as I sat facing the Blue Ridge foothills that so beautifully framed Cowpie Manor. Only a silly spoof, yes, but oddly enough its ludicrous approach to the seriousness of life had, at the time, a more beneficial effect on my attitude than a dozen pious sermons. For it suggested light-heartedness, rather than gravity. In any event, I made use of its goofy message, and for the next couple of days as I sat at my outdoor headquarters under the spreading elms with clipboard in hand I kept telling myself, "What I'm struggling with is not the end of the world for me or anyone else. So lighten up, buddy. Lighten up."

My most immediate concern was a very commonplace one: the need for money and finding a way to acquire it. Throughout my life as a businessman I had produced good income, starting with the earlier years spent in advertising and, after that, during a 21-year period that ended two years before when I resigned from British Trade Corporation, an Anglo-American firm whose primary function was to act as liaison and as expediters between British and American companies with common interests. During my long tenure with British Trade I had been vice-president in charge of U.S. operations, and my resignation was provoked because of my objection to our policy of introducing what I was convinced was an unworthy and poorly engineered product to the American market. Unfortunately, I was now reaping the effects of standing up for principle... a man without a job and very little money left in the bank. The last of the installment checks in payment for my stock interests in British Trade that had been coming my way during the past two years would arrive in about three weeks, but those funds wouldn't stretch far enough or long enough to provide anything other than temporary relief. After that, zero income.

As the sun rose ever higher in the sky, the top sheet on the clipboard, aside from the bit about life being only a test and a few meaningless doodles, was almost as blank as when I first sat down, and I was inwardly scolding myself for being better at drinking coffee and watching circling vultures ride the up-drafts than I was at spawning any red-hot constructive ideas. Then it dawned on me. For a long time I had been eligible for social security benefits, but had never signed up. For many years I had sounded off to whoever cared to listen, declaring unequivocally that I would never, ever, accept such a thing as a monthly hand-out from the government. When it was pointed out, as it always would be, that I had put money in for most of my working career and therefore deserved to get something in return, it still didn't matter. In my view, it was too much like being on welfare. Now, in light of the new set of circumstances, I decided such a lofty attitude had to go, and the Department of Social Security would soon have an enthusiastic new recruit. I suspected, however, that it would be some time before I actually saw the color of their money and I hadn't the foggiest notion what my benefits would be once the bureaucrats agreed to include me. Based on what little I did know, I felt certain that whatever the payments amounted to they would be nowhere near enough to sustain me without a considerable amount of additional income, and the only way to produce that would be to work for it.

So I kept asking myself over and over, "What can I do to earn a living?" I pondered every possibility that came to mind, including some that were totally impractical and, for that matter, even downright frivolous. Hanging in my closet was a splendid tailcoat with white tie accessories, plus a midnight blue dinner jacket and a white one for summer. Yes, but damn it, I was too old and ugly to act as a gigolo on an ocean liner, so that was out. Well, what about a job as a maitre d' or headwaiter somewhere? I soon concluded, however, that much of the dining in my area seemed to require the wearing of a baseball cap, macho style, while eating out, and the drinking of beer, macho style, straight from the bottle. A guy in fancy duds would only scare away the customers, so that too was out.

"Nice going, Lewis," I said to myself. "Most guys your age with your level of past earnings are sitting on their butts living off retirement benefits. Your crazy notion that some pie-in-the-sky entrepreneurial venture would leave you in high cotton has once again backfired, only this time you've gone through much of your savings and there's no sustaining income with which to re-fatten the kitty. And, just to make things worse, you're a so-called senior citizen." (I hated the label). "Throughout your entire working life you've earned money as a business executive of one sort or another, but with no specific marketable skills. You can't walk into a place where people are being hired and say: 'I'm a shoemaker' or 'I'm a computer programmer' or 'I'm a brain surgeon.' Even if you could find employment, the first day on the job you would probably unintentionally offend somebody by saying the wrong thing to the young office manager or the kid who's the foreman or chief ditch-digger or head-bottle washer or whatever, and end up getting fired before you even get started. No, hiring yourself out doesn't seem like the best solution to the pickle you've suddenly found yourself in. You've got a real problem, old man."

Because my business experience had been so general over the past forty or so years and so lacking in specialization, my mind kept returning to the disturbing question: Who on earth would want to hire me? Try as I might, I couldn't come up with an answer. The more important question, however, was: Who on earth would I want to work for? The answer to that one was easy. Nobody! All my life I had basically been my own boss and could come and go and do as I pleased without needing anyone's permission. During my early years in advertising I was one of the two owners, and even during my long association with British Trade Corporation, ninety-nine percent of the time I called the shots on a daily basis when it came to the projects under my wing on my side of the ocean. This urgent requirement for independence and autonomy applied now more than ever. I was spoiled. And in all honesty, I knew that I would make a lousy employee and would, in fact, do the world of management a great favor by not even bothering to ask anybody for a job. But money had to come from somewhere. And if not as a result of someone paying me a salary, then I would need to generate income on my own through some entrepreneurial enterprise. But the problem is that it takes money to make money, and I didn't have enough left to start anything much grander than a shoe-shine stand.

Even so, I began to give considerable thought to what I would like to do if money was not part of the equation. That was the question I asked myself. A few frivolous suggestions crept in, but were quickly dismissed as not being worthy of serious consideration, but the one nagging thought that kept running through my mind was that I would very much enjoy being a serious painter - in all probability a landscape painter.

The life of the professional painter had always impressed me as being an enviable occupation. I had had a lifelong interest in art, and for years, while living in Washington, I had owned a successful major art gallery as a sideline venture, and I did know how to draw reasonably well and had dabbled in watercolors as a hobby. But I had never, ever given even a fleeting thought to the possibility of earning my living as a painter. As I sat fantasizing about what such a life entailed, I scribbled out the following list:

Life of A Painter:
1. Challenging: Considerable skill required for success.
2. Sky's the limit for those with ability.
3. Communication with an audience through output of work.
4. Freedom.
5. Ideal work combination of mental, physical and spiritual.

After jotting down these quick impressions, there was no doubt left in my mind. If I could earn my living as a painter, it would be the happiest and most rewarding life imaginable. But common sense quickly told me to put a stop to such pointless daydreaming, for I had neither the experience nor the financial cushion to even consider such a possibility. No matter how appealing the thought of starting a new life as a painter might be, it was not in the cards for me. Over the years I had experienced, and was still experiencing the hard way, the penalty for not always being practical. I knew it was a foolish waste of time even for one minute to think seriously about earning my living as a painter. Nope. No way. I just plain couldn't do it.

"Who says you can't?" an inaudible inner voice seemed suddenly to come out of nowhere. It was, of course, my own alter-ego piping up, demanding equal time. "What do you mean you can't be a painter? it continued. "And what's all this talk about not having any money? It's all around you. You're eating off it. You're walking on it. You're looking at it. You're riding in it. Get with it, brother. You have all you need right here." I had learned from past experience that this silent voice was the uninvited herald of contrary opinion, as sound asleep as Rip Van Winkle most of the time, but almost always wide awake and rarin' to go anytime I was on the verge of making an important decision. All too often, to my later regret, I had failed to listen.

I was quick to respond. "What are you saying? Yes, I eat my meals on a rare early American butternut draw-top table and I walk on fine old Oriental rugs. I see French and American Impressionist and Old Master paintings when I look at my walls. For years I've driven a beautiful green Jaguar. All these things have value. Are you suggesting that I sell all this, that I sell my belongings? No! I could never do that. They're way too much a part of me."

I was a man who for many years, in spite of financial ups and downs, had had the pleasure of surrounding himself with some of the finest the past had to offer. The meal might consist of nothing but beans, but those humble beans could be eaten, if I chose, off an antique table with Georgian silver as my flatware, my feet resting on a fine old Heriz rug, a bonnet-top flame finial Philadelphia highboy with cabriole legs behind me, period Hepplewhite to the right, Queen Anne and Chippendale straight ahead with old Sheffield, armorial Lowestoft, and other goodies just sort of hanging around. To me, the good life had always been much more than just some money in the bank or securities in a drawer.

Yes, I loved the beauty of my trappings and never tired of their presence. They were my silent companions. It had never occurred to me that I would ever part with any of these old friends. But it was too late. The thought had already gotten a foothold in my mind. I did have some substance that could be turned into money if I so chose. For years I had lived in a large and impressive house in Washington, D.C., but it had been owned by the corporation. And I was now only renting the present place, so there was no house to sell. Yet I did own personal effects of considerable value. If I liquidated everything at even a fraction of their worth there would perhaps be enough, if I lived very frugally, for me to get by until I could begin to earn money as a professional painter. But what if I sold everything only to end up as a dismal failure as a painter? What if it turned out that I was so lacking in talent that my paintings never sold or I ran out of money before I became good enough to produce sustaining income? What if? What if? It was downright scary.

While in the midst of this dilemma it suddenly dawned on me that one of my very good friends was a man named William Woodward, a professor of fine art at George Washington University who just happened to be a very successful, highly regarded master painter and whose studio was only about a thirty minute drive away. "It would make sense," I told myself, "to pay Bill Woodward a call." Maybe he could give me some sort of an assignment that would help me determine if I possessed enough natural talent to ever hope to succeed as a painter. I waited for a day when he was not teaching at the university and climbed the steps to his studio occupying the entire top floor of a commercial building. Upon entering, I thought at first that Bill might have stepped out, for he was nowhere to be seen in the part of the big main room where he customarily stood at the easel and painted.

"Hello, Maestro!" I called out, thinking perhaps he was in one of the adjoining smaller rooms. The handsome face of a man in his mid-fifties suddenly appeared from around the side of a huge frame of stretched canvas and, upon seeing me, broke into a warm smile.

"My friend," he said, stepping forward and shaking hands. "I don't mean to be in hiding, but the dear lady who commissioned this work has a home that can accommodate paintings of this size. As you can see, it's allegorical and, at her request, the subject is Time. Speaking of time, I think it's time for a break and a cup of coffee. I'm interested in what you said on the phone about wanting to learn to paint in oils. I know you once dealt in art as a sideline, but I don't know much about your painting background. Tell me more."

As we sat sipping coffee and relaxing, he on a high stool near the easel and me sprawled out in an old butt-sprung overstuffed chair that had seen better days, I told him how I had always had a side-line interest in art, and how, at an early age, I was influenced by a very talented older brother who, without even trying, was an unusually gifted watercolorist. I went on to say that throughout most of my life, in a manner similar to that of a camera-nut, I had played around with watercolors as a hobby, often taking a small pan of paints, together with some brushes and a block of watercolor paper, along with me on vacations, or sometimes even on prolonged out-of-the-country business trips, knocking out quick sketches in far away places. I then added that because of some life drawing sessions here and there, I pretty well knew how to draw, so I felt that I had the foundation for being able to paint more seriously, and that I believed I could handle oils if I knew how to start.

At the completion of this brief resume I asked, "So, Bill, is there some way for me, working alone and at my own pace, to get off on the right foot?"

Bill offered me more coffee and poured some in his own cup. "Yes, I can suggest a way that will help you get started. But first, tell me, which of the great painters of the past do you admire the most?"

" That's easy," I said. "I'd start the list with the French Impressionists and put Claude Monet at the top, followed closely by Camille Pissarro and Alfred Sisley, then the American painters William Merritt Chase, Childe Hassam, Theodore Robinson, John Singer Sargent, after that more Frenchmen: Eugene Boudin, Pierre Bonnard, Charles-Francois Daubigny, should I keep going?"

"No, that's enough," Bill said approvingly, as if he enjoyed my recitation. "That's a good list. I like all those guys too. Here's what I want you to do. Find a good color reproduction of a painting you like by one of the artists you've named and copy it as faithfully as you can. After you've completed the drawing, start brushing in an underpainting composed of burnt sienna and burnt umber thinned down with turpentine to an almost watercolor consistency. Once that has dried, and before brushing on the color, bring it by and I'll have a look."

Remembering my childhood response when asked by a grownup to show them something I had drawn, I said "All right, if you'll promise not to laugh."

I was halfway down the steps when Bill called out, "Hey, do you have an easel?"

"No I don't,"I yelled back.

"There are three big professional class easels in the closet just inside the front door. I'm no longer teaching private students and don't need those easels anymore. So take one, my friend, and good luck with it."

After expressing my gratitude, I headed straight for the nearest art supply store to buy everything necessary for producing my very first oil painting.

From having read biographical accounts of some of the great painters, I knew that it's good practice to copy the work of masters, and copying was always part of the standard curriculum in centuries past when training to become an artist was perhaps more structured. Manet wasn't above going to Spain to copy Velasquez. Picasso did his share of copying works in the Prado. Renoir became discouraged with his own work and went to Italy to copy Rubens. But I didn't think it was done anymore except for the few people that receive special permission and are occasionally seen copying works in museums. Perhaps most would-be artists don't want to bother. Well, I wanted to bother, and was thankful to Woodward for putting me on to what I felt sure would be an effective shortcut to learning some of the basic characteristics of painting in oils.

My own home library contained a large collection of art books, so reference was easy. After looking at many color plates, I finally settled on a work by William Merritt Chase, a beach scene with figures, painted on Long Island in 1892 and measuring 20 by 34 inches. It seemed to me that few 19th-century artists had his flair for choosing appealing subjects and then painting them with such dash and verve. At The Seaside is a scene showing ladies with their young children and nursemaids relaxing on a sunlit beach. They are clustered in small groups and, for the most part, are sheltered beneath brightly colored Japanese parasols that add touches of brilliance to the composition. It is summer, and soft fluffy clouds drift in from the sea. Puffed sleeves and sashes; lace, ribbons and bows adorn the white and pastel ankle-length dresses of the women, and their Gibson-girl hairdos are ornately crowned with flower-laden hats and bonnets. Only one pretty young girl wears anything so revealing as a knee-length dress. Unlike the others, she and two infants are actually barefooted. Yet, it was precisely because of such Victorian standards of elegance that Chase was able to imbue the painting with a mood that portrays the grace and propriety of the good life of that period, a charm which otherwise would have been impossible to achieve.

After setting up my new easel in the sunroom, I followed Bill's advice, painting everything in by using mixtures of only two colors, burnt sienna and burnt umber. Once the under-painting was thoroughly dry I took the partly finished canvas back to Bill, who gave me high marks for the work done so far and, to his credit, didn't laugh once except while telling an uproariously funny joke that had nothing to do with oil painting. Now, after several days of adding color, I was nearly finished with the painting and had gotten to the fun part, adding the final touches and trying as best I could to match the hues, tints and shades of those shown in the color reproduction.

I found that each day while standing at the easel I became so absorbed in what I was doing that little thought was given to my critical financial situation. Typically, I would start the morning with selections from my collection of classical music, choosing pieces like Chopin's second piano concerto; Mendelssohn's Midsummer Night's Dream; the sixth symphony by Beethoven and, perhaps, Bach's Sheep May Safely Graze. No heavy stuff by Mahler or Wagner. Rather, music to keep the mood peaceful but exalted was my aim. Music to paint by.

Next, I would fling open the door to the large, outdoor fenced in area that I called "Dogpatch Haven" and shout, "Time for painting class!" and suddenly a thundering horde of three yelping, nipping, ecstatic dogs would bound headlong into the sun room, each determined to get to privileged places on the sofa or frayed Oriental throw rug near the easel before the others. As always during these permission to enter sessions, there was urgent competition for attention, with each dog doing its best to crowd out the other two in hopes of being treated as the one and only dog the master really gave a hoot about. And each dog had its own way of trying to earn this most-favored status.

Daisy, a little black and tan almost-border collie, a shameless flirt, invariably headed for the corner of the sofa near the library door and closest to the easel. Her half-brother Abner, always a little clumsy and confused, would race the others for the right to plunk himself down in the opposite corner of the sofa, only to then realize that most of the action would take place closer to the easel, so he would move back and forth on the cushions, his curly black wool glistening like a Persian lamb coat fresh from the furrier's. Dexter, the almost-golden retriever, because of his size was not permitted on the couch, but he made his presence known at the start of every painting session by sitting on the floor on his haunches, with front paws limply crossed and tongue dangling stupidly out of one side of his mouth, looking as silly and goofy as a comic character but inordinately proud of himself.

These were my "students." Daisy would soon be half asleep, lying on her back with heavy-lidded eyes gazing vacantly off into space. Dexter, not one to exert himself any more than necessary, lost no time in getting comfortable on the rug, snoring away hour after hour. Only Abner sat up in class and paid attention. Throughout each session he positioned himself quietly on the floor, watching every stroke of the brush.

Eventually, the painting was as completed as I knew how to make it. Copying Chase had been a splendid challenge, demanding all the skill I could muster in an effort to make the replica look as much like the master's hand as possible. After some last minute brushstrokes and a few highlights here and there, I signed my name: Wm. Covel Lewis after Wm. Merritt Chase. As I brushed on the signature, it entered my mind that I had fallen heir to a good news/bad news situation. The bad news was that I still had to find a way to earn a living The good news was more comforting. In less than a week from a standing start I had completed my first oil painting, a reasonably accurate facsimile of a masterwork permanently on display at the Metropolitan Museum of Art. A well-trained eye could certainly tell the difference between copy and original, but I doubted if most garden variety art buffs would be so discerning. At day's end I knew, without being told, that I had done a surprisingly good job. In fact, much better than I had anticipated.

Clean and refreshed after taking a shower, it occurred to me that it was high time to reward myself with a sundowner, so from the liquor cabinet I removed a bottle of Famous Grouse scotch, placed it, along with a carafe of water, on the old-Sheffield tray and headed for my private sanctum, the big white lawn chair on the terrace. On my way there I remembered the words I once saw printed on a card behind a bar, "Work is The Curse of The Drinking Class." Income-producing work as a painter, I thought, would not be a curse for me but a blessing.

Sitting quietly on the terrace in my big white lawn chair, I drank in the enchantment of the twilight scene, with gently rising hills stretching westward to the mountains. From day to day, from moment to moment, depending on the clarity and nature of the light, their character and contour seemed in almost constant change. A summit vanished; another one appeared. A misty veil turned piney patch to noble cypress grove, and shafts of golden sunlight converted simple orchards into lush exotic gardens. As gold and purple twilight moved slowly westward on its endless journey, I sat relaxed, savoring the musky taste of fine scotch whisky. It was good to sit quietly and enjoy the splendor of the view, to forget my problems if only for a moment. It was a special triumph to have successfully completed my very first stab at oil painting. In such a setting, with a good drink in hand and the muted tones of a gold and crimson sunset softly crowning the western hills, it would be a foolish mistake to waste time brooding over my financial problems. There would be time enough for that in the morning.

Soon after daybreak I once more put coffee carafe and mug on the Sheffield tray, but this time I left off the legal pad, clipboard, pens and cordless phone. So far as I was concerned, I was through with brainstorming, and I needed to concentrate and not be disturbed by phone calls. The time had come to make a serious decision, and a yes or no answer was in order. Should I, or should I not, bet everything on getting to the place where I could support myself as a professional painter? That was the decision I had to make.

As I sat pondering the pros and cons a story came to mind about a king who had a favorite horse and told the court magician that he had exactly one year in which to teach the horse to fly. If successful, he would be rewarded with bountiful jewels, a mansion and a retinue of servants. If he failed, well, his head would be chopped off. A year passed, and after the poor magician's unfortunate session with the axeman, the magician's assistant went to the king and said he could teach the horse to fly, but only if he were awarded all the goodies beforehand. The king reluctantly agreed. A friend later asked the assistant why on earth he volunteered to do something so stupid.

"A year is a fairly long period," the novice replied, "and during that time, while I'm living in grand style, the king may die so I won't be punished, or, I may die and it won't matter, or, the horse may learn to fly!"

The odds of me learning to paint well enough to earn my living as a painter were, I felt, a little more favorable than teaching a horse to fly. If I failed, my head wouldn't be chopped off, but spending whatever capital I might get from the sale of my belongings without having first turned the corner as a successful painter would leave me in even worse shape than I was now.

But once again the inner voice made its climb back onto the soap box. "You say you would like the life and career of a painter. Then, damn it, be one! Whatever it takes to accomplish it, do it. Forget about the temporary pain you may experience in selling all your treasures – they're replaceable. Forget your present lack of qualifications – that's correctable.

Just make sure you try ten times harder than anyone else and the day will come when your work will start to sell. It won't be easy, but life may begin to be a lot more fun. In fact, you may find that the best phase of your life still lies ahead. What do you say? Have you got the guts to give it a try? Think for a moment about your possible alternatives. You're seventy-one years old.. If you go back into business, you'll be pushed around as an old cricker. You'll start thinking that the good life is all behind you and spend what's left of it rotting on the vine. Why not break away from all that? Why not fill your remaining years with challenge, with action, with doing something new and exciting?"

My thoughts naturally drifted to a man who embodied that attitude, my grandfather, a physician who took daily horseback rides until he was ninety-seven and lived to be a hundred. If he were still around, he would no doubt say, "Get up off your gluteus maximus, Bill. Start a new career. Go find some adventure."

The image of a radically new life was beginning to take shape in my mind. I could take a chance, leave the nest, buy some more art supplies, learn to paint, hit the road, go to faraway places, stumble along with strange languages, chase some women, eat the food, drink the wine, start a new life, have some fun!"

I said to myself, "Let's give it a try. Maybe this old horse can learn to fly."

CHAPTER TWO
Farewell To Cowpie Manor

I sat looking out over the landscape, thoughts racing through my mind. A part of me wanted very much to believe that my brainstorming had paid off, and that I now had answered the problem of how to generate future income. But the course of action suggested during my heart-to-heart talk with myself, while convincing in many ways, still left room for a whole array of nagging doubts. Perhaps I shouldn't be too hasty. Perhaps I should keep trying to figure out a way to make money without rocking the boat too much, to not do anything drastic, in line with the saying, "Better the devil we know than the angel we don't." To sell everything I owned and stake my future livelihood on the slim chance that at such a late age I could somehow become skilled enough to produce a sustaining income by painting pictures seemed way too risky and irresponsible – even downright foolish. The expression "starving artist" could damn well apply to me once my small nest egg gained from selling my things was used up.

But enough of this gloom and doom. "Think positively!" I told myself. "What if I don't fail? What if I succeed? Others have succeeded, why not me? They all had to start somewhere. If I take whatever God-given gift of talent I possess and through instruction, study and endless practice, along with self-discipline and determination, cause it to grow, why shouldn't I be able to do it? Yes, it's taking a big chance, but it could be the best decision I've ever made. I'll never know unless I give it a try. That's the only way I'll ever find out."

I was in an endless dilemma, a mental tug of war. The conservative, practical side of my nature was urging me to be cautious, to not be sucked in by the flimsy notion that, at this stage of my life, I should bet everything on succeeding in a field where very few ever make their living from the sale of their paintings. But, in opposition, the adventuresome, more trusting voice within me seemed to be insisting, just as emphatically, that life was perhaps opening a new door, beyond which were rich rewards waiting to be claimed. I remembered the old proverb that I had heard all my life, "God never shuts one door but another one opens." Reassuring, yes, but would it specifically apply to me? I felt that in my case God hadn't merely closed a door gently, he had slammed it shut.

As a child growing up, the rest of the family and I frequently would hear the floorboards creaking from what seemed like ceaseless footsteps overhead as my father paced back and forth in his study. It was his conviction that a man can think better when he's walking, and, in his case, walking it through was always the prelude to any important decision. I put aside the pen and clipboard and got up from the chair. In my father's mode, head down, hands clasped behind my back, I began pacing the flagstones of the terrace. Back and forth, back and forth, back and forth. I had no idea what to expect as a result of the exercise, certainly not a voice booming through the clouds or thunderbolts from heaven, but my mood was receptive to any hint of spiritual guidance that might present itself. Back and forth, "Should I, should I not?" Back and forth, "Should I, should I not?" Time dragged by as I paced, and I seemed to be getting nowhere, when a quotation I hadn't thought of in years popped into my mind: "Whatsoever your hand finds to do, do it with your might." I wasn't sure of its origin, though it sounded like something from the Bible, and I was about to dismiss it as being vague and inappropriate since it didn't specifically say, "Do it" or "Don't do it," when it suddenly struck me that the words did indeed contain a message, a strong message that could well be aimed right at me. The phrase, "Whatsoever your hand finds to do," clearly implied, and even seemed to encourage, the freedom to chose an occupation – in my case, choosing to become a painter, and "do it with your might," was telling me that success would be assured if my whole heart, mind and energy was poured into the work. I sat back down, knowing I had been blessed with an answer. My mind was made up. I would sell everything I owned in order to become a painter.

Filled with a sense of quiet victory, I sensed having just made the most exciting, and perhaps the most meaningful, decision of my life. In a little more than a week I had altered course a hundred and eighty degrees. Instead of the highly paid executive position I had been destined to fill only a little over a week ago, I was now on the first leg of a new heading that would take me through uncharted waters as an unpaid, unskilled, beginning would-be painter at the age of 71. The prospects of what lay ahead were both exhilarating and frightening. Exhilarating because I would be embarking on a challenging new endeavor with all the implications of possible adventure. Frightening because I saw what little there was left of my security blanket going up in smoke. My umbilical cord was being severed.

First of all, I would need to move out of Cowpie Manor, for I would no longer be able to afford anything but the cheapest of living accommodations, and moving away from such a pleasant home struck a sad note. Although an ideal base of operations if all had gone as planned, now there was no reason to be within driving distance to Washington, D.C. and close to air transportation. My first impulse was to start thinking about relocating into much smaller and less expensive living quarters in the same part of Virginia that had long been familiar territory to me, an area in which I felt at home and enjoyed having friends. But, would staying put geographically be best for the purpose I had in mind? Virginia winters could range from mild to harsh, but in either case I couldn't envision myself standing outdoors painting for very long. And, with the typical summer haze, the light wouldn't be landscape-painter friendly during much of the warmer months. An even more important consideration than the weather, however, was the realization that if I remained connected with my present surroundings it would be almost impossible to maintain a schedule amounting to total immersion as a beginning painter – there would be too many distractions, and half measures wouldn't get the job done. No, it would be better if I made a clean break, like a student leaving home to dedicate himself to his studies.

Because it no longer made any difference where I lived, I was free to live anywhere I chose, within reason. So why not let it be an attractive setting where the weather would be as near perfect as possible, the food good, the wine plentiful, the natives not too unfriendly and, most importantly, the U.S. dollar enjoyed good buying power. The Provence region of France came to mind immediately. "Yes," I thought, "Why not?" I had been there, off and on, perhaps a dozen times. And while communicating with the French in their own language had, on occasion, caused them to either look upon me with pity or else threw them into gales of laughter, I still had always been able in the past to handle anything French that came my way and I had full confidence I could certainly muddle through again. But it would be several months before I could settle all my affairs, not till fall, in fact, and that might not be the best time of the year to relocate in France where winter weather could be uninviting. Also, the exchange rate was unfavorable at the time. Better rethink.

"Why not Mexico?" I wondered. I had been there twice as a tourist and had found it interesting. And, in talking with any number of people who had spent a fair amount of time there, they had, for the most part, given it good marks. Living expenses were considerably less than in the States, and in many parts of the country the weather was said to be near perfect the year round. It might well be the ideal place, a place where I could concentrate on painting without all the pleasant distractions I knew I would encounter in France. Yes, France could wait until later. But for now, Mexico would be best.

And so it was that before the day was over I had made three decisions that would have a long-lasting effect on the rest of my life: (a) I would sell everything I owned; (b) I would use the money derived from the estate sale to live on while I trained myself to become a painter; (c) I would move to Mexico.

Each passing moment brought with it the realization that every aspect of my life would, in one way or another, require rethinking. A beginning painter would have no reason to wear the expensive London hand-tailored three piece pinstripe suit just home from the cleaners, so it might as well be put away in moth balls. I was gradually beginning to get the point that a totally different lifestyle was in the offing. The number-one priorities on last week's list could now be taken off the list entirely. And, although the prospects of starting a new life as a novice painter in a strange land were challenging and appealing in many ways, at the same time I had to face the fact that by doing so I would be inviting a whole pot full of unwanted changes. At a late age I would need to abandon many of the things that had become an integral part of my life. I would have to walk away from friendships, some quite deep and built up over the years. My attraction to the horse country of Virginia and my acquaintance with many of the people living there would need to be put on hold. Yes, such a major change in my life would mean saying goodbye to familiar faces, sights and events. I would be giving up my occasional tennis weekends at Farmington, the country club in Charlottesville where I had been a member for a good many years, and I would miss the tailgating parties every spring and fall at point-to-point races. The things we've become accustomed to, both good and bad, offer a degree of comfort and security, and a part of me dreaded making the adjustments that lay ahead even though I kept affirming, over and over, that it was all for my own good and reminding myself that, as my British friends might have said, "You cawn't have it both ways."

Another area of grave concern was the welfare of the three most lovable and personable dogs ever to win a tender place in a human's heart. They would need new homes, and eventually there would be the sadness of separation. Becoming something of a gypsy would mean less frequent communication with members of my family, especially my sister Laura in Atlanta and my brother Dick in San Diego. And, of course, pulling up stakes would signal the end, on a day-to-day basis, of the long and valued friendship I had with Lisa. We had shared many memorable experiences during the years of our association. Leaving her would be difficult.

Lisa and I first met soon after my return from a meeting at British Trade's corporate headquarters in London. For a couple of years I had been dealing in paintings, strictly as a sideline. Early on a Saturday morning before my plane's departure from Heathrow, I took a cab to Portobello Road where I found two small paintings. Both were oil on panel and both were unsigned. One looked to me like a murky George Moreland coastal scene, and the other, because of its subject matter and stylistic treatment, caused me to think it might have been done by the Barbizon master, Charles Francois Daubigny, or one of his followers. There was paint-loss on one painting and the other badly needed cleaning, so once back home I took them to a restorer in Bethesda whose shop adjoined an art gallery. After leaving the resorer's, I stopped to look at the paintings in the gallery and was soon in conversation with the attractive young woman who was working there and whom I soon learned was the daughter of an art collecting couple that were friends of mine. When she found out that I bought and sold paintings, she let it be known that she was not in love with her present job and asked if I needed an assistant. My luck as an art collector had recently been good, for some months before I had bought an unsigned Benjamin West from a private dealer in London for $10,000, and its subsequent sale to a dealer in Chicago brought me $44,000. It was a gamble I had taken and done well on. As a result, I had been giving some thought to becoming more seriously involved in fine art as another business instead of just a lucrative hobby. Lisa and I agreed to meet and discuss the possibility of us carving out a job for her. As I left her that day, I remember thinking: "Be careful. There may be an empty head behind that pretty face."

An after-work interview was scheduled, and a few weeks later we sat before the fire in my Georgetown living room. In the process of discussing her job qualifications, I noticed that she kept looking at a painting hanging above a small Chippendale chest. It was a *fete gallante* subject and purportedly done by the Frenchman with a German first name and Italian sir name: Adolph Monticelli. A few weeks before I had taken it to the acknowledged expert on this 19th century painter. He had studied the work carefully for some time before telling me that, in his opinion, it was not as advertised, but was instead by the hand of an imitator.

During a lull in the conversation, Lisa suddenly asked: "What are you doing with that fake Monticelli?"

I was enormously impressed. This young woman was bright. From the painting's subject matter and style she had identified it, from across the room, as the type of painting Monticelli would have done. But, at the same time, she rejected it as not being a genuine work by that painter, a point that I had missed when I bought it and one that took the expert some time to figure out. But the best was yet to come. A little later I saw her eyeing the worn but handsome Oriental rug beneath our feet. "Do you like it? I asked."

"Yes, very much. It's a beautiful old Kazak. Or is it a Kazak? I don't know what it is. Anyway, I like the colors."

"Oh, so you know something about rugs?"

"No. No, I really don't. I just made a wild guess, that's all."

"Well your guess was exactly right. What can you say about that one?" I asked, pointing to a small throw rug, one of my favorites.

"I really don't know. I suppose it could be a Shirvan. But I'm sure it isn't."

"Yes, it's a Shirvan all right. Keep going. You're batting a thousand. How about that big one over there?" It was the best I owned, a very old and valuable Heriz.

She didn't want to answer. I begged her to try. She protested, saying, after all, Oriental rugs were not her field. Finally, tired of my urging, she reluctantly murmured, "Heriz?"

There were about ten more rugs in the house, but I was beginning to lose interest in the game; the contestant was making it look too easy, and I was already more than convinced. She had gotten three right out of three tries in an extremely complicated subject totally outside her field of expertise. She obviously had grade A-brains. But one thing still needed to be determined. We were talking about it being a full-time job for her and she and I would be working closely together when I was not involved in British Trade business and, from time to time, the two of us might even be traveling together. I certainly didn't want some overly serious, deadpan egg-head casting a gloomy pall over my normally happy existence. Because of this, I felt it was important to find out if she had a quick wit and a sense of humor.

"What's the difference between ignorance and indifference?" I asked. From the way I said it, she could tell I wasn't looking for a dictionary type of definition.

"I give up. Why don't you tell me? What is the difference between ignorance and indifference?"

"I don't know and I don't care."

She laughed instantly. "That's funny. I'll have to remember that one."

Perfect. She was fast on the uptake and enjoyed a good laugh. Here was an intelligent and attractive young woman with a college degree in fine art, fluent in both French and Italian, and ready to report for duty. There were so many good things in her favor, how could I go wrong? So, with Lisa Johnson's help, the two of us, together with a staff of several others that were added later on, had some exciting years in the art business, snooping around in much of America and half of Europe in our search for fine paintings. Jim, the ever proper Englishman and senior partner in British Trade Corporation, liked her from the start and made it plain that in his view, she could do no wrong. Once part of the team, Lisa attended many of our B.T.C. business sessions wherever they were held. And on those occasions when Jim and I would clash head-on over policy matters, she used her time wisely by sitting quietly and saying little, saving energy until meal-time when she became a dedicated connoisseur of wine, taking full advantage of us both by claiming that anything less than the finest (and most expensive) *grande cru classe* Bordeaux gave her a headache.

Soon after Lisa came on board, the corporation bought a big house near the National Cathedral. It had once been the bishop's house, and we called it Smartbarton Elms, a spoof on the name of the nearby grand and historic estate, Dumbarton Oaks. Lisa and I both moved into Smartbarton and lived there for the five years before I resigned from British Trade Corporation and the house was sold. During that time, she occupied her own suite in the north wing. After my severance from BTC, she put her talents to work and soon established a reputation as one of the area's finest decorative painters, and settled into her own condominium near Georgetown at the same time I moved to Cowpie Manor. Now that I was planning to move to Mexico, I realized how very much I valued her friendship and knew that I would certainly miss her.

Most of the past few days I had left the phone unplugged so I could reorganize my life without distractions. I plugged it in and made a call to Lisa. When I told her of my plans to sell everything and move to Mexico, she was plainly upset.

"What you're saying doesn't make any sense," she said somewhat firmly. "You told me a couple of months ago that Jim had called from London asking you to reconsider, to pick up where the two of you had left off and come back with British Trade in your old job as vice-president in charge of American operations. What's wrong with getting paid a good salary every month, and having an expense account, and flying on the Concorde, and going to annual meetings at fancy resorts? Why on earth don't you just forget about painting and Mexico and take him up on his offer? He wants you back."

"Quite honestly, Lisa," I replied, "I haven't even given any thought to such a possibility. Jim's a wonderful guy and one of the best friends I'll ever have. But the direction in which he wants to steer the corporate ship brings out the mutineer in me. No, I'm sorry, Lisa. It wouldn't be fair to him, or to me either for that matter, if I went back now just because I need the money. Anyway, I've made up my mind. I've decided that the best thing for me to do is sell all my pretty doodads, move to Mexico and learn to be a painter." It was a lot for her to absorb all in one quick shot.

There was silence for a moment. Then, in a strained voice, "Boss, you can't do that! What do you mean move to Mexico? That's crazy. You can't move away from here. You belong here. Have you thought about what you're doing? I don't want you to go."

I was touched. But in spite of her protests, my mind was made up and I knew that nothing would change it. To show compliance, however, I agreed that we should meet for lunch in a few days and talk it over. She urged me not to carve anything in stone until then. It would be pointless, I felt, to tell her that the stone had already been chiseled. Before hanging up I purposely mentioned that while she would be losing a friend with a place in the country to visit on weekends, she would be gaining a friend with a vacation spot in Mexico, where the winters are warm and sunny. Nobody is happier than Lisa at the prospects of foreign travel.

Next, I called my sister Laura in Atlanta. I was positive of her full support. Sure enough, once I began informing her of my plans, her pleasant Southern voice was lilting with excitement as she gave me her wholehearted support.

Moments later I was on the phone with my brother Dick in San Diego, telling him about the nosedive of the big project. He had had enough of his own low blows and disappointments over the years to be sympathetic. Eleven years my senior, Dick had been a talented watercolorist all his life. Midway through a successful advertising career he threw in the towel and carved out a new life for himself as a fine artist with a widespread reputation as a cityscape painter. Apparently we both shared the same genetic defect: an addiction to paint brushes..

"What are you going to do?" he asked when I had finished.

" I've decided to become a painter."

"A house painter?"

"No, a picture painter."

"You must be kidding. You'll starve to death."

"Yeah, well it might be good for me. I need to lose some weight."

"Seriously, Bill. I hope you know what you're doing.".

"Yeah. Well why change now? I've gotten by all these years without needing to."

"What in the hell's gotten into you, old boy? You must know how tough it is to earn a living as a painter. Very few ever make the grade. At this late stage of your life, of all things, why that?"

"Because of Titian. I recently remembered the Titian limerick and figured that had to be the life for me."

"What's Titian got to do with it? What limerick?"

"Gee, what cave have you been living in? I thought everyone who had ever lifted a paintbrush was familiar with that oldie. The first time I heard it I was so young and I laughed so hard I kicked the slats out of my cradle."

"Well come on, damn it. Don't keep it a secret. What is it?"

"As Titian was mixing rose madder,
His model sat perched on a ladder.
Her position, to Titian, suggested coition.
So he climbed up the ladder and had her."

At the end of a long and hearty belly laugh, brother Dick came back on. "That's a good one, Bud. Sure, go ahead and be a painter. You can do it. Why not? Sometimes a man fights best with his back to the wall. Give it a try. Never say die, say damn. I'm all for you."

With a plan of action firmly in mind, a thousand and one details begged for attention. For the next few days I spent many hours on the phone making arrangements of one sort or another and following through on the things to do notes to myself I kept jotting down on slips of paper. My long-time friend Bob Carter and his wife Suzanne dealt in fine art, antiques, and also handled estate sales, so I entrusted them to dispose of all that I owned, except for the few things I intended taking to Mexico, and the sale of my beautiful green Jaguar, which I would take care of on my own. Bob's schedule was filled until mid-September, so we set a date for the weekend of the 15th, 16th and 17th and agreed that he would send out a mailing and run substantially large ads in The Washington Post and the local papers.

Until Martin, a friend who had spent considerable time in Mexico, pointed it out, it had not occurred to me that my Jaguar had no business showing its pretty face south of the border. Instead, he advised, I should buy an uncomplicated American make that could be repaired by any shade-tree mechanic. He suggested that I would do well to look for a used Ford, Chevrolet or Plymouth with a good engine, but a ratty-looking body was to be preferred over one that was too neat and trim; otherwise I might find myself walking instead of driving. I listened carefully, took it as wise counsel, and went to see my friend Gerry.

Gerry owned several rent-a-car and leasing franchises and I figured he might be able to help me out if one of the fleet cars was ready for retirement. Sure enough, he had one that fit Martin's description to a tee, a six-year-old Plymouth Reliant station wagon painted a dark and dingy blue. Although the odometer showed only forty-four thousand miles, the body looked as if it had undergone a rather hard life. There were no big dents, but scuffs, dimples and scratches abounded and the paint finish was accommodatingly dull and oxidized. In addition, all four hub caps were missing. I felt confident that Martin himself could not have made a better selection for the purpose I had in mind.

"It's got a good engine," Gerry told me, "but it may be a trifle out of timing. The mechanic tells me it runs a little rough."

"Who was it leased to?" I asked. "A little old lady, I suppose, who only drove it to church on Sundays."

"No, but you're close. Since the day it was new it's been leased to a rabbi. For all I know he only drove it to the synagogue on Saturdays." We both laughed. From then on I never referred to it as anything other than the "Rabbi Roadster."

While awaiting the house sale I spent every spare minute concentrating on learning how to paint in oils. I had benefited a great deal from following Bill Woodward's suggestion that I copy a work by a master painter. But now it was time to try winging it on my own. My interest lay primarily in landscape painting. So everyday, weather permitting, and with all three dogs as enthusiastic passengers, I threw supplies and gear into the back of my newly acquired four-wheel vibrator and, after briefly studying the detailed county map on the seat beside me, I poked the Rabbi Roadster's dingy blue nose down some hidden back road, all the while looking for the perfect combination of appealing vista and off-the-road parking space. The area of Virginia where I lived was so filled with natural beauty there was never any shortage of subject matter.

Each morning, bursting with well-intended resolve, I set forth to create the charming landscape painted with great verve that would magically emerge upon the canvas and be my reward by day's end. Instead, more than half of all the charming landscapes were scraped off the canvas with the cold hard edge of a palette knife and reduced to what looked like the oversized droppings of a very sick bird, then dumped ingloriously into the plastic garbage bag attached to one of the easel legs. Mine was a problem common to most beginners, although at the time I was convinced that the messy evidence of my own ineptitude was a unique experience. And, in spite of the many "damn its" and other assorted expletives I chose to utter throughout the course of a day, I still seemed unable to make the brush behave to my liking or produce any of the myriad wonderful effects I had in mind.

With almost every fresh attempt I only added to my already high level of frustration. I was getting my nose quite thoroughly rubbed in the simple fact that having a burning desire to paint is far different from actually knowing how to paint. Day after day, at the end of long hours of standing in front of the portable French easel I had bought, I would return home, chugging up the driveway to Cowpie Manor in the Rabbi Roadster, alone and discouraged, wondering if I had taken leave of my senses in ever thinking I could eventually earn my living as a professional painter. Homes for the blind might be the only market for my work if I didn't drastically improve, I told myself at the end of one particularly disappointing day in the field. Something had to be done. It was high time for one of my twilight brain-storming sessions on the terrace.

Firmly believing that one should always go into a meeting well prepared, I made straight for the cabinet that once housed the delicious but costly Famous Grouse. Now, because of belt-tightening austerity, the liquor store's cheapest version of Old MacSludge resided there in its place. The scotch bottle, a tumbler and a carafe of water were placed on the customary silver gallery tray and, together with a yellow pad and clipboard, carried to the Big Elm Conference Center, so conveniently located only a few yards from the house with a splendid view of the mountains. Once seated in my special chair, the barn cat Phaideau came slinking over and was soon rubbing lazily against my leg and purring softly. All three dogs, exhausted from lying in the shade all day and watching me paint, were now getting some rest in Dogpatch Haven, so Phaideau and I were the only ones present when I called the meeting to order to outline an agenda and put some thoughts on paper.

One thing was certain. If I was going to stick to my announced gameplan, I needed to analyze what was wrong and correct it fast. The luxury of just fiddle-faddling around, playing with paints as a diversion while killing time before the cocktail hour might be an excellent modus operandi for countless others, but had no place in my own scheme of things. No, my objective was to speed things up, take shortcuts, and learn all I could as quickly as possible. I had made a commitment and there could be no middle ground. It was becoming increasingly clear: I'd damn well better either learn to chirp or get off the limb.

These one-man policy meetings of mine typically involved nothing more complicated than a simple question-and-answer session. My customary procedure was to start with a question, write it down, scratch my head a little, have a sip of scotch, think up as many feasible answers as came to mind, and write each one of them down. Then, one by one, eliminate all but the final answer, the one that seemed to be the best of the lot under the existing circumstances. Voila! Problem solved! (I hoped). That particular evening my questions and final answers were somewhat as follows:

Q: Why am I having such problems with learning to paint?

A: Because, you're expecting too much in a short period of time. There's a lot to learn. Be easy on yourself while still knowing how important it is to be critical of your own work. If painting were an easy way to make a living, people would quit their jobs in droves, buy a few art supplies, throw away the keys to their place of business, say to hell with any further commuting, and take up painting. So, get used to the fact that success won't come easily.

Q. By following Bill Woodward's prescription for copying a masterwork, I produced a remarkably good replica. But that was painted over a period of time under studio conditions, and Mr. Chase had done all the thinking for me, so I didn't have the problems I'm now encountering while trying to do things on my own out in the field. I can't afford the cost of lessons, so I've got to keep trying to search out the right way to proceed entirely on my own. What's the best way for me to do that?

A: Possibly, through books. Go to a well-stocked art-supply store and hope to find some good how-to books.

Q: Assuming the how-to books give me the key to the step-by-step process of building a painting, there still is the matter of helpful criticism normally coming from a teacher, and that is not accounted for by reading a book. What do I do about that?

A: I'm lucky there. Those years spent buying, selling, and dealing in fine art should provide me with a fairly high level of self-criticism. Watch out that it doesn't cause me to be too critical of my own work. Most beginners fall into the trap of doing something god-awful and thinking that it's great. I'm more apt to do something mediocre and scrape it down or throw it away because it's not perfect. Once in a while I might run a painting past Woodward for a quickie critique, but make sure I don't take advantage of his friendship by doing it too often.

Q: Am I under a serious disadvantage in not seeking out formal instruction even though I can't presently afford the expense. There's a saying among attorneys that a lawyer who represents himself has a fool for a client. Does something similar apply to self-taught painters?

A: Benjamin West, second president of the Royal Academy; Winslow Homer, one of America's finest; Vincent Van Gogh, the great post-impressionist, and others like them who had little or no formal training, have already answered that question.

It was almost dark. Phaideau had gone to sleep. My glass was empty. It was time to bring the meeting to a close.

In the days and weeks that followed I began to make slow but steady progress as a would-be landscape painter. The books I bought the day after my brain-storming session were of much practical help, and because of their instructive guidance I started paying more attention to the process of building a painting. And, with it all, I did my best to be a little easier on myself on those occasions when my work fell short of the goal. The object of the exercise is to learn and have fun while I'm doing it, I kept telling myself. Most of the hours spent painting away, out in the open, knee deep in nature, were happy and care free, and more and more frequently I found myself chugging home in the Rabbi Roadster with a feeling of inner reward as a result of the day's painting effort coupled with an increasing awareness that slowly but surely I was gaining ground and on the right track.

Dexter, Daisy and Abner were especially pleased with the new lifestyle, as we were spending far more time together than before. Dexter was always close by, for I had to keep him tied or he would end up in China. The other two would not wander too far from their Rabbi Roadster-bound Alpha dog or, if they did, I would start blowing the bugle and they would come scampering back to headquarters, an obedience lesson I taught all three of them while they were still very young. Well before the approach of Mexican D Day I had flyers printed announcing that the dogs were available for adoption. The headline read: Can You Qualify To Adopt The Best Friends You'll Ever Have? The body copy that followed described each of the dogs and a color photo of all three was hand pasted on every sheet. I took the sheets around to veterinary clinics, supermarket bulletin boards and local animal shelters. The notice was rather professionally done and I fully expected that in very short order my phone would be ringing and all my time spent in interviewing applicants. It wasn't quite like that, though the poster was at least partially successful. For an excellent home was found almost immediately for Dexter.

Tom, a young lieutenant soon to depart for foreign duty and his wife Carrie, in need of a pet companion while Tom was away, fell in love with Dexter at first sight. They impressed me as a fine young couple and I knew I could rest easy as far as Big Yellow was concerned. But damn, I sure hated to see him go.

It was quite different in the case of Abner and Daisy. First of all, I didn't want them separated, since they had been side by side since birth. I therefore had to turn down several offers from people to take just one or the other. So the weeks flew by and they were still in Dogpatch Haven at the time of the house sale. Several people saw them then and expressed interest, but they failed to measure up to the standards that I was determined to see met, so I refused to give them the dogs. One obnoxious woman, an ax-handle-and-a-half-wide across the butt, began to mouth off something about equal opportunity and acted as if she might sue me for some perceived injustice on my part when I as much as let her know that she, or anyone like her, would obtain possession of those two little charmers over my dead body.

The situation was one of increasing concern, for I was absolutely determined that I was not going to compromise even if it meant delaying my departure. But all ended well. Only a few days before I was scheduled to vacate the property, Lisa's friend Spencer called and informed me that he would like to take them both. They were treated like rare and precious Dresden dolls ever since.

It rained relentlessly throughout the entire day on September 15th, the first day of my house sale, and a mere handful of people showed up. The next day brought angry black clouds with howling winds that turned the rain into blinding sheets of stinging pellets, so that by late afternoon only a dozen or so die-hard house-sale bargain hunters had showed up. By six o'clock closing time, after two full days, the inside of the house looked almost untouched except for a few bare spots here and there. The combination of dreadful weather and the distance of sixty-five miles from the city had kept potential buyers away.

"We'll have a good day tomorrow, Bill, and make up for lost time," my house sale agent Bob Carter said reassuringly as he and Suzanne were leaving at day's end.

"It will need to be more than just a good day," I replied, looking around me and making a sweeping gesture with my arm. "All this has to go, Bob, or I'll have a bigger problem than I'll know how to handle. If we need to give stuff away, I'd rather do that than have anything left at six o'clock tomorrow night. I've no intention of paying storage on things I may never see again. There's only one option: twenty-four hours from now this house has got to be so empty there'll be nothing left but the dust on the floor."

"What about donating anything that's left over to a charity and having a tax write-off?" he asked as I walked with him toward their van.

"You must be kidding," I shot back. "Look, Bob, I'll draw you a picture. For a long time to come I won't have any income except social security, so I desperately need every cent of cash I can get my hands on in order to live, and my only source of cash is inside that house. So tomorrow accept offers, cut prices, make deals. Near the end of the day, you can even give things away! Do whatever you need to do to move everything out of there and have the place completely empty by the time the last person leaves."

The next evening while Bob and Suzanne did their final adding machine tallies at the card table they had set up on the summer porch, I sat on the steps, weary and depressed, trying my best to suppress the sadness of a day spent watching my cherished possessions disappear before my eyes. Once they finished their summary, Bob was to deduct their twenty percent commission and write me a check for the balance. I had no idea what to expect, but I recalled how several years earlier I had had my household furnishings and personal possessions appraised, item by item, by Peter Columbo, a reputable Washington appraiser and antique dealer, and the assessed value at that time totaled just under $250,000, and I had given Bob a copy of this appraisal at the time we first talked about having the house sale. I turned to see him walking toward me and I shifted position so as to stand up.

He spoke before I had a chance to move. "Why don't you stay seated, Bill. The news isn't good, and you may be more comfortable hearing it sitting down." He handed me some sheets of paper listing the sale price of each item and, along with the list, a check for the total amount. I looked at the check, and my heart sank.. It was for $43,654.28. That was all. On a good day, the highboy alone might well have brought that much.

"I'm sure sorry that it's not for a lot more, Bill," Bob said sympathetically. "Suzanne and I did all we could. It was a rotten break, the bad weather, and having to cut prices to get rid of it all on the last day. I hope you're not too disappointed."

As I sat, staring at the check, I had the feeling that I was for all the world like the man in the Bible who had stupidly sold his birthright for a mess of pottage. But, the deed was done, and there was no way to put the egg back in the shell. The only option left me was to adjust downward on all future expenditures until someday, God willing, the need for austerity would be over and income would start coming my way again. On the good side of the ledger, I had managed to find a buyer for the Jaguar without having to reduce my asking price by as much as I had anticipated. And, quite surprisingly, nine of the dog-entourage, small field-trip paintings done within the past couple of months had sold during the sale for several hundred dollars each. One woman, a total stranger, bought three. The sale of these first-attempt paintings was a good omen, and served as mental life support to my otherwise badly sagging morale.

Sitting on the steps of the now empty Cowpie Manor, I watched as the Carters drove off in the fading daylight. I was on the verge of feeling sorry for myself, when some fragments of an earlier message slowly found their way into my consciousness *".... the easier you play the game of fortitude, the more relaxed you become to each challenge, the more you control your destiny.. .A frantic spirit is a stupid one."*

These words of wisdom deserved reflection in a far more convivial setting, I decided, so I locked the front door of the empty house, got in the Rabbi Roadster and headed for the good French restaurant three miles down the highway. Once there, I would start with a Martini and some paté campagne, then some boeuf bourguignon for an entree, along with a half bottle of that delicious troisièmes crus Margaux, Chateau Giscours.

"This is the first night of my new life," I told myself. "It's time to celebrate."

CHAPTER THREE
The Trail Of The Blivit

From the moment I announced my intention to move to Mexico and paint, friends and acquaintances familiar with that part of the world, almost without exception recommended San Miguel de Allende as the town for me. There, they assured me, I would find what I was looking for. They described it as an attractive colonial town about four hours' drive north of Mexico City, a place where artists congregated and two facilities devoted to teaching art were located. It all sounded like the ideal habitat for my purposes, so, from the very start, San Miguel was my destination.

Friends invited me to sleep in their guest cottage and make their horse farm my staging area for the days remaining before my scheduled departure for San Miguel on October 5th. While there, I spent my time wrapping up an assortment of last-minute details and packing and re-packing both the station wagon and the small trailer generously donated to my cause by a couple I knew.

There were problems I had not anticipated. The Jaguar had supposedly been sold but, in spite of my daily phone calls, the money from its sale had yet to become more than a promise. The place where I bought new tires for the trailer told me that it was only a garden trailer and warned me against driving it over forty-five miles an hour. Gordon, my host, emphatically agreed with that advice. At this late date I was getting the message that garden trailers aren't designed for heavy loads, long distances and high speeds. It soon became obvious that the sides of the trailer were not high enough hold the intended load, so I had to drive into Warrenton, buy more lumber and quickly devise a way to build extensions for the sides so that a top consisting of waterproofed plywood could be secured yet easily removable. I installed hasps and heavy duty padlocks on all four sides with a fifth padlock securing the oversized chain connecting car and trailer.

On the afternoon of my scheduled departure, I was hard at it, stuffing the last few small items into the tiniest of the nooks and crannies when the phone rang. It was Walt, the guy who had bought the Jaguar. He said he had finally gotten his financing taken care of and had a certified check in his possession ready to turn over to me but that he was on such a tight schedule I would need to be in his office by four o'clock or else wait until the next day. He was twenty-five miles away in Front Royal. I looked at my watch: it was three-twenty. I said I would be there.

Although it was still early in October, the day was scorching, and with sweat pouring off of me I would have given anything for a shower, a cold beer, a change of clothes and a chance to say a proper and grateful goodbye to my host and hostess. As it was, I called to Gordon who was over by the horse barns and told him I had to high-tail it out of there *tout de suite,* not even time to run down to the big house and say goodbye to his wife Jackie. He came over and we shook hands. As he looked at my overloaded rig his expression became one of grave concern. Both the Rabbi Roadster and trailer were so heavily loaded that in profile they together formed a V, with the rear bumper of the station wagon almost dragging, and the hitch for the trailer only a couple of inches off the ground.

We stood for a brief moment, side by side, staring silently at my intended means of international transport.

"Your trailer springs are almost flat against the axles," he said shaking his head. "I sure hope you make it, Bill."

I slid in behind the wheel. "Don't worry, Gordon. I'll be O.K.," I answered, doing my best to sound unconcernned and confident. Then, waving goodbye, I presented the best smile I could manage.

He stood there watching as I slowly pulled away, a former fighter pilot ace, looking for all the world as if he would rather face enemy fire again than to trade places with me.

As I inched the half mile or so down the winding gravel lane to the hard surface road, the trailer hitch, at each slight depression, scraped bottom. I knew Gordon was right to be so apprehensive. Perhaps I should turn around and go back. But instead, I continued, giving myself a pep talk filled with some of the old bromides: "Nothing ventured, nothing gained. Faint heart ne'er won fair lady" (I figured Dame Fortune qualified as a lady) and, of course, "No guts, no glory." On and on I crept until I reached the asphalt road. Sure enough, I was soon clipping along at a reasonable pace, still keeping my options open, ready to turn back if necessary, but first going far enough to have a basis for judgment. After about a mile I came to a key intersection. If it will go one mile, I reasoned, this poor excuse for a moving van ought to go five. If it'll go five I'll shoot for twenty-five and I'll then be where I want to be, so let's turn left and head toward Front Royal. I arrived with a few minutes to spare, picked up the check as promised, took one last wistful look at my lovely British racing green Jaguar with golden pinstripe down the sides and climbed back in behind the wheel of the dowdy little Plymouth whose implausible responsibility was to get me to Mexico. I started the chugging, under-powered engine and began my journey.

The next day as I drove on south I had plenty of time to collect my thoughts and reflect on recent events. There were friends I thought of that I should have said goodbye to, but I had been too busy to cover all the bases. And there were those who asked me to join them for dinner before taking off, but in most cases that hadn't worked out either. By late afternoon I was breezing along, mostly unaware of the fact that I was driving a severely handicapped tandem rig. On the monotonously smooth surface of the interstate I had let the speedometer needle creep up past sixty. My fool's paradise was soon destined to end, however, as the sun settled over the rim of the Tennessee hills and I made the descent toward a tributary of the Cumberland River.

Frequently, roadbeds and bridges join at an asphalt hump that allows for the contraction and expansion of the bridge structure. My abrupt comeuppance happened with lightning like speed just as I left the bridge and hit the roadbed again. The ribbed joint between bridge and road surface proved too much for the overloaded trailer. There was a sudden sharp noise, and a quick glance in the sideview mirror showed a dense spiral of blue smoke close on my tail. It took all my concentrated effort to brake safely onto the shoulder of the highway. Inspection showed that the probable had become the actual. The leaf spring on the rightside had snapped like a dry twig, permitting a metal side brace to fall down on the tire, retarding its rotation and scraping the tread down to its intermeshed fabric. I stood looking at it helplessly. At least, I thought, I'd better get the hazard lights flashing so I don't accidentally get clobbered. To my dismay, they no longer worked on the trailer. Well, dammit, Gordon was sure right and I was in one hell of a predicament. Unless St. Christopher came riding by on a bicycle, things were apt to get even worse, for I was out in the middle of nowhere and it would soon be dark.

I was crouched down to see if there was anything conceivable, anything at all I might try that would make it possible to limp into the nearest town, when a nasal voice behind me said,

"Looks like that there spring has broke plumb through."

Without me having seen him do it, a passing motorist had pulled his pickup truck off the road and was parked in front of me with the engine still running. His wife and two kids sat quietly inside cab. There have been few times in my life when I have been so glad to converse with another human being as I was at that moment. He told me I was about eight miles east of the nearest town, that there was a 24 hour filling station there with a wrecker and he would have them send it to help me. I thanked him profusely, tried to give him money, tried to give a buck to each of the kids but he would have none of it.

It was dark as the inside of a cow by the time the wrecker arrived. The driver could well have been the twin brother of my earlier benefactor. While waiting for the wrecker to show up I had been wondering how an emergency vehicle without an inventory of spare parts could make it possible to get the wheel turning again. Wreckers certainly don't carry springs for garden trailers. But I had underestimated the country smarts of the driver. Within seconds of analyzing the problem he had the wrecker turned around and then, quite miraculously I thought, produced a two-by-four of exactly the right length which he somehow wedged in between the axle and the broken spring. In nothing flat he had me moving again, the two of us using the shoulder as our own private lane with his mars lights flashing behind me for protection. As we drove along in the darkness I gave considerable thought to the improbability of the necessary repairs being available in the little town where we were headed. The driver had told me its population was only about a couple of thousand. Garden trailer leaf springs of exactly the right size and strength would surely be something so unusual as to need ordering, probably from Nashville. It was now Saturday night and supply houses would all be closed until Monday morning. It seemed logical to expect that I might need to hang around and waste several days, and I dreaded the prospect of doing so.

In due course we arrived at the all-night station. After paying for the wrecker's round trip, a mere $18, my first question was, what could I do about getting new springs. "Well that shouldn't be no problem," I was told by the proprietor. "Buddy Atwood has a place just around that there curve. He makes trailers and does weldin'. I seen him drive by here just a few minutes ago. He's home now. Whyn't you go ast him?"

I headed off in that direction and no more than a hundred and fifty yards around the curve and up the hill from the station was a crudely lettered sign: R.M. Atwood-Welding. Scattered about on his property were numerous bits and pieces of old trailers as well as some new ones that were freshly painted. Atwood soon sized up what was needed, told his dog to shut up, turned on some more outdoor lights and began poking about in his inventory of spare parts. Nothing but junk until needed, I thought, and then pure gold. Finally he came back from an old work shed carrying two leaf springs that looked sturdy enough to support the wheels on earth moving equipment.

"These here's a bit heavier than what's on there but they's the best I've got. I'll guaran-by-damn-tee yuh they 'ont give out on yuh. Only thing, they's gonna give yuh a stiffer ride, but they ain't gonna break on yuh."

I assured him that I had no objection to the stiffer ride, as I had no intention of riding back there myself. The cause for rejoicing was that springs were available in such an unexpected and out of the way place. But I knew that there had to be some bad news as well. The matter of when and how much was yet to be discussed. Reluctantly, I asked him how soon he could install them and how much it would cost. Well, he allowed, he could start right now, but a lot of work would be involved to make the springs fit, lots of welding, special parts would need to be fabricated to accommodate existing fittings, all of which might need to be secured with new braces, and maybe a whole hell of a lot of other things he hadn't even figured on might slow him down and cause him more work. The way he was building his case I was prepared for a price quotation only slightly less than the national debt with delivery scheduled, if everything went well, two weeks from Wednesday. Eventually, after thinking and scratching and spitting tobacco juice he more or less forced himself to declare, "Well now, hit's like I say, they's a lot of work involved, so I reckon hit'll run yuh right about sixty, maybe sixty-five dollars." I did my best not to register my reaction of joyful surprise. There was still one possible fly in the ointment. He had said nothing about time. When I finally got up enough courage to ask, he rather matter of factly said, "Oh, hit'll be ready 'bout seven in the mornin'." Bright and early the next morning, after buying a new tire from the overnight station, I was on my way again, Buddy Atwood, skilled craftsman and entrepreneur, sixty-five dollars richer, and me with trailer springs that could make it across the boulder strewn bed of the Grand Canyon.

A couple of nights later I stood looking at the bridge crossing the Rio Grande that would lead me into Mexico the next morning and a new way of life. Brother Dick's words came to mind, "I hope you know what you're doing, Bill." I wasn't at all sure that I did. Mostly I was optimistic and filled with confidence. But there were dark moments when I felt my future was overwhelmingly precarious. There was only one way to find out what the future held in store. Cross that river in the morning.

Driving across the Rio Grande into Mexico, I wondered what might be expected from the Mexican Immigration authorities and was more than a little apprehensive about carting so much stuff into their country. According to everything I had read, much of what I was carrying with me fell into the category of permissible imports only for those who had lived in Mexico for at least five years. There was good reason to believe I was not violating any serious law, yet an overly curious official or one looking for a handout could delay me for hours while things were unpacked and re-packed in exactly the right way, as they would need to be, in order for the station wagon doors and the lid on the trailer to be closed again. On the other hand, I had been assured by several people who claimed to know the Mexican ropes that surveillance tends to be lax and, with luck, I should be able to get all my belongings into the country without a problem.

I had the luck I needed. Nothing was questioned or examined. I was free to proceed onward toward the interior of the country that I knew almost nothing about but had nevertheless chosen as the place where I would start my life anew.

After some coffee and a routine quick check of car and trailer couplings, I was soon bouncing along on the frequently rough surface of the Pan American Highway leading to Monterey, with San Miguel my eventual goal. Before going to bed the night before I looked in my Spanish-English dictionary so I would know how to say "Soy pintor" (I am a painter). I had been told that artists and writers are looked upon favorably by the Mexican government and I thought the phrase might prove useful. Sure enough, after an hour or so of driving, a checkpoint appeared up ahead. A car and a van had been pulled off the road, for some reason, and were being examined. As I handed the beefy guard my papers I gave him my most confident and cheerful,

"Buenos dias, senor."

"What are the contents?" he asked, looking first at the car and then at the trailer.

"Personal belongings," I replied, and then foolishly added, "Soy pintor."

He shook his head like I was some kind of a nut, sighed deeply and muttered, "O.K., go on." Microwave, stereo system and other no-no's remained unchallenged.

The portion of the trip from Virginia to the Mexican border had been child's play compared to what was soon to confront me as I drove further into the country. To begin with, I was so heavily loaded that all reactions, including braking and steering, were far more pronounced. In Dallas I had investigated the possibility of overload springs for the car, but the dealer couldn't accommodate me. He told me that the light Plymouth station wagon was designed to carry a maximum weight of 350 pounds. About three times that amount of weight was crammed into the car itself and it was pulling another five or six hundred pounds.

The overstuffed condition of car and trailer brought to mind a boyhood chum named Arnold Lockett. He was a precocious kid who was forever impressing the rest of us by, among other things, bragging about how rich he would become when he grew up by gaining control of the automotive industry. Arnold never disclosed to us exactly how he proposed accomplishing this grandiose objective. One day he gathered a group of us together and shared with us a bit of his esoteric knowledge: the definition of a blivit, which he announced was two pounds of whatever (Arnold preferred using the S word) in a one-pound bag. Arnold would be pleased to know, I felt sure, that I now remembered him by thinking of my bursting-at-the-seams vehicular twosome as The Blivit.

With each mile of driving on the rough and uneven Mexican highway it became more and more apparent that the trailer had a mind of its own. Like an obedient animal it would go along for a while in utmost docility, willfully submitting to its tether, only to suddenly become a force of obstinate rebellion, whereupon a series of violent bucking, lunging, swaying and jerking motions would ensue, causing me serious concern about the possibility of it coming unhitched and taking off on its own. From the start, even before leaving Virginia, the various tail-light functions never all worked properly at any given time, even though the wiring was checked and re-checked by professional mechanics and, almost constantly, by me. Of grave concern was the fact that the safety latch attending the ball-and-socket joint was, to say the least, somewhat erratic in its dependability. On several occasions, fortunately at relatively uncritical times, the union parted company and the trailer tongue became unhitched of its own accord. My greatest fear was that this might occur while going downhill with the heavily loaded trailer becoming something of a loose cannon, capable of causing a major disaster.

Soon the flat desert wasteland began to give way to more rolling terrain with a trace of mountains on the distant horizon. The guidebooks stated that San Miguel is at an elevation of nearly 6,300 feet, so there would be plenty of Sierra Madre Mountains to negotiate before I got there. I had no idea how my four-cylinder tandem rig would perform when put to a test in the mountains. Well, I would soon find out. As I neared Monterey I could see a steep grade ahead with a long line of trucks and cars snaking their way up the mountainside. I spotted a Pemex station and pulled in, eventually making the attendant understand that in addition to a full tank of gas I wanted him to check everything – oil, brake fluid, water, steering fluid, the works. As it later turned out, it was good thing I was so thorough. As I drove out of Monterey I could look ahead and see the stark and jagged saw-tooth peaks of the mountain range I was about to cross.

Mexico is a land of big, ponderous, slow-moving trucks, many of which belch out huge clouds of smelly black smoke. And I quickly learned that trucks could be a special problem on winding, two-lane mountain roads that present an endless series of *curvas peligrosas (*dangerous curves.) Underpowered trucks often creep along so slowly as to barely make it uphill, causing succeeding vehicles to line up behind, waiting for a chance to pass. But passing is not easily accomplished because the lead slowpoke speeds up each time the road flattens out and, also, the distance between the *corvas peligrosas* is often too short to permit overtaking the guy in front.

I was well into the mountains when I found myself somewhere near the center of a long daisy chain of cars and trucks, all of us constrained by the motorized snail at the head of the line. My poor little Plymouth didn't like what was being asked of it, pulling a load that was way too heavy at a speed that forced it to almost constantly shift back and forth between second and high gear. With increasing concern I watched helplessly as the temperature gauge rose steadily until it was almost into the red. If the needle got any higher I knew the engine might seize up on me, and that would be curtains for the Blivit as far as the rest of the trip was concerned. I hoped for a shoulder so I could pull off, but there was none. Whether I liked it or not I was hopelessly pinned in, front and back, and had to keep my place in line. There was one little trick I employed that may have helped slightly in saving the day. At every opportunity when the engine was not actually pulling I would shift into neutral and bear down on the gas pedal, hoping the speeded circulation through the radiator would help cool things down. Even so, the needle had climbed well into the red when at last, thank God, my opportunity came to pull off the road.

They were only a couple of furrowed tracks in the rocky red dirt and I didn't have the foggiest notion where they would lead me, but they got me off the highway, which was essential to survival, so I didn't hesitate. Following these deep ruts, the Blivet coasted down into a clearing, coming to a stop in front of an abandoned, boarded-up restaurant. I sat for a moment, wondering what was best to do: leave the engine running, hoping the circulating water would have the desired effect or, in the event the engine had gotten so hot the water had evaporated, turn off the key, raise the hood and let the engine cool down gradually from the air, a longer but safer way. I decided on the latter course, leaving the key in the ignition and flipping it frequently to get a reading from the gauge, which showed the needle at the top of the red. The thought went through my mind that I might be sitting there for quite a while when something caught the corner of my eye.

On what had been a sort of raised concrete outdoor deck running across the front of the building, there stood a skinny, stringy-haired woman in a tight black dress. Within seconds after seeing her I heard the sound of a car coming up from behind and turned just as two Mexicans in an ancient, red Chevy convertible came alongside, almost, but not quite, stopping. The one on my side was a mean-looking man of about thirty. He sported a droopy mustache and the welt of what appeared to be a recent knife cut across his right cheek. The guy behind the wheel leaned forward so he could get a better look at me. The skin on his face gave the impression of fitting too tightly over its bone structure and his half-opened mouth displayed sharp, uneven teeth. The two of them stared at me silently as their old jalopy inched slowly past. I sat for a few moments feeling a trifle uneasy, but enormously relieved that they had not caused any trouble. Soon my mind was back on the temperature problem. One hand was on the door latch and I was about to get out and go lift up the hood when I saw her again, the woman in the black dress. She was looking out beyond me.

A split-second glance in the side-view mirror told me, in military parlance, it was time to Close station! March order! On the double! Scarface and his buddy had circled around and were coming back. An instant later I had the engine started, the car in gear and the gas pedal flat against the floor. As the accelerating Blivit neared the point where what had once been the exit driveway rejoined the highway, there seemed no way to get back onto the hard surface without first crossing a rain-washed gully that would surely do untold damage to the springs and axles of the car and I would almost certainly lose the trailer. I quickly figured that my one and only hope was to take a chance and veer off through the bush, betting on the ground being level enough beneath the foliage to get me across. Luck was with me as I went crashing through the tangle of low vegetation and came shooting out in front of a surprised truck driver leading his own private parade up the hill. The two hombres in the red junk-heap were nowhere in sight.

In the excitement of the moment I had completely forgotten about the over-heated radiator. Now, moving along at a good clip on a downhill grade I saw, to my great relief, that the needle on the gauge was back where it belonged and the danger past. As I descended the mountain and neared Saltillo the events of the recent half-hour ran through my mind. Perhaps I had over-reacted. Scarface, his friend with the rat mouth and the skinny woman in the black dress were all three probably very nice people, with the two guys going to all the trouble of coming back so they could offer their assistance in the event I needed help, or maybe they just wanted to invite me to a fiesta their church was having that afternoon. Also, driving like a crazy man through a mountain thicket was probably a foolish thing to have done and might have seriously damaged the car or trailer, or even me.

My stomach told me it was time for lunch. Inside the restaurant I was greeted by Carlos, the owner, who I soon learned had worked for his uncle up in Chicago and saved enough to come back and open his own place in Saltillo. The decor was garishly fancy, with lavender walls and elaborate chandeliers. Carlos spoke perfect English and was friendly, coming over to the table to chat. As we were talking he looked out through the front window and saw my overloaded car and trailer with the V profile, he asked if I had had any trouble making it across the mountains. I followed his glance and there, stuck to the trailer fender on the passenger side was part of a rather sizable young tree, a souvenir from my involuntary fling at bush-hogging while making my hasty getaway.

I told Carlos about the engine overheating and how I had been forced to pull off the highway to let it cool. He asked me how come there was so much green stuff stuck to the trailer fender, so I told him about the two guys in the old jalopy and my speedy departure through the bush. He said he felt sure I had done the right thing in leaving without saying goodbye, that there were bad guys who hung out in the mountains hoping for motorists in trouble. Possibly much more serious, he ventured, was the fact that there had recently been news on local radio and T.V. of a prison break with some inmates still at large. In my case, no crime had been committed and there was nothing to go on but my gut feeling that the two guys, in coming back, had some kind of mischief in mind. Nevertheless, Carlos thought it would be a good idea, once the lunch traffic was out of his hair, for him to call the police just in case my description of the two characters driving an old red convertible fit anything the law might be looking for.

We had said goodbye and I was halfway out the door when I suddenly remembered. "Oh, and Carlos, one more thing."

"Yeah?"

"Tell the cops to be sure and look inside the old boarded-up restaurant. I believe they'll find a skinny woman in a black dress. She may be part of the act-if there is an act."

"Gotcha."

As I drove on toward San Miguel I thought about how for years I had heard the term, "mountain top experience." I had been in Mexico for less than one full day and I had already had one, didn't like it, and had just as soon not have any more. The next afternoon, the Blivit did the slow bumps and grinds over the cobblestone street leading into San Miguel, coming to a dead stop at each of the numerous "topes"- speed bumps stretched across intersections to keep traffic from going too fast. The San Miguel section of the guidebook with its map of the town showed the Posada de las Monjas, a recommended modestly priced hotel, to be close to the center of things, so I headed there, parked in their private lot, checked in, showered, put on fresh clothing, and was soon ready to start poking about on the streets of my intended new home.

I had heard good things about the town. But then one always hears good things about blind dates, yet it's a well known fact that they seldom turn out to be as fabulous as described. I was like a person with a package to unwrap, but hesitating to do so because the package was non-returnable and the contents might not measure up to expectations. For months I had fantasized about the new life awaiting me in San Miguel. What if that new life turned out to be a disappointment? What if I found out, after coming such a long distance, that I just plain didn't like what I found in San Miguel? My combination wise counselor/tough drill-sergeant inner voice suddenly barked: "Well damn it, shut up, lock the door, put the key in your pocket, go take a look and find out."

From the very start it was evident that traversing the town as a pedestrian was not an easy or relaxing activity. Most of the busier sidewalks were so narrow that two or more people couldn't pass each other without someone either hugging the building or else giving way and stepping out into the street. The alternative meant walking on the sometimes treacherously uneven cobblestone surface of the street itself which required shoes with heavier soles than the ones I had on. I soon discovered that the town was built on a hillside with both its flanks dipping downward, so that no matter where or in what direction one walked, at least half the time it was an uphill climb involving a significant amount of huffing and puffing. Street by street, block by block, I covered the territory, taking it all in as attentively as if I had been an enemy spy.

Within the first twenty-four hours I had a pretty good feel for what the community did, and did not, have to offer. Some factors were appealing. For example, one got the impression that, in general, there was a rather more interesting and better-advantaged-than average-group of Americans who had chosen this locality as a place to spend all or part of their time. One evidence of this was the high mark they had imparted on the local library, endowing it with many fine reference books and, to my great pleasure and astonishment, a classical tape collection of what I estimated to be nearly a thousand cassettes, all available on a loan basis. Also, the little city had what seemed to be a reasonably good scattering of shops and restaurants, especially those clustered near the Plaza Principal with its bandstand and shade trees. Flanking the plaza were hotels and business establishments and the spectacular centerpiece of the town, La Parroquia de San Miguel Archangel, the parish church and spiritual soul of the community.

Much of the next few days was spent talking to realtors, checking ads in the English-language newspaper and studying the notice boards, all with a view to finding a suitable place compatible to my very limited budget. One American real-estate lady who had been recommended by a stateside friend rather smugly informed me that what I was looking for was available at a mere $2,100 a month, but the owner wanted to reserve the right to use it periodically on weekends. My reply was not too kind.

Since my principal reason for considering San Miguel as a place to live was because the art facilities in the community had been given such high praise, my top priority, along with housing, called for checking out the two institutions that specialized in teaching fine art. My goal was to find a source of expert instruction in the basics of painting, specifically, the painting of landscapes and genre scenes in oil in the manner of the Impressionists. I especially hoped that a teacher providing such instruction would be so accomplished and so aligned with the Impressionist tradition that I could view that person as a mentor. I was not the least bit interested in wasting time and money in anything other than fundamental, time-tested basics. Let others occupy themselves with doing the clever stuff and expressing themselves to their heart's content, but that had nothing to do with my objective. The traditional approach to painting that was good enough for Alfred Sisley, Camille Pissarro and Claude Monet was good enough for me, and that was that.

So, in a clean shirt, fresh khakis and high hopes, I set forth on my inspection tour. At the first place I was greeted by a pleasant member of the staff, given a copy of the curriculum and ushered into a room where examples of students' work were on display. For what it was, some of what I stood looking at was quite good, but I could see at a glance that the emphasis was on design, abstract painting, art with a message, avant-garde art in varying degrees, but I did not see, as I had hoped, any worthwhile examples of *plein air* (open air) landscape painting.

The next institution was bound to deal more in the type of painting that held my interest, I told myself optimistically, and I was pleased upon arrival to be told by the receptionist that there was an exhibition of works by faculty members on view in the gallery. Although much of what was on display was similar to what I had seen at the place I had just left, the subject-matter for the paintings by one instructor – several landscapes, and one scene showing people – was more down my alley. But, even though I considered that those particular paintings had been done with a reasonable degree of competence, they didn't have verve and were by no means outstanding, as would have been the case if my friend Bill Woodward or others of his stature had been wielding the brush. My enthusiasm was ebbing. It was becoming disappointingly apparent that the instruction I was looking for was not available in San Miguel. Maybe I was expecting too much. After all, it was unrealistic to hope to find the modern day reincarnation of a great teacher like Thomas Eakins, William Merritt Chase or Frank Duvenek holding court in a small town in Mexico. I needed to have a beer and re-think.

While enjoying the malty flavor of a second bottle of cold Dos Equis at an outside table beneath a canopy of lavender jacaranda blossoms, I began to arrive at some conclusions. My intention, from the very start, had been to learn to paint landscapes and genre scenes (scenes of everyday life) well enough to start producing income before my little dab of money ran out. I could not afford to waste time and money on any course of study not aimed at that target. I knew better than anyone else the way in which I wanted to paint, and where I wanted to end up.

That line of thought led me a step further: maybe I should be my own teacher. Back in Virginia I had made considerable progress in the dual role of teacher/student in just a few months. Why not keep on wearing both hats for a while, at least until something better came along? Right off the bat I would save money. Proceeding under my own steam would necessitate me, and me alone, having to ferret out the best ways to achieve the results I envisioned, so I would be forced to work a lot harder and, in the long run, I might be all the better off because of it. Also, it slowly began to sink in, if I was not going to take any art courses, there was no longer the need to find accommodations in San Miguel where the cost of living was too pricey for my tiny nest egg. Perhaps I would do well to consider looking in some more affordable community.

It was lunch time and the tropical downpour just ended had turned the narrow streets into knee-deep torrents of rushing water. Almost directly across from what had been my storefront shelter was a restaurant named Lucy's, so I hopped and waded my way over. Within minutes the sun was beaming down and I was seated, as the only customer, under a canopy at a table in the outdoor garden with some seafood wonton on order.

I could hear their two voices even before they entered from the sidewalk, all of her vocal energy expended in berating him, to which he was replying, "Spare me. Spa-a-a-re me." They wound their way through the decorative trees and flowering shrubs and settled at a table next to mine. I couldn't help but notice her wide-brimmed straw hat covered with artificial fruit and flowers with a cross-looking little yellow bird affixed by means of a spring steel wire, permitting it to swing and sway each time she moved her head. It was impossible not to overhear their conversation, from which I gathered that a piece of property was involved, with her now directing an unmerciful barrage of I-told-you-sos his way because they hadn't sold it when the market was better. Upon each outburst he would go through the same routine. It consisted of him rolling his eyes upward, both palms extended in a manner of supplication and, as if beseeching the mercy of some unseen deity, soulfully and pleadingly intoning, "Spare me. Spa-a-are me," the second "Spa-a-a-re me" accentuated by the injection of his own hammed-up bleating vibrato. I was impressed. He was really quite good at it, I decided.

Right in the middle of one of her more vitriolic blasts he turned to me and asked, "Are you enjoying your visit?" I assured him I was. He then asked me where I was from and within a few moments we were engaged in a conversation, during which I mentioned that I had come to San Miguel to paint. He introduced his wife and himself as Lucille and Harold Somebody-or-other from Ohio. As we talked, his wife set about refocusing her attention and I could see it was going to be on me.

"Is your wife here with you?" she asked.

I made the fatal mistake of saying, "I don't have a wife."

Suddenly, like a war horse darting into the fray, she wasted not a moment. "Oh, do I ever have the perfect woman for you," she declared. "She'll be here in a few days and she just loves art. She'll be absolutely perfect for you. You've simply got to meet each other."

"Who the hell are you talking about?" Harold wanted to know. "I hope you don't mean Marge."

Well, of course, Lucille said, she did mean Marge. After all, she reminded him, Marge was her very best friend. So now the two of them were at it again, with Harold demanding equal time.

"You're sure right about one thing," he stated. "She's perfect all right. A perfect pain in the butt." I gathered that Harold thought that there were only two things wrong with Marge: everything she said and everything she did.

Lucille was undeterred. We would all have dinner together after Marge arrived, she announced, and that was that. Harold said I would need to bring along some extra handkerchiefs to wipe away the tears after hearing all of Marge's sad stories. Well, he would have some sad stories to tell too, Lucille assured him, if he had all the physical problems poor Marge had suffered from in recent years.

As I stood up to leave I said how much I had enjoyed talking with them both and would certainly look forward to meeting Marge, at the time not realizing it was to be my last day in San Miguel. After paying the check I turned to wave and say one more goodbye. I couldn't make out what Lucille was saying, but whatever it was was being said emphatically, for the frantic motions of the little bird were quite animated. I could, however, hear Harold's plaintive reply: "Spare me. Spa-re me." As I walked toward the posada I reflected on the fact that I had come all the way to San Miguel hoping to find a painting mentor but, instead, my closest human contact had been with a couple from Ohio having a domestic squabble.

About mid-morning of the next day I decided to abandon my fruitless search for acceptable housing in San Miguel and, instead, drive over to the Pacific Coast by way of Guadalajara to see what Puerto Vallarta had to offer. I planned to investigate the outlying areas, hoping to be near the sea but away from the tourist crowd and still have the advantage of decent restaurants and the P.V. airport. As the day wore on my luck did not improve. Most of the afternoon was spent creeping along at little more than five or ten miles an hour on the old road to Guadalajara, now no longer in use, instead of traveling at a more normal speed on the currently used highway. The frustrating part was that the two roads paralleled each other, but for countless miles there was no access to the modern four-lane stretch where I could look over and see traffic happily speeding along at full tilt. Except for a few farmers with their tractors, horses or burros I found the Blivit to be the only vehicle on this relic of a road, yet my full attention was required at all times in order to negotiate the unending obstacle course of potholes, some of which I felt were large enough to merit consideration as tourist attractions. I had gotten into this fix partly because my Spanish was so poor that even though I sometimes knew how to ask questions, I couldn't always understand answers. But, in addition to that, a key sign at a key junction was missing, so half a day was wasted while I crept along watching the roadside crops grow.

It was late afternoon by the time I was back on the main road again and, with darkness approaching, I began to hope and pray for a motel. But, as daylight finally faded, there was still no sign of any place offering overnight lodging. My headlights had barely been turned on when, to my enormous relief, amid the shacks and shanties cluttered along a particularly shabby stretch of roadway I spied it...what had to be the world's oldest still-in-service, almost-out-of-gas neon sign resolutely trying to get its message across with a pulsating M, flickering O, steady T, missing E, and blinking L. Thank God, my refuge for the night had appeared in the nick of time.

The unshaven proprietor in the dirty undershirt seemed surprised at seeing a real live gringo enter his bare-light bulb reception lobby, but within minutes I had handed over to him the peso equivalent of $7 in American money and he was yelling "Ignacio!" at the top of his lungs until, in due course, a surly looking boy showed up to take me to my room. After climbing the four full flights of outdoor fire-escape steps terminating at the building's roof, the kid turned on a flashlight so we could see to step over pipes and other functional impediments until we reached a metal door that opened onto an enclosed flight of stairs that connected to a floor below. At the bottom was a small landing with three doors, mine being one of them.

Inside the room was a sagging bed, a chair and a single window opening onto a dank air shaft. In one corner was open space designated as the bathroom, a bathroom, however, with no hot water or seat on the toilet. This adapted portion of an old factory building now serving as a three-room motel was about as dismal a home away from home as one could possibly imagine, yet I felt incredibly lucky to have found it when I did. It was too dark and perilous, I decided, to try to make it out and back across the roof, so I contented myself with the promise of food and drink sometime after daybreak the next morning. The soggy pillow, I deduced, had rested several heads since its last washing, so I got a shirt out of my bag and spread it over the lump beneath the coverlet, wedged the chair in between the floor and the door-knob to prevent any surprise attack, and with my clothes still on to avoid bodily contact with the dirty bedding, turned off the overhead light bulb and slept like a baby.

In the process of pulling away the next morning I noticed that the flea-bag of my night's repose was lacking a name, so I decided that La Cucaracha (the Cockroach) fit perfectly.

Memories of some of my overnight hosts of years past, places like The Connaught and The Savoy in London, the Hotel George Cinq in Paris (dinner only) and the Negresco in Nice for some reason came to mind, but were quickly dismissed. "Learn to paint well enough and someday maybe you can stay in places like that again," I told myself as I drove along looking for a much needed cup of morning coffee.

West of Guadalajara on the road to Puerto Vallarta is the town of Tequila, where the firewater of the same name has been distilled since the 17th century from a cactus-like plant of the amaryllis family called Agave. Surrounding the town and stretching as far as the eye could see on either side of the highway were the rolling contours of agave plantations, blanketing the earth in a soft faded viridian, while the adjoining roadsides and fields lent borders of bright cadmium-orange wildflowers, all beneath a pure cerulean sky crowned with cobalt. Van Gogh, I felt, would gladly turn over in his grave for a chance to see and paint this uniquely beautiful landscape, a combination of colors of exactly the right hue, so straight from his palette.

Puerta Vallarta was as I expected, overrun with gawking tourists and deadbeat resident loafers. In addition, it was steamingly hot and humid. However, it didn't take long to turn thumbs down on my earlier notion that I might choose to set up housekeeping in one of the outlying villages. The living conditions there, I discovered, were way too primitive even for someone like me receptive to an el cheapo lifestyle. Instead, I focused my attention on finding a place to live right in Puerta Vallarta, and while doing my house searching I stayed in a posada near the ocean in the older part of town.

Staying in the same inn was a dish-faced guy from New York named Melvin who told me that for over a month he had been looking for a house similar to what I had in mind, going out each day by foot and covering a wide area of realtors and notice boards, but to no avail. As in San Miguel, one realtor I spoke with said she could accommodate me with a rental for over $2,000 a month. Another realtor showed me snapshots of an accessible-only-by-boat, thatched roof, open-on-three-sides job. Absolutely perfect for Robinson Cruse, I told him, but for my needs too ridiculously impractical to even consider. He was, however, a very nice young guy with a Mexican mother and an American father and, because of that, easy to communicate with

41

and most helpful. His advice was for me to partially backtrack and look near Guadalajara in the Lake Chapala area where, he assured me, there would be enough options to find what I wanted. Optimistically, yet reluctantly, I decided to take his advice, and the nose of the Blivit was soon headed back in the direction from which it had come only a few days earlier.

A split second has been defined as the amount of time that transpires between the light changing and the guy behind you blowing his horn. My reactions may have been even faster than that when I saw what was coming my way. It was on the road leading back through the mountains when on a sharp, blind *curva peligrosa* there they were; two huge trucks abreast and blocking the entire road. Blue brake smoke and skidding tires was the mode of the Passee, while full speed ahead was clearly the intention of the Passor who was aiming straight for me. There was no shoulder (there never is) and a long, deep drop-off on my side of the highway. For the second time in as many weeks I had no choice but to head for the bushes, this time trying to steer the thin line between staying partly on and getting mostly off the road. As the speeding semi brushed past me, I had enough of a fleeting glimpse to see that it was one of the gargantuan double-trailer chicken transports loaded with thousands of factory-raised birds.

Rocks, thick brush and my foot on the brake all combined to bring the Blivit to its stop, perched on the outside edge of a mountain curve. I quickly jumped out to see if I still had the trailer and if all six tires had remained inflated. Grateful that no apparent damage had been done, I was about to scramble back in behind the wheel when I noticed a single white feather floating down in a slow, lazy zig-zag motion from the thermal that held it aloft. As I pulled back onto the road the facetious thought crossed my mind that what I had just experienced was such a close call that my guardian angel had lost one of his wing feathers.

That brought to mind the Jimmy Stewart movie shown each Christmas in which he is rescued by a novice angel named Clarence. I imagined that if Clarence decided to pay me a visit he might well say, "You've been keeping me awfully busy lately, Bill. It was only a couple of weeks ago that we did the Tennessee Waltz when the trailer spring broke. A few days later we had that crazy 'mountaintop experience' as you call it. And now this – almost being done in by a Mexican chicken truck. Haven't you had enough of the perils of the open road? You came down here to paint! Surely, you can't get into too much trouble doing that. I sure hope you'll hurry up and find a place to live and settle down so I can get some rest."

As I drove on toward Chapala, suddenly and from out of nowhere, the Blivit and I were greeted by a light shower and with it an incredibly beautiful rainbow, the symbol of promise. "A good omen,"I told myself. "Maybe Clarence will soon have his wish."

CHAPTER FOUR
In Search Of The Wild Tortilla

Some twenty-eight miles south of Guadalajara, my right foot began alternating between the accelerator and the brake pedal as the Blivit descended the winding mountain road leading down into the lakeside town of Chapala. My plan was to drive around, look the place over and, in case I encountered any ex-patriot Americans, ask questions about living in the area, and if I liked what I saw and heard, talk to a realtor. Several hours later as the sun was setting, with the western mountains silhouetted against a gold and purple sky, I sat signing lease papers and handing the rental agent the equivalent of $650 for the first month's rent. After nearly a month on the road and living out of a suitcase, I had finally found a place I could call home.

The town of Chapala, I learned, had a population of about thirty thousand, and was the largest of the communities bordering the lake. The wide main street, Avenida Madero, boasted a parkway down its center with trees and decorative plantings and even a fountain. Contiguous to a park with a bandstand was a sizable mercado that offered shoppers a wide variety of fresh produce, flowers, meat, fish from the lake and the usual selections of plastic trivia. On either side of the main thoroughfare I saw a scattering of reasonably attractive Victorian vintage hotels, banks and civic buildings interspersed with numerous mom and pop hole-in-the-wall stores and shops. The entire scene was punctuated by sidewalk cafes with such names as Cafe Paris, Cafe Superior, Beto's Cantina and Nido's, each of them no doubt destined to provide the final resting place for their own permanent contingent of antiquated loafers. I was told that a couple of blocks away on a parallel street, T.S. Eliot holed-up long enough to write one of his books – no one seemed to know which one. Farther along on the main drag was the twin-spired parish church, across from which was a large dance pavilion and beer garden where if, by chance, the devil's work is done on Saturday night it may be easily absolved by merely crossing the street to the church on Sunday morning. One of the town's most attractive features, so far as I was concerned, was that it dozed in the sun on the shores of a sizable lake.

Lake Chapala is a natural, stream-fed, fish-filled body of water roughly fifty miles long by fifteen miles wide. It is almost completely surrounded by mountains that level off enough near their base to provide plenty of flat land for home sites, villages and farming. The climate is claimed to be the world's most perfect and I truly believe it is. As a result of constantly sunny days and temperatures dependably in the mid to upper seventies there is an abundance of lush, tropical flora to enjoy, much of which seems to rely on botanical time clocks as well as weather, so there is an interesting visual change taking place much of the time, resulting in nature providing a wide variety of blooming trees, shrubs and flowers of every description.

The house I rented was located approximately a mile west of the town. It sat on a rise far enough back from the water to offer a splendid view of treetops, a wide stretch of lake and the mountains beyond. Mixed in with palms, orange-flowered tulip trees, lavender jacarandas and crimson, mauve and vermilion bougainvillea were tall, slender ornamental cypresses that added a Mediterranean flavor to the view from my veranda. The two-year-old white stucco and red-tile-roofed tri-level structure was designed to let in plenty of light to an interior design of arched doorways, beamed and vaulted ceilings, tiled floors throughout and generous use of marble in its two-and-a-half bathrooms, all of which came equipped with seats. The furniture was what I would call Mexican casual and was liberally accompanied in each of the rooms with terra cotta jardinieres of decorative plants, some of ceiling height. The overall effect was quite pleasant and I was extremely pleased to have found such a comfortable home situated amid beautiful vegetation and within sight of both water and mountains.

One of the more rewarding aspects of the long journey's end took place within minutes after Jose Luis, my new gardener and handy man (who came with the place), and I carried the last packing box into the house. I practically flew down the twenty-two steps to the street-level carport in my eagerness to unhook the trailer. "Hooray!" I felt like shouting. "No more Blivit!" Now empty and with no load to pull, the trusty Plymouth was back to being called by the name I gave her when I first bought her – The Rabbi Roadster. By the next afternoon she was all tuned up and, as a reward for her yeoman's service, waxed and polished. So far as I could determine, her only casualties consisted of two missing hubcaps that had been stolen in Puerto Vallarta and, as a result of the too heavily loaded low-slung rear end scraping across potholes, rocks and speed bumps, the tailpipe had come loose. As it banged and rattled against the body framework, it sounded for all the world like an angry tap dancer was chasing along behind doing a loud and animated dance; all of which was soon brought to an end by a local shade tree muffler mechanic who, after about an hour's work involving much welding, charged me the unbelievably low price of only $3.50.

I soon had paints and brushes unpacked and, before attending to anything else, went to work on assembling the studio easel and getting ready to do my first painting from my own veranda. The builder of the house must have had me in mind, for this area of my new home with its red tiled floor and covered ceiling made it a perfect indoor/outdoor studio, sheltered from direct sunlight in fair weather and water damage during the rainy season. I decided not to worry about leaving painting equipment and supplies outside the locked front door at night, for it seemed reasonable to assume that any thief with the brains he was born with would be on the lookout for things with an easier cash reward than what was to be found among my painting paraphernalia. It was with a feeling of great reward when, a few days later, I finished my first Mexican painting, a view of the lake with mountains rising up from its western shore.

During the next few weeks there was ample opportunity to become acquainted with the many ways in which life in Mexico differs from what we are accustomed to in the States. To my dismay, I found out rather abruptly that some of the Mexican-made products were Micky Mouse in nature and apt to fail in performance. Early on a Saturday morning I was inserting a full magnum bottle of drinking water, of the type and size used in office water fountains, into the tubular steel frame that permits it to tip for pouring. The sleeve brace, intended to support the heavy glass bottle gave way and fifty or more pounds of hard-edged dead weight came crashing down on my left foot, mutilating some of the toes. Bellowing like a wild bull, plus shouting a string of choice expletives, may well have caused some of the neighbors to sit up in bed. For several minutes I hopped about on my right foot with the injured one gushing blood out through the shoe. I must say, the impressive example of Abstract Expressionism left on the kitchen floor by my bleeding foot would have made Jackson Pollack, the originator of the drip and splatter technique, extremely put out with me, for what he would have charged millions of dollars to do, I had done just as well for free. Somehow I managed to hop the two flights up to my bedroom, cut the toe out of a tennis shoe, hop back down and drive roughly a mile to the indescribably grubby little twenty-four hour store-front clinic.

It was just after eight o'clock when I banged on the door and was admitted by a sleepy-eyed young Mexican doctor nearing the end of his graveyard shift emergency duty. As he examined my foot he asked, "Can you move your fingers?" When I complied by wiggling the fingers of both hands, he exclaimed, "No, no! I mean your foot fingers." From my very scant understanding of the Spanish language I am led to believe that there is no discrepancy in the matter of pronunciation, and that words are consistently pronounced as they are spelled. So, applying this very sensible and logical rule he pronounced *oun* in the word *wound* like the ball of string is *wound*. To say the least, it sounded somewhat ludicrous when be gravely announced, "You have badly wounded foot fingers," to which I felt like replying, "Well, damn it, it's up to you to unwind them."

The operating room measured no more than about eight feet in either direction, with even less than that amount of usable space because of being located in such a position within the building that traffic from the other three tiny rooms must pass through it to get anywhere. As the anesthetic began to take effect I had a chance to more closely observe my surroundings. I was stretched out on an economy size operating table, my head touching the wall at one end and my feet sticking over the edge of the operating table at the other. To my right was a cabinet containing what looked like basic medical supplies while above and behind my head, I had noticed earlier, was a little niche with a figure of Christ on the cross. Over the years the ravaging effect of mildew had turned the originally snow-white plaster surroundings into what presently looked like some underground grotto with unsightly blotches of discoloration ranging from grey to soot-black. But by far the most disturbing part of what I saw were the large and extensive cracks on walls, floor and ceiling. Having had a civil engineering academic background I remembered enough about differential settlement to realize I was witnessing a near critical example of its effects.

Meanwhile Elia, the young nurse, had come on duty. She and I had gotten acquainted from my earlier visits to see the resident internist, Dr. Garcia, about my gout and some intestinal miseries. And, because of what had turned into nearly unbearable earaches, I had had several sessions with Dr. Marin, the specialist in that field. In the past, Elia had always seemed bashful and subdued but now she was most animated, obviously having quite a crush on Dr. Reynosa, the young medic who was carving up my toes and doing a sewing job on open wounds and waiting for overactive blood vessels to calm down a bit. The two of them became so absorbed in the mirth they were sharing that I feared Reynosa might get so unraveled as to inadvertently sew some of my toes together. It took considerable restraint on my part to keep from asking them to please stop playing doctor and nurse long enough to allow my patchwork to be completed. Instead, I once again concerned myself with the differential settlement cracks.

Directly overhead and framed into the ceiling was a grouping of six glass bricks permitting a vague, gauzy view of what appeared to be a very old lady with a reed broom sweeping what was evidently a patio above the operating room where the three of us were clustered. Taking another good look at the gaping fissures traversing walls and ceiling I began to see the overall pattern of potential structural failure. There was no question in my mind but that a stress analysis study would verify that at almost any time a dangerously heavy slab of tired, old, un-reinforced concrete ceiling could suddenly collapse. For some reason the entire situation in which I found myself struck me as being so preposterous as to be downright humorous. So, with Elia and Reynosa chattering away and giggling every other breath, I pulled a ballpoint pen from my shirt pocket and a scrap of paper from another and scribbled out:

> *"Sweeping granny falls through plaster,*
> *Causing operating room disaster.*
> *Doctor, nurse entwined 'neath rubble.*
> *Gringo's foot still gives him trouble."*

Because of the need for daily dressings and, subsequently, a persistently nagging bronchial or amoebic condition, I went back to the clinic on an almost daily basis and was alarmed at the rapidity with which the differential settlement cracks were expanding. I expressed my concern to Dr. Garcia who admitted that he and the rest of the staff were so apprehensive about the possibility of the roof caving in on them that they were soon moving to another building. They sure didn't measure up to the standards of the Mayo Clinic, but they were extremely nice people who had been most kind to me.

Soon after unpacking and getting organized I set about doing what I had moved to Mexico to do. From dawn to dark, seven days a week, health permitting, I painted. The Chapala area, far more than San Miguel, offered a wide and appealing variety of landscape subject matter. The lake, because of its receding shoreline, was disparagingly referred to by some as a mud hole. To me it was just the opposite. The reclaimed terra firma along the shoreline being, for the most part, verdant and pleasing to look at, was made all the more interesting because of the grazing livestock. And, since water, unless overly disturbed, will do its best to take on the color of the sky, the lake was nearly always blue throughout the day, becoming kaleidoscopic in the early morning and again at sunset. The mountains, quite different from our Blue Ridge were, nevertheless, pleasant to behold with their mesquite covered contours rising and falling in a series of deep, irregular ravines fanning out from the crest of each promontory. The farms, homes and villages that rim the lake presented an inexhaustible supply of paintable subjects. My favorite of these was a Japanese nursery where I went to paint on three or four occasions. It was a botanical gold mine that occupied what I would guess to be about thirty acres, stretching from the Jocotepec road to the base of the mountains. I liked going to the nursery, not only because it was peaceful and beautiful, but also because I could paint relatively undisturbed and to me that, in itself, outweighed many other considerations.

Before going to Mexico I had decided that with daily helpings of warmth and sunshine it would be foolish not to paint outdoors, *en plein-air,* as was the mode of the Barbizon painters and later the Impressionists, rather than inside under studio conditions. Also, I was determined not to use a camera but, in the more old-fashioned way, make drawings or watercolor sketches on the spot to serve as studies for larger more serious paintings. The problem with this out-in-the-open approach is that it is virtually impossible to set-up and paint outdoors without attracting a crowd of gawking, sometimes noisy, always distracting onlookers. To me it amounted to an unintentionally rude invasion of privacy and I hated it but, for the sake of being a purist, I reluctantly learned to subject myself to being viewed as something akin to a freak in a sideshow almost every time I went out to paint. Frequently I was more curt and unfriendly than I wanted to be, but otherwise I ran the risk of having unwanted all-day visitors. The kibitzers that got to me the most were expatriate Americans who typically would arrive on the scene and upon seeing a nearly completed canvas of, let's say, a church, with the church itself located directly across the street, would start a conversation by asking, "What are you doing, painting that church?" I always felt like replying, "Hell no, you fathead, I'm painting Goldilocks and the three Bears having luncheon on the grass." It's what I have mentally catalogued as: "Needless Question with Obvious Answer Number One."

On several occasions I had some interesting encounters while painting on-location. One day I drove off in a different direction from my customary route. I set up outside a small village near the lake and was soon painting a most pleasant scene of farmlands with haystacks in the foreground and fields separated by shrubbery and stone fences in the middle distance. The day was gorgeous, there were no kibitzers to annoy me, the painting was going well and altogether I was as happy as if I had good sense. But, in keeping with the saying 'all good things must come to an end', there was in due course a shadow on the ground beside me and I turned to see a rather clean-cut young Mexican intent on watching me paint. I looked at my watch and saw that I had been standing at the easel for several hours and needed a break. With his reasonably good English we were soon in a conversation with me asking him what the village was like and whether it was a good place to live. He said he would soon be leaving it; that it was a "hard" village. I didn't understand his use of the word and asked him to explain. He told me that a lot of drugs were smuggled through the town on their way north and that there had recently been drug-related killings. As he left I wished him well and went back to painting, soon dismissing our conversation from my mind.

A couple of hours later there was an even bigger shadow on the ground. This time I looked around and stood face to face with a tall man who bore a striking resemblance to the British actor, Peter Ustinov. Instead of Needless Question with Obvious Answer Number One he made a couple of intelligent comments about the painting on the easel. The glare from the afternoon sun was making it difficult to continue and I was getting tired from standing so long. I offered to buy him a beer at the cafe and bar that was just across the road from where we stood. He accepted, saying he was going there anyway to meet the man who was to bring him the fish for his two sick pelicans. As we sat at the table drinking the cold and welcome Dos Equis he told me he had a house nearby and had moved to Mexico from Switzerland. In talking about his native land I mentioned the Beaux Rivage in Montreux where some years before when Lisa and I were on the trail of what we thought might be a missing El Greco, I had picked up the tab for a German con man and his girlfriend. At that time it was considered to be one of the finest restaurants in the world, certainly one of the most expensive. This guy said he had been there many times which, if true, let me know that he was no Swiss cotton picker.

As we sat talking he abruptly left the table and was soon exchanging agitated words in Spanish with two men who had entered the bar. Although I couldn't understand most of what was said, I caught just enough words to know it was about fish. Turning his attention back to me he said he was very upset that the fish had not arrived; none yesterday either. He said his pelicans were very sick and would die without fish. After the second beer I was about to tell him goodbye when he said he had to run back to his house and would I mind going along and giving him an opinion on two paintings he owned. I agreed to go take a look. It was an impressive piece of property with a large house, a big kidney shaped swimming pool and a near football-field-sized pond with ducks, geese, goats and burros all hanging around it. Sure enough, standing there on the bank were two pelicans. After attending to whatever it was he had returned for, he rejoined me as I stood looking at the pond and its barnyard menagerie. Pointing to the two pelicans he asked, "What do you think? They look pretty sick, don't they?" I assured him that he was talking to the wrong guy, since all pelicans, except those in flight, look very sick to me.

Driving home I pondered the events of the past few hours. First of all, without any overt effort on my part I had been offered privileged information about drug activity, which could no doubt be easily pinpointed. Secondly, I began to think about how easy and altogether logical it would be to scoop the guts out of fish and put ampules of cocaine or opium in the empty cavity; then deliver them to a runner or dealer with a sick pelican problem who could justify daily commerce in baskets of fish. Better forget about it as far as any local discussion was concerned, I figured, or else the title of this story might be: "A Funny Thing Happened To Me On The Way To The Mortuary." It had all been dumped in my lap so easily and without one iota of effort on my part; and that caused me to wonder if it wouldn't be a good idea to train a few undercover narcotics agents in the use of brush and palette and send them out into the field where drug activity is suspected. Their first assignment might be to investigate "The Case Of The Sick Pelicans."

Some of my kibitzer encounters were of a humorous nature. One morning in the nearby town of Ajijic, I was well along with a rather large canvas when a very portly lady huffed and puffed her way over to where I was standing. After watching the free show for a while she asked, "How did you happen to become an artist?" I was in a jocular mood, so I told her that as an infant my parents had high hopes for me becoming a man of substance when I grew up; a doctor, a lawyer or a successful business man. But, while yet a baby I got dropped on my head, whereupon my father morosely said to my mother, "Well, dear, there's nothing left for him now but to become an artist." The dear lady took me seriously. She remained silent for a while and then gravely shook her head and said, "That's too bad, but there are other options you know. I have a cousin in Omaha and he's not very bright either, but he does quite well as a home products distributor. You might want to consider that as an alternative possibility." It was my turn to remain silent for a while. Eventually, all I could think to say was, "Thank you. That's very kind of you. I'll give it some thought."

Other than brief conversations with onlookers or discussions with the doctors at the clinic, there were days on end when I went from morning to night in almost complete solitude. From time to time I would meet some well meaning individual who would suggest that I make myself available for a hand of bridge, or consider joining the local country club and start playing tennis or golf again. "Thanks, but no thanks," was my answer to all such offers. I had a mission, one mission only – to totally immerse myself in the daily act of painting. Someone tried to convince me that I should join the local Art Association. Again, thanks, but no thanks. My mission was not to talk about painting but to paint. I knew I couldn't afford to fool around and be sociable. I knew that I must, come hell or high water, teach myself to paint well enough to make people want to buy my work. My entire future depended on that one thing. It was a case of root hog, or die.

Lonely holidays came and went, and while others were quite rightly taking time off to celebrate, I painted. On Christmas Day I stayed home and set up an easel on the third-floor sun deck just off my bedroom. About midday as I stood painting a view of the lake, one of the little girls splashing about in the pool a couple of doors away looked up at me, smiled, and said, "Merry Chreestmas, Senor." I smiled back. "Felice Navidad, Senorita," I replied. Those three words were the only ones I spoke that entire day.

Throughout much of the time spent living in Chapala I suffered from what I imagined to be a combination of bronchitis, malaria, walking pneumonia, and a disease I invented in which all the iron in one's system turns to lead and settles in the butt. Dr. Garcia frankly admitted that he was puzzled. One day he asked, "Have you ever had anything like this before?" Vaguely remembering a time years before when I suffered from a siege of symptoms that had left me feeling like death warmed over, I replied, "Yes, once." He was silent for a moment. Then, his face brightening as if a diagnostic breakthrough had at last been achieved, announced, "Well, now you've got it again!" Although Dr. Garcia never did figure out what it was I had come down with, he was, however, able to determine that, whatever it was, it was quite serious. Armed with that knowledge, I gave my condition the new and important sounding medical name of "Enfermedad Indeterminado Serio." There were days when I felt too sick to paint, and I would lie in bed in a pool of sweat. Such was the nature, I told myself, of Enfermedad Indeterminado Serio.

By late winter I had begun to think about vacating at the end of my lease term and taking the paintings that had by then been completed back to the States. It would be best, I decided, if all of the works were framed and ready to show. I needed to find a framer, and I had mentioned this to my next door neighbors, Rosemary and Pieter van Goyen. I was on the veranda painting one afternoon when Rosita, who insisted that she be called Rosemary, suddenly appeared, dressed like she was on her way to a garden party at the Buckingham Palace. She was a tall, willowy woman in her late forties who forever reminded me of either Zazu Pitts or Carmen Miranda (actresses of the 40s and 50s) or, better still, her own zany combination of the two.

Rosemary was Cuban by birth, a chatterbox by nature, and inseparably bonded to the daily practice of personal adornment. Long, gauzy, billowing dresses with dramatic sashes, bows and ribbons; white cotton gloves and wide-brimmed floppy picture hats formed the basis for her uniform of the day, which was always accentuated with a generous display of costume jewelry. She had oversized feet and, as if to prove it, she wore long, pointed, brightly colored shoes that made her feet look even bigger. In a locale where there were still plenty of pack burros trudging along dirt roads, numerous remnants of outdoor plumbing, a place where the inhabitants, regardless of ethnic origin, were not noted for pickiness in the matter of their dress code, it made no sense to get all dressed up each day with nowhere to go and no one to impress once she got there. But dressing up made her happy, so she did it.

"Come on, Beel. We be late," she said emphatically.

"Late for what?" I asked.

"Late for see Xavier. I tell you Sunday we see Xavier Tuesday. Today is Tuesday. You forget?"

"Xavier?" I repeated the name quizzically.

"Xavier is man who make picture frames. I tell him we be there at four. Maybe four-thirty." I looked at my watch. It was four twenty-two.

"Where does he live?" I asked.

"Beyond Ajijic. Is quite far." She was certainly right. It sounded like about a ten mile drive, so we would be late. I wiped the wet paint from the brushes I had been using, took the nearly finished landscape off the easel and placed it just inside the wide arched doorway of the living room, not bothering to lock the house.

"Will Pieter come with us?" I asked. But the answer was obvious. A quick glance across the shrubbery-lined walkway that separated our two houses showed Pieter, her former boss and now her husband, Dutch ex-patriot, American middle-management retiree, spending the afternoon in his accustomed mode: stretched out in the hammock on their veranda absorbed in a paperback, a lit cigarette dangling from one hand and a bottle of Corona beer within easy reach of the other. "Don't get into any trouble, you two. I'll stay here and guard the property," he called out, waving the beer bottle in a farewell salute as Rosemary and I descended the twenty-two steps to where our cars were kept in the street level carports.

The road from Chapala through Ajijic had its rough spots and there were places where it was being repaired. With cars pulling in and out the going was slow. But once past the village we again picked up speed and were making good time until we were abruptly slowed down by a big double-trailer semi blocking the right-hand lane. The driver had his left turn signal flashing, so I dutifully fell in behind him although the passing lane was clear.

"Pass him. Pass him, Beel," Rosemary said authoritatively. "In Mexico, big trucks like him is tell you is O.K. to pass by making left turn signal."

"No," I said. "Where I come from turn signals mean the driver intends to turn. We'll stay put until he turns left."

"No, Beel, no. Is different here. In Mexico if they want you to pass, like is now, they make the signal to tell you is O.K. Is different here."

She and Pieter had lived in Mexico for over four years and I had been in the country only a few short months. Pieter had recently given her their older model gas guzzler and purchased a shiny new compact for himself. So she did drive her own car. Maybe there was reason to believe she knew what she was talking about. Anyway, the passing lane was clear. My what-the-hell, let's-give-it-a-go attitude succeeded in getting us about halfway past when the sudden sound of airbrakes and a towering wall of steel rapidly cutting across the left hand lane told me it was time to hit the brakes. As I did so, a quick flash of reason suggested that the

Rabbi Roadster might well be side swiped by the second trailer if I stayed on the road. In an instant we were off the highway and onto the dirt, our roadside entry accompanied by a loud bang as the left rear tire blew out.

As we wobbled to a stop we were greeted by a series of other unaccustomed sounds. A blue-eyed goat tethered to a nearby tree decided it was time to bleat. Bantam hens clucked away, scratching the dirt and kicking up chicken goodies as their half-pint lord and master flapped his wings and crowed. The resident cow, thin and Rhone colored, turned her head in our direction, made a gasping sound and then produced a long and soulful moo, while the confused young dog tied to a house post did his initial duty by bursting forth with a couple of tentative woofs, only then to decide it was more fun being friendly, and during the remainder of our unscheduled visit he occupied his time by wagging his tail and begging to be recognized. The Rabbi Roadster had come to rest on a somewhat rural homestead consisting of a main shanty and several secondary shanties. Other than the small coterie of domestic animals, it appeared as if no one was at home to invite us in for tea.

"Are you all right?" I inquired of Rosemary who appeared to be so unnerved that, for once, she seemed at a loss for words.

"Why you drive like crazy person, Beel! Look what you do. You have crush-ed my hat." She was clutching her hat in both hands and had twisted it out of shape. She held it up for me to see.

"Well, tomorrow you'll just have to wear another one." I replied. "And, I might add, thanks to your driving advice, you have crush-ed my tire. Now I've got to get busy and change the damned thing."

While tightening the lug nuts on the spare, a bantam hen came our way cackling and carrying on in a manner one might expect if a chicken her size had just given birth to an ostrich egg. Rosemary kept playing with the radio, from time to time joining in on the vocal part of any song that struck her fancy. Her off-key and out of sync accompaniment led me to believe that my ears would like it better if I engaged her in conversation.

"Do you like eggplant, Rosemary?"

"Si, why you ask?"

"Have you ever seen a walking egg plant?" I continued.

"Walking eggplant? No. Course not. Everyone know is not possible for eggplant to walk. That silly!"

"It's not silly. Look," I said pointing to the little hen. "Here, right before our very eyes is a genuine Mexican walking egg plant. I'm not saying she's an eggplant, Rosemary. I'm saying she's an egg plant; two words. The kind of plant where things are made, like cement plant or power plant. She makes eggs, so she's an egg plant. Don't you get it?"

She sighed with weary exasperation. "No, Bill. Believe me. That is not eggplant. That is chicken."

It was well past five-thirty by the time we got to Xavier's house. His wife told us that he had gone out just before lunch and had not returned. No, she didn't know where he was, but we were welcome to wait.

As I pulled the car back into the its carport, Rosemary remarked, "Is very rude for him to be late for a so important meeting. I tell him that when I see him," ignoring the fact that we ourselves had been over an hour late.

Pieter had not budged an inch from the time we had left except to light more cigarettes and open more beer. His face expressed amusement as Rosemary indignantly launched into the story about the awful truck driver who should be arrested for having caused so much trouble and how poor Beel had nearly wreck-ed his car. After she had gone in the house, Pieter said with a chuckle, "If you want to live a long and healthy life, Bill, for God's sake, don't take any more driving advice from Rosie. It's true that sometimes the Mexican truckers use their left-turn signal to indicate that it's O.K. to pass. But most of the time it means just what you would expect: that they're about to turn left. The trouble is, there's no way to know for sure which is which. As for Rosie, I'd have to say that after Lourdes and Fatima, the next most important miracle is her own survival in spite of what may well be the world's craziest driving when she's behind the wheel of a car. What about a beer?"

"No thanks, Pieter. The last one was on you. It's my turn. Anyway, I'm in the mood for something a little more powerful. A few days ago I bought a jar of Mexican jalapeno peppers, so let's go to my house and I'll mix a pitcher of one of my famous Hell Fire and Damnation Martinis."

He called to Rosemary to tell her we were going next door.

"Wait a momento," she said, coming back onto the veranda holding what looked like a large cookbook, fancy enough for a coffee table. "Here, Beel, I want to show you something." She opened the book to a double spread picturing an array of vegetables in full color. With one hand she held the book and with the other she pointed to what looked like a purple gourd and announced in a most informative tone of voice, "This, Beel, is eggplant. You see, is not same as chicken."

"Thanks, Rosemary. I'll try to remember the difference," I said as Pieter and I headed to my place to enjoy my favorite jalapeno pepper recipe.

It was springtime up north, the days were getting longer and in a few weeks it would be time to pack up and move out. On the third try I managed to succeed in having a meeting with Xavier. He was a pleasant young man who appeared to be filled with the spirit of willing cooperation. For starters, I asked him to make six frames to my size and design specifications.

"No problem, Beel," he assured me. Yes, yes, he understood everything perfectly. Don't worry. Yes, they would be ready for me in one week, next Wednesday, to be exact, all of them fine sanded and ready for me to gild.

I went back to pick up the frames on the date promised. Xavier was, as before, smiling from ear to ear. The frames? Well, he hadn't been able to start on them yet, but don't worry, he would have them for me Monday. When I finally did get my hands on the six frames, none was made from the type of molding I had requested and three were the wrong size, forcing me to alter the size of my paintings so they would fit his frames - a bit bass ackwards, to say the least. After poking around and learning that he was about the only game in town for custom-made frames, I gave him an order for ten more frames, this time insisting that he write down my verbal instructions in his own handwriting so he would be sure to get everything right. It didn't matter. As before, he got it all wrong and was five days late to boot. But instead of being embarrassed or chagrined he simply ignored my obvious displeasure and with a happy and enthusiastic expression exclaimed, "They look good, don't they Beel! Didn't I do a good job!" Working with this guy, I decided, was like trying to nail a custard pie to the wall.

To my great relief and as a result of what, in my opinion, amounted to a minor miracle, he did manage to perform pretty much as promised on the final batch, so that I had the last of the frames in hand barely in time to get them gilded before I started packing. Because of everything from gout to foot-finger mutilation to prolonged sieges of Enfermedad Indeterminado Serio, my painting productivity was well below original expectations, and in this regard I was somewhat disappointed. But, unless I had contracted some incurably malignant disease, the physical drawbacks would be only transitory and therefore not worth worrying about.

I remembered how an elephant was reported to have chided a mouse for his utter worthlessness, scolding him by saying, "You can't push over buildings. You can't pull up trees by their roots. You can't shake bridges. You can't do any of the things I can do."

The little mouse pondered for a while and then replied, "Yes, I know. You're right. But, well, you see, I've been sick!" That, I decided, was partially my excuse.

The important thing was that from the very first day of standing out in an open field, brushes in hand, canvas on the easel, a dome of clear blue sky above and the whole world out in front, I knew without question that I was doing what I should be doing and, because of that, I felt an inner satisfaction that goes with doing what one is doing by choice rather than necessity. Picking up speed, developing skill, making more painterly judgments would require time and a lot of hard work. But those were details. The thirty-two canvases, all of them in hand-crafted and gilded frames that I would be taking back to the States were, in a sense, a certificate of having passed the freshmen tests. I knew that insofar as the quality of my work was concerned I had turned a vital corner and that the path ahead would be on firmer ground as time went on. "Now," I told myself, "instead of saying, 'I'm going to be a painter,' I could truthfully say, 'I am a painter.'" Unless hard pressed to do so, I would simply neglect to add, "But one with an awful lot yet to learn."

It was Blivit time again. As I went about the job of packing paintings in either the back of the Rabii Roaster or the trailer and, with Jose Luis's help, carrying the items to be left behind to their storage space in his tool shed, I mentally reviewed the past seven and a half months spent in Mexico. Moving to Mexico had been a good decision. The perfect climate had made it possible for me to paint out in the open day after day, or at least on those days not spent in sick bay. Lack of friends, except for Rosemary and Pieter, had made for a lonely life, but a far more productive one than would have been the case otherwise. Days and evenings of feeling sequestered and alone, except for the occasional beer or Hell Fire and Damnation Martini with Pieter, had at times drawn heavily on my resolve and determination to keep plugging ahead on my own. The thing I missed most, I had decided, was the stimulation that would come from being around others on the same path; not just arty people, who can be found in abundance most anywhere, but practicing, professional painters devoting their lives to painting as a means of earning a living. I had improved enormously during the time spent in Mexico and had reached a point at which I needed to start swimming in deeper water.

There was an obvious solution. France was the answer. Those painters whose work I admired the most were the French (and American) Impressionists. In France I would find the kind of stimulation I was looking for. Driving through the South on the way down from Virginia I had seen a sign in a shop window which read, "If you can't run with the big dogs, stay on the porch." I didn't want to stay on the porch. I wanted to run with the big dogs. It was becoming clearer by the minute that when I got back to the States there was only one sensible thing to do. Pack up all my paints and brushes and head for France.

CHAPTER FIVE
The Cat's In The Apple Tree, N'est-Ce Pas?

My first introduction to France, or rather the French language, occurred at the tender age of nine. My mother had a dear friend, a Scots woman named Mrs. Murdoch who, in younger years, had spent considerable time in France and professed to be fluent in the language. So mother and Mrs. Murdoch contrived that my older sister Polly and I go to Mrs. Murdoch's home three afternoons a week and be tutored in French. Well, as seemingly good ideas of this sort often work out, it proved to be an almost total waste, especially so since Mrs. Murdoch was deaf as a post and, in spite of cupping her hand to her better ear, she understood only a fraction of what Polly and I shouted back at her when asked to recite. Regardless of our answers, Mrs. M. would respond with her habitual mannerism of first sucking in her breath in a gasping sound quickly followed by, "Yes, yes, yes, quite so, jolly good." About all I gained from those afternoon sessions was learning to count up to ten, names of the basic colors, how to order coffee with or without cream and sugar, and asking the waiter to bring me either a bottle or a glass of red or white wine. This latter was pretty heady stuff for a kid of nine still mostly in knee pants. Along with it all, this somewhat eccentric lady taught us sentences of her own composition which, because we had no text to follow, Polly and I were expected to learn by rote. For some crazy, unexplainable reason, one of these sentences remained stuck in my mind years later: "*Regardez, Monsieur, le chat est dans la pommiere.* (Look, sir. The cat's in the apple tree.)" It's hard to imagine a more useless sentence to remember for one who would years later have need of speaking French. Fortunately, my many trips to London and from there on to France for both business and pleasure, had left me with a rudimentary understanding of the language, so I felt sure that once in France I could survive and make my wants known.

While still in Mexico, I had called Fogelsville, Pennsylvania to tell my old friend, Charlie Dent, that I was coming back to the U.S. enroute to France. Charlie invited me to stay with him for a couple of weeks before taking off for Europe. With a fairly large house and a big barn and other outbuildings there was plenty of space available for storing the paintings I had brought back from Mexico as well as a parking space for the Rabbi Roadster. Because of my hermit-like, penny-pinching life in Mexico devoted entirely to painting, I had managed to stay within a tight budget. I reasoned that if I followed that same formula in France, I could afford to live there for four entire months, June 1st through September 30th. Whether or not I could stay within the same restricted budget in France remained to be seen.

It was raining cats and dogs when the plane landed in Paris, causing the long taxi queue outside the terminal to move forward slowly. In the process of waiting my turn I managed to get drenched from head to toe. Finally, a cab to Montparnasse Station, but then another long wait in the ticket line. With all my past visits to France I had never been to the Brittany part of the country. The guidebooks had good things to say about Nantes, touting it as the Paris of Brittany. So it seemed a sensible idea that this small city should be my first destination. One of my guidebooks described Nantes's historically important royal chateau, famed as the seat of the dukes and duchesses of Brittany, and recommended a small and inexpensive hotel directly across the street from the palace grounds. I decided to make it my first stop.

As the express train sped through the French countryside near the banks of the Loire River, I was overcome by a strange feeling of deja vu. Scene after scene was remarkably familiar, yet I sensed that somehow there was a missing ingredient. At last I realized that I was looking at settings that were the subject of numerous paintings by American expatriates such as Daniel Ridgeway Knight and Charles Sprague Pearce or their French counterparts, Jules Breton and Jules Bastian-Lepage. Missing were the nineteenth century peasant girls in full skirts, Breton caps and wooden shoes, all so typical of paintings of that genre. With nose to the window, even with the unrelenting rain, it was good to be in this special part of the world, so favored by many of the great painters of the last century. A rare privilege had come my way, an opportunity I was determined not to take lightly.

In the process of negotiating the few steps between taxi and hotel entrance, I became as thoroughly doused as if someone had sprayed me with a garden hose. In this half-drowned condition I managed, in between wheezes and sneezes, to register for a room, wishing that Madame LaFarge, the nervously well-meaning young owner could speak even a few words of English, as she seemed completely incapable of understanding anything I had to say in French. She assigned me number nine, a tiny room at the end of the hall on the walk-up third floor. It was, to say the least, somewhat Spartan, with only bed, table, and chair, which left barely enough room on the floor for my oversized luggage. On the plus side was the fact that there was a bathroom, and while not much larger than a phone booth it was, nonetheless, still a bathroom. The floor-to-ceiling window occupied the entire exterior wall and invited a superb close-up view of the most regal chateau in all of Brittany. But a quick glance in that direction showed the rain to be so persistently heavy that even the ducks afloat in the moat appeared in ill temper because of it.

As I closed the wooden shutters I knew without doubt that the grand view from my window would need to wait to be appreciated by some future occupant of cubicle number nine. For a Gallic version of Enfermedad Indeterminado Serio had struck again, this time without the for-better-or-for-worse, till-death-do-us-part involvement of Dr. Garcia and staff. I had come down with a severe case of multiple symptoms to which, in honor of my French surroundings, I named, *"Malaise Majeur Extraordinaire."* For the next four days I remained in the small closet of a room that now served as my infirmary, its interior darkened by the tightly closed outside wooden shutters and the heavy inner draperies. With great effort I got out of bed only for trips to the bathroom. The injunction always advocated by physicians came to mind: Drink lots of water and stay in bed. Anyone who has ever tried to do this is soon struck by the absolute impossibility of carrying out two such contradictory pursuits at the same time.

Each morning my fidgety young landlady would knock on the door and ask if I was all right. I would respond by telling her from my side of the door that I did not need anything, that I still was not feeling well but nevertheless, O.K. I suspect that the only portion of my answer that she understood was the expression, O.K. for it seems to enjoy universal acceptance.

Her daily inquiry caused me to remember a time when, many years before, I was briefly interned in a twenty-eight man ward in St. Thomas Hospital in London. The nurses, called sisters, attended to their various duties from a station in the center of the ward. My bunk was at one end of the long narrow room and directly across from that of a man whose face I never saw:

a Captain Mumby. Three or more times a day a young cockney orderly with the food cart or tea caddy would stop at the foot of Mumby's bed and make the same high pitched inquiry: "Captain Mumby, are you all right, sir?" A deep voice, always sounding a bit impatient, I thought, would answer: "Yes, yes, I'm all right."

Time after time, it was always the same: "Are you all right?" "Yes, yes, I'm all right." After several days of the same routine, the orderly was making his breakfast rounds and appeared at the foot of the bed as usual. In a bright and cheerful manner he inquired: "And how are you this morning, Captain Mumby, sir?" No response. This time, reaching down to shake the patient's foot and in a slightly apprehensive tone, "Captain Mumby. Captain Mumby, sir. Are you all right?" Complete silence. Then, in a treble voice that rang throughout the ward, "Sistah! Sistah! I think we've lost Captain Mumby." It now occurred to me as I lay suffering in this tiny French hotel, staffed only by its owner, if Mme. LaFarge might wonder, with some trepidation, if I was to become her Captain Mumby.

After four days with no food and lying on bedclothes soaking wet from my own feverish perspiration, I decided it was time to follow old Horace Greely's advice and go west. As I was paying the bill, my ever jittery young hostess wore what I interpreted to be an obvious expression of relief upon seeing that I was at last on my feet and leaving. I was every bit as glad as she that I hadn't Mumbied out on her, so to speak. In an attempt to be polite and show interest she asked where I was headed next. "Quimper," I told her (Pronounced Cam-pear) with the accent on the last syllable). She didn't understand, and I couldn't seem to make her understand even though I repeated the name several times, as well as adding that it was a city in the west of Brittany. After fumbling through luggage I eventually produced a map and pointed to Quimper. "Ah, Quimper!" she exclaimed, pronouncing the word exactly as I had been doing for the past five minutes. Such is the lot of the linguistic dummy who, even after many trips to France, has gotten little further than "The cat's in the apple tree" stage of development.

My eventual destination was the tiny village of Plogoff located near the western tip of the Breton peninsula. I knew absolutely nothing about the place and was going there only because the guide book listed the name and address of a small hotel and described it as offering the attractive combination of being on the ocean and having clean rooms and decent food at inexpensive prices. It sounded like my kind of a place. From the map, Plogoff appeared to be about twenty or so miles west and south of Quimper. Since the train terminated at Quimper I would need to connect with a bus in order to get there. The schedule showed about a two and a half hour interval between the train's arrival and the bus's departure, enough time to permit poking around a bit in a town whose name was familiar to me because of the character and high quality of the beautifully hand painted ceramic faience that's been produced there since the seventeenth century.

Quimper is a charming little city set like a gem within a rim of gentle hills, steeped in Breton history and legend, seat of kings, dukes and bishops since the Middle Ages and site of the largest Gothic edifice in Brittany. For all of this and more it rightfully deserves its place in the sun. Upon seeing the old city for the first time, I marveled at the Gothic tracery of the twin spires of Saint Corentin's Cathedral, was fascinated by the antiquity of the eleventh century nave in the Church of Notre Dame, and succumbed to the age-old appeal still present along the labyrinth of narrow winding streets, alleys, lanes and squares, each flanked with their storybook half-timber houses complete with corbels, beams and overhangs reminiscent of lives and events that took place there on center stage many centuries ago.

My heavy, unwieldy luggage was right where I had left it on the sidewalk in front of the bus station. Near it sat a pretty young French girl. She looked up and smiled as I approached.

"Bonjour, Mademoiselle."

"Bonjour, Monsieur. Are you English?"

"No, as American as they come," I answered as the bus pulled up to the curb. The door opened and she at once began to pick up the heaviest of my three pieces. "No, no, no, I protested. Perhaps this smaller one. You are most kind and I thank you very much," I said, feeling a trifle guilty that I welcomed her help as much as I did.

We sat next to each other and immediately fell into an easy conversation. She, a college student, had hopes of becoming a writer. In answer to my question, she told me that Emile Zola was her literary idol and seemed pleased when I mentioned that he had been a good friend of my favorite painter, Claude Monet. Some half-hour later the bus pulled up in front of her family home, a Breton style white stucco house overlooking the sea. She walked several steps toward the house, then turned and blew me a kiss. "Not too bad a day," I said to myself, "for a so-called senior citizen (ugh!) just out of bed after a very trying siege of *Malaise Majeur Extraordinaire*."

As the big Citroen bus snaked its way along the coastal road, I couldn't help but wonder what on earth lay in store for me. I had made no specific plans before leaving the States. All I knew was that I wanted to go to France and paint. Not for reasons of self indulgence, but something akin to what a devout Christian must feel in wanting to visit the Holy Land. Impressionism, the style of painting I had always admired the most, was born and nurtured in France. Something within me seemed to be urging me to go to the source of it all as the next step in my development as a painter. Like a person who claims to be called to enter the ministry or priesthood, I felt convinced that it was something I had to do. The fact that I could ill afford to survive financially for four months in a country noted for high living expenses would just need to be dealt with in one way or another. The old saying, "God takes care of fools and drunks," might need to be expanded, in my case, to include "and cash-poor itinerant painters poking about in foreign lands."

The bright June sun had finally chased away the low-swept seaborne clouds and now the tip of Brittany was bathed in friendly warmth. My ailment, whatever it was, had failed to gain a permanent foothold and had beaten a cowardly retreat. For the first time in almost a week, my stomach was begging for some solid food and good French wine. In fact, the world was beginning to take on its former luster and, once more, it felt good just to be alive. Best of all, nearly four months of painting in France lay ahead; a painter's dream waiting to be fulfilled.

Before leaving for France I had learned from Bill Woodward that he would be in Brittany for the first half of the summer. He said he had put together a group of Americans who had signed up for his painting classes and that they would headquarter in the big chateau owned by his long-time friend, Philippe. During my short walking tour of Quimper I bought a map of Finesterre, the western part of Brittany. I unfolded the map and studied it. The chateau, I saw, was no more than twenty miles from where I was staying. I was soon on the phone talking with Bill Woodward.

"What the hell are you doing in Plogoff?" Bill wanted to know.

"Beats me, I said, Everybody's got to be somewhere. Why? Where should I be?"

"That's up to you, but Plogoff is halfway out to sea and pretty isolated. Tomorrow morning is my mid-week morning off – no class until two-thirty in the afternoon. I'll come pick you up around ten. In the meantime, I'll talk to Philippe. We should be able to find a place for you here. I think you might be a lot happier being around other painters. It's a good group this year. We work hard, but we have a lot of fun doing it. Glad you're in France, my friend. See you tomorrow at ten."

It had rained again during the night, but by the time Bill arrived with Dandy and Lucille,his two golden retrievers, the skies were again clear and there was promise of a warm spring day ahead. Although it was still early June, Bill's clean-cut features had already acquired a healthy, tanned look from painting outdoors.

"So, have you given up on Mexico?" He asked as we drove the winding road that cut through age-old farm fields and linked together the ancient villages along the way. His rich, modulated voice and easy style of talking invited the pleasant conversation that was taking place between good friends.

"I'm not quite sure," I answered. "In many regards I had the ideal set-up in a place where the weather was perfect for painting. I lived in a nice house, and there were certain other advantages. But I may not go back because…"

"Let me guess," he interrupted. "You may not go back because you found it boring. There was no cross-painter dialogue. It was not stimulating enough to sustain your interest as a painter."

I looked at him in surprise. "You are absolutely, one hundred percent right. How did you know all that?"

"Years ago, I went there to paint. It wasn't long before I threw in the towel and headed for home after what amounted to something of a painting siesta. As I left, I swore that I would never, ever look another tortilla in the face." We both laughed. Then, more seriously, Bill asked, "What are your present plans? How will you spend your time in France?"

"Frankly, I don't yet know enough about what my options are to have any plans, but I do have an objective," I replied. "My objective is to paint, and when I've finished doing that I'll just paint some more. Exactly how and where I end up doing all this painting is anybody's guess. One problem I'm faced with right off the bat is the matter of having more luggage than can easily be transported. I intend to stay almost four months, until the first of October, so I packed enough clothing to accommodate changes in weather. Between basic day-to-day necessities and painting supplies and equipment, there must be seventy or eighty pounds of stuff I'm lugging around."

"I believe you," Bill said. "Just helping lift that big bag into the trunk is enough to give a guy a double hernia."

I continued, "It's entered my mind that one solution might be to rent a small boat and live aboard it while drifting along on the Seine or the Oise or the Loire, using the boat as a floating studio in the manner of Monet or Charles Francois Daubigny. What do you think of that idea?"

"Not a hell of a lot," Bill said without hesitation. "Both the guys you're talking about had boats that were too small to live on. We know from Manet's painting of Monet's boat that it wasn't much more than a rowboat with a canopy. Also, back then, for peanuts you could hire some lackey to pole the thing through the water. Today, with fuel in France costing between four and five dollars a gallon, traveling any distance in a boat that's big enough to live on would eat a hole in you pocket in no time. I think I'd forget that one if I were you. You would probably be better off buying a car. Have you considered that?"

"No I haven't. Wouldn't that cost me an arm and a leg?"

"Maybe. Maybe not. Let's talk to Philippe about it. He's got connections. You never know, he may be able to find you some cheap wheels so you can get around on your own. First of all, you'll need a place to stay. How much can you afford to pay for monthly rent?"

"As little as possible," I said. "I was paying only six hundred and fifty dollars a month in Mexico for a nicely furnished three- bedroom house. I know I can't get much here for that kind of money, but that's about as far as my budget will stretch."

"You're dead right," Bill said. "You'll be lucky to find a doghouse here for six hundred dollars a month. Especially during the next few months when this entire area is filled wall to wall with summer tourists. There's a slim chance that Madame Bouchet might have something. I'll call her when we get to the chateau."

"Who's Madame Bouchet?" I asked.

"She's an old gal who owns a waterfront saloon. She lives above the bar and she's been known to rent, from time to time, a small apartment on the third floor. The trouble is, it has no private entrance, so a tenant has to walk through the main part of the house in order to get to it. For that reason, she's a little touchy about who she rents it to. If it's available and if you can pass muster with her, it could be an ideal pad for you. Her place is right in the middle of all the nightlife along the waterfront strip. The best part is, there's plenty to paint within walking distance. I'll give her a call right away."

"That sounds great, and thanks in advance," I said. "But for the immediate future, what do you propose I do about a roof over my head? It seems to rain here rather frequently and some type of shelter might come in handy."

"Well, at present, there's not even temporary room at the chateau," he said. "Philippe has leased out the entire east wing, and upstairs remodeling is under way in much of the remaining portion. Do you remember a guy named Fred Baker? He remembers meeting you."

"Yeah, I think so," I said. "Isn't he a doctor who owns a chain of clinics?"
"That's the one," Bill said. "He just sold out for something like a hundred million bucks and is over here killing time waiting for his wife to join him, but she keeps postponing her arrival. Philippe owns a cluster of time-share units on the same property as the chateau. Benning is occupying one of them, a three-bedroom apartment. He says you're welcome to sack out in one of the bedrooms for a few days. Meanwhile, Philippe has asked Michel, a young guy who lives on the property, to clean up the extra bedroom in his cottage. You can stay there until we can find you your own permanent place.

"And, while you're living on the premises you might as well paint with the group. You'll meet some good painters. About half are professionals, in one form or another, including a portraitist, a watercolorist, an illustrator who wants to learn landscape painting, and then there's Susan, a woman who's here in a master-of-fine-arts program. Several others are advanced amateurs who probably could turn professional if they wanted to. Mostly, they're people in their thirties, forties and fifties. We were just now talking about the lack of any like-minded painters to rub elbows with while you were living in Mexico. Well, you'll find all the cross-painter stimulation you can handle right here. So, after you've checked in at Fred Benning's, put together whatever painting gear you'll need and be ready after lunch to leave on a field trip with the rest of the gang. It's intensive painting. We don't fool around. There's no better way to make progress. You're my friend. It won't cost you anything. It's a chance you shouldn't miss."

"Thanks Bill," I said. "You're a good man and a good friend. Believe me; I appreciate your kind offer. And I'll gladly accept your help in finding me a place to stay, since you don't make a business out of locating rental properties for friends. But you do earn your living as a highly skilled and widely esteemed professional artist and teacher, Professor Woodward. I have always felt that it is never right to accept from a person, free of charge, that which he earns his living by doing. I'd like to say yes, and fall in with the troops after lunch, but I can't afford to pay and I'm not a free-loader, so I gotta' say no. But, Bill, I sure do thank you for your generous invitation."

Bill told the two dogs to settle down and quit barking at whatever it was they were excited about and then said, "Look, my friend, don't be silly. I would never have gotten to where I am if, along the way, a lot of people hadn't helped me. If I make it a little easier for you to learn to paint better, further down the line at some future date maybe you can help somebody else. That's the way it works. You've chosen a tough assignment, Bill, starting out late in life from an almost standing start and betting everything on the slim chance that you can make a living as a landscape painter. Normally, I'd say that the odds for a guy in your position succeeding would be about equal to that of a snowball in hell. But, from what I've seen of your work, you do have some talent and that helps, but beyond that you seem determined to put forth all the time and energy and focus it takes to be a winner, so you'll probably end up doing O.K., and I hope you do. But still, no matter how you slice it, you're off on a perilous journey. You're not a kid anymore, Bill, and you probably feel the need to make up for lost time. If as many as a dozen well-meaning teaching professionals, like me, offered to help you, gratis, it would make all kinds of sense for you to simply say, 'Thanks, pal. You've got a deal. I accept.'"

I turned in my seat and extended my right hand. During the handshake I solemnly said, "Thanks, pal. You've got a deal. I accept with much gratitude. You're dead right. I need all the help I can get and I guess I shouldn't be too up-tight and stuffy about my inability to pay for it right now. With about the same chance that one has of winning the lottery, if I should ever make a name for myself as a painter I'll make sure you're given full credit for your part in helping it to happen."

A little over a mile beyond the last of the villages, Bill turned off the main road and onto the grounds of the estate granted to the Marquis de Ploeuc by King Louis XIV, still in the hands of the same family after nearly three centuries. An avenue of ancient trees led past the overseer's stone cottage and, after a slight curve to the left, we came into full view of Chateau Gilguiffin, stately and serene in its park-like setting. As Bill swung the car down the gravel driveway leading toward the imposing edifice we were about to enter, he extended his arm in a sweeping gesture while wearing a contrived expression of gravity and, in a tone of voice intended to express solemn profundity, he declared: "Be it ever so humble, there's no place like home."

"Yes, I see what you mean. And since you've been coming here every summer for the past twenty-five years, it's evident that your life's not been an easy one," I said consolingly.

As the car came to rest in the rear courtyard separating the chateau from the long chain of outbuildings that at one time housed the living quarters, stables, granaries and workshops essential to the chateau's household and its retinue, Philippe's dog Charlotte, a big mahogany colored Braque Allemande with oversized feet came loping out to greet Lucy and Dandy, giving me a cursory sniff and a tail-wag of approval while she was at it. Bill looked up toward the top floor of the largest of the out-buildings.

"From about midway out to the end is the space we use for a studio," he said pointing. "We keep our canvases, easels and painting supplies up there. And on rainy days that's where we paint. After lunch we'll pick you out a little area that you can call your own and a place where you can leave things when you're not out in the field painting. I have quarters here in the chateau. But all the painters are staying at an auberge several miles from here. They get shuttled back and forth in the two vans we've rented for field trips and will show up a little after two, and by two-thirty we'll be on our way for an afternoon of painting. Sound like fun?"

"Sure does," I replied. "Thanks again for including me."

"Well, come on, let's go inside; it's nearly lunchtime," Bill said, opening the door that led us through the family entrance and the few steps down onto the massive stone slab floor of a large and antiquated kitchen. A round wooden work table of sturdy build occupied the center of the room. Cupboards and cabinets were spaced around the walls and, in one corner, boards with hanging pegs held up oversized cooking utensils. A lofty ceiling supported by heavy, rough-hewn timbers accounted for the overhead. I followed Bill out into a hall and on to the room where we would find Philippe, Bill's longtime close friend and lord of the manor, only, in this case, not just a manor house but a large and important chateau.

The centerpiece of the room we entered, which I soon learned was Philippe's "headquarters", was the huge walk-in fireplace in which an oversized log crackled, hissed and sputtered. Charlotte had somehow gotten there ahead of us and lay sprawled on the ledge behind the fire, from time to time making strange groaning noises. High above the mantle, securely fastened to its wooden shield, hung the head of a ferocious wild boar, its tusks protruding angrily, as if determined to protect the hearth below. On a low, square coffee table in front of the fire were stacks of magazines, journals and art books of French, British and American origin. Twin lounge chairs, made all the more comfortable from well-seasoned usage, and a long divan of leather, smooth and soft as a baby's bottom, formed a grouping around the table. A full-height trestle-based library table ran the length of the divan's backside; more books, more magazines, a beautiful epergne of Quimper faience and an enormous silver serving tray made one end of the tabletop their home. Beyond the butler's cart with its array of whiskey and liqueur bottles, past the double doors leading to the great hall, my eyes focused on the grouping of small paintings and memorabilia interspersed with armoires, bookcases, bombe chests and other period furnishings, then continued round the corner and along the stretch of the three foot thick exterior wall with its deep-set casement windows until, at the far end, the room terminated with an oval table of generous size suitable for private dining. To the left of the table and beyond the fireplace, Philippe sat at his desk studying what looked like a ledger pad. From us having met once before, I remembered him as a trim man of military bearing with grey-green eyes that twinkled when he laughed. As I recalled, he especially enjoyed making risqué remarks in the presence of women who, for some reason, seemed to not be offended by his colorfully French accented naughty-boy language and witty repartee, usually accompanied with a devilish grin.

"My friend," he said, smiling broadly upon looking up and seeing me, then rising from his chair and coming forward. "Welcome to Guilguiffin," he continued, as we stood shaking hands. Then, in a tone of mock sincerity, "Where are the women? When I see you at the Virginia Gold Cup races two years ago you are with beautiful women. I hope you bring them with you to France."

"They're not with me now, Philippe, but I'm sure they will be coming over soon. When the word got out that I was on my way to visit you, there were so many of them, including some perfect strangers, all kicking and screaming and trying to get on the plane that there wasn't going to be enough room left for the regular passengers, and so the airline…".

"Hi, Lewis. That sounds like a crock if I ever heard one."

I turned to see Fred Baker who had just entered the room and was in the act of putting a bottle of scotch on the butler's cart. "As Bill may have told you, I have an extra bedroom, and until Jennie comes over a few days from now, you're welcome to stay there," he said, filling a glass half full, setting the bottle down, stepping forward and shaking hands in a friendly manner.

"Thanks, Fred. That's most kind of you," I said. "I promise not to be a bother, and to get my self out and into a place of my own at the first opportunity. I understand from Bill that congratulations are in order, that you sold the chain of clinics and are now a gentleman of leisure."

"Yep, he answered." Then, stealing a line from a late-show comedian, he continued with, "I decided I would rather have a full bottle in front of me than do another full frontal lobotomy." He had a receptive audience and the line got a good laugh.

The door from the hall opened and a young woman in a cotton shirt and blue jeans appeared. "Excuse me, gentlemen. Sorry to interrupt, but I'm making a run into Quimper. Anyone need anything?" Spotting me, she walked over and said, "Hi, I'm Susan, one of Bill's students. I hear you'll be joining our group. I drive one of the vans and you're welcome to ride with me this afternoon. No one needs anything?" she asked again, looking from one to the other. "O.K., see you later."

Her face was exceptionally pretty, I thought, and, to steal a line I once heard, "her torso more so". I followed her with my eyes as she left the room, an act which did not go unnoticed by Philippe.

"That won't do you any good, my friend. She will tell you that you remind her of her father. I know, because that what she tell me," he said with an impish grin.

"Well," I said, "If her father's like either one of us, he has a very dirty mind and ought to be ashamed of himself. Anyway, a man can dream, can't he?"

Later, stomach-filled and happy, I sat next to Susan as the two vans rolled slowly through a network of sleepy country roads, past tiny villages where old men sat at open tables sipping wine and spinning yarns until, eventually, we pulled into the snug pocket of a turn-around, barely leaving space enough for other motorists to get by. Before us lay a broad, stream-fed estuary, now at the flood stage of the tide, its ripples lapping gently against a sea-grass shore. Across the waters, a panoramic sweep of slate-roofed, whitewashed, double-chimneyed houses stacked themselves against the hillside, until those perched along the summit near the village church with its Gothic spire met, in bold profile, a sky of periwinkle blue.

"This is beautiful," I said to Susan as we stood looking at the view. "Where are we?"

"I'm not sure," she said. "But I think it's called Pont Croix. Bill mentioned yesterday that he wanted to come here, that it's one of his favorite painting sites. It's easy to see why."

Soon, there were twelve of us stretched out along the high ground of the bank, setting up our field easels, squeezing paint onto palettes, adjusting canvases, selecting brushes, studying the landscape, making compositional decisions, and starting the process of roughing-in with brush strokes.

Woodward, filling the dual role of painter and teacher, positioned himself near the center of the group, making running comments as he painted. As thoughts came to mind, he expressed them for the benefit of those on either side. He pointed out that we had but four hours in which to complete a painting. During that time the tide would begin to ebb and the water recede, so allow for it. The scene before us offered a lot of information. It would be easy to get bogged down in detail. His advice: Don't. He suggested that it would perhaps be best to select only a segment of the overall view and focus on that, remembering to work toward emphasizing a center of interest. Keep in mind, he told us, the importance of painting everything once before painting anything twice: cover the entire surface, so that no blank canvas remains, before working on details or adding more brush strokes to any portion of the painting. He asked us not to forget that every painting should have an abstract design idea behind it. He talked as he painted. I listened. I hung onto every word. This was what I had been needing.

Severral times during the afternoon, Bill laid aside his own brushes and spent a few minutes with each painter, offering an on-the-spot, mini-critique of the work in progress. He had a good easel-side manner, in every case offering encouragement as well as constructive suggestions. One of the things he said to me was that I should learn to paint faster. At the time, I found it hard to equate good painting with fast painting, but since he was an expert and I was still learning, I decided to take his advice seriously and try painting faster. There was an almost immediate improvement in my work.

That night, before falling asleep, I looked back over the events of the past few hours and counted my blessings. I had climbed out of bed that morning a stranger in a foreign land with little command of the language, no prior housing arrangements, and no specific game-plan insofar as painting was concerned, but only the determination to somehow, one way or another, paint. Though not willing to admit it, even to myself, I had been in France only about a week and had already begun to feel lonely, disconnected, and at loose ends. Suddenly, everything changed. I had been warmly welcomed by friends. Because of them, I had emerged in the midst of enjoyable company in as enviable a setting as one could hope to find. Best of all, I had been invited to set up my easel alongside other serious painters, all under the aegis of a good friend who was one of the very best of professionals. The promise of a happy summer spent painting in France was fast becoming a reality.

I fell asleep with a smile on my face.

CHAPTER SIX
Life On The Waterfront

The proprietorship of le Colombier, the waterfront bar above which I lived, was a rigid matriarchy composed of three generations of females. The commander in chief was, of course, Madame Bouchet herself. She was a broad-framed and fleshy woman with a face that had seen better days before her eyes had lost their luster and her cheeks had become soft and flabby. But, despite the passage of time, her chin line remained positive and determined. She was the boss. There was no question about it; she was a tough old biddy, as one would need to be to operate a waterfront gin mill such as the one she owned. Yet, I suspected it was a toughness born from the necessity for survival rather than any mean-spirited attitude. Each Saturday evening, and again on Sunday morning, a taxi would pull up in front of the bar and Madame Bouchet and another woman, her skinny, pointy-faced old friend, would laboriously climb in and out on their way to and from the church up on the hill. The ironic possibility entered my mind that this flesh-pot proprietor, whose livelihood depended on raking in every small increment of profit she could get her hands on, might well be one of the most generous contributors once inside the doors of salvation.

Next in the line of command was Madame Bouchet's pretty daughter, Chantal. She was the working manager, and the one with whom I communicated much more easily than I did with her mother. Then, there was Chantal's teen-aged daughter, Yvette, who more or less helped tending bar but otherwise spent much of her time learning to smoke, flirting with sailors and fussing with her makeup. Last of all was Annie, Yvette's little red-haired sister who contributed her high-pitched screeches and childish laughter to the more normal range of barroom noise.

I was not one of the bar's steady customers. First of all, there were ways of spending spare time that I found to be much more enjoyable than hanging around le Colombier as a barfly. But, aside from anything else, an eight ounce glass of beer with a much-too-deep head of foam cost eight francs, roughly a buck and a half. For the same amount of money, I found that I could buy a full liter of the same brand of bottled beer at the store only a couple of blocks away. So the store got the major portion of my beer-drinking expenditure, and the eight-franc glass of le Columbier suds was reserved for rare occasions. There were times, however, when the ladies of le Colombier would happen to see me walking by on my way back from a field trip with all my gear and a freshly painted picture in hand and, on such occasions, I would be invited in so they could have a look at what I had done. Madame Bouchet especially seemed to enjoy viewing my paintings, and it was not unlike her to continue staring intently at one of them after the others had lost interest and gone on to something else. This struck me as being out of character with the stone-faced visage that she normally projected.

Most days, if the weather was compatible with outdoor painting, I would gather up my equipment and supplies, make my way past the two yapping little ankle-biters on the second floor, and head for where I had parked the Houlotmobile the last time it was driven. The Houlotmobile was the name I had given the twenty-three year old Peugeot I bought half-interest in from Michel, who had been ordered by Philippe to find me a car. The name had come to mind because the car looked so humorously decrepit, with its smashed-in roof, its amateurishly spray-can- painted body and spindly appearance that it reminded me of the funny-looking little car driven by the great French comedian, Jacques Tati in the movie Les Vacances de Monsieur Houlot (Mr. Houlot's Holiday). Michel and I reached an agreement whereby he would have full possession of this motorized relic when I was out of the country, which was, of course, most of the year, but I would have complete custody and full use of it if and when I was in Brittany the following summer. But with gasoline nearly five dollars a gallon, I frequently sought out paintable settings close by to which I could just sling my combination easel/paintbox over my shoulder and walk.

There was plenty to paint near my own waterfront domicile; no lack of subject matter for an outdoor painter. There was the old port itself, its inner harbor edged with aging buildings like the one I lived in, each different from its neighbor. Here, a proud edifice with dormer-bordered mansard roof, and over there, perhaps a scaled-down version of a small palace with inset balconies overlooking the vista of an endless sea, while countless chimney pots, and gabled roof-lines, and heavy-shuttered windows, and ornamental trim, and variance of color all combined to provide each home and building, regardless of its size or importance, a look of total individuality. Nesting in the bottom floors and stretching along the entire length of the Rue du Vieux Port were the vendors, the bars, the creperies and cafes, the more prosperous ones adding eye-appeal with their brightly colored awnings and parasol shaded sidewalk tables. From the extremity of one of the several jetties extending well out into the harbor, it was an easy matter to set up an easel and paint this architecturally venerable, often vibrant, sometimes raucous, forever changing view of life along the waterfront.

A narrow spit of land running perpendicular to the Rue du Vieux Port formed a natural breakwater and offered protection from the sea forvthe old inner harbor. Along its length on the seaward side were the commercial canneries supplied by the wide-ranging fishing fleet, now much smaller than in years gone by. A Frenchman told me a story about how the fleet at one time netted fish as far away as the coast of South America and how, during what he called a storm from hell, nine hundred boats were lost. In order just to ply the waters of their own Breton coastline, which accounts for roughly one-third of the French total, they have had to be expert sailors. For there are tides of up to thirty feet of variance, off-shore shallow draft rock formations, treacherous undertows and currents, and weather that can rapidly spell disaster for those unprepared for the sudden fury of a North Atlantic storm. Because of all the commercial fishing activity, however, there were always vessels aplenty waiting to pose for the painter's brush.

Some days I found myself wandering along the quays, field easel slung over one shoulder and hand on the other side holding a blank canvas in search of its subject. What would it be? Work boat? Factory ship? Trawler? Tug boat? Maybe the best place to paint that morning would be the marine railway at the dry dock. I'd better go there and take a look to see what was being worked on that might make an interesting picture.

One of my favorite close-to-home subjects was the old harbor itself, jam-packed with boats of every description, many flying the colors of nations halfway around the globe. For not only were the local waters home port for the commercial fishermen, but they supplied safe haven and port-of-call for an almost endless succession of vessels ranging from ancient windjammers – the lugger rigged and full-rigged barkentine training ships for cadets – to modern power yachts.

They all came and went within full view of my two big windows, and on days when the entire harbor was the subject of a painting, I stood before the easel in my living room with as fine a visual perch as any harbor master could ever wish for.

Madame Bouchet's daughter, Chantal, was, as a poet of the romantic period might have described her, "a comely lass." She had auburn hair that fell down over her shoulders, blue-green eyes, and lips that were teasingly pouting. Her figure was trim and well-endowed, unlike the more chunky peasant variety. I suspected that she, more than any other reason, accounted for le Colombier's bar being one of the more popular ones along the waterfront stretch.

Soon after my arrival as third floor resident, I noticed a woodworking shop on a side street near my living quarters. I took some stretcher bars there to be shortened by means of a splice or scarf joint. The proprietor was a nice looking young man who did the job well. When I pulled money out of my pocket to pay him, he waved his arm in a negative gesture and said something like "de rien." I later took him a bottle of wine as a token of my thanks. And though we never actually became friends, we did speak when we met on the street or saw one another in Madame Bouchet's bar. From the way he stared at Chantal, it was obvious that he had a crush on her. But she was married to a sullen looking man who rarely showed his face, so the woodworker had to content himself with nothing more serious than standing silently at the bar, gazing at Chantal and watching her every move.

In Brittany, during the summer, the evenings are long, with daylight lasting until ten-thirty or eleven o'clock at night. Depending on my mood, I would either set up the easel by the open windows of the living room and work on a painting, or go below and kill time over a beer and watch the world go by. Either way, I had a full view of the waterfront street and harbor. A couple of times a week I would see the woodworker go to the sea wall, climb down the ladder to where his small sloop was moored, cast off the lines, and then scull his way out to the fairway, hoist canvas and head for open sea. Upon his return several hours later, he would climb back up the sea wall ladder with a string of fish and go directly to the bar. There were never as many fish on the string when he left the bar as there were when he entered.

I had been living above le Colombier for several weeks when there was a knock on my door one morning and I opened it to see Chantal standing there smiling. She was holding a serving dish with both hands. On it was a large plump fish. It was for me, she said, and I accepted it gladly. That night I poached it in white wine over potatoes, onions, celery and carrots, and after I had put aside a sizable portion for myself, I filled a casserole and took it down for the bar-ladies who ate their meals on the middle floor, the one just below mine. It was nice listening to their rave reviews the next morning and, from then on, I always shared with them the fish brought to me by Chantal once or twice a week. Before long, I put two and two together. In the evening I would see the woodworker sail forth on a fish-catching mission, and the next morning there would be a knock on my door, followed by fish for dinner that night.

I was taking a shower one morning when the pilot light of the little hot-water-on-demand gas-burning unit in the kitchen poofed out on me, leaving the water so cold I might as well have been swimming in the Bering Sea. To save gas, the pilot light was set so low that when the unit's thermostat decided that the coil of metal tubing above had had enough hot flames, the sudden surge in air pressure extinguished the pilot light. At least, that was my theory. To get things going again, I kept a box of matches in a handy place, for more than once while living there I had left the shower to go re-light the unit. Dripping wet and clad only in my birthday suit, I entered the kitchen. At precisely the same moment Chantal was about to put the fish in the refrigerator. Plainly startled, she took one quick look at me.

"Excusez-moi, monsieur!" she said in a trilling French voice.

"Pardon me," I blurted out in English, quickly doing an about-face and hastily retreating to find a bath towel.

When I returned to the kitchen, I found that the fish had been left on the counter next to the refrigerator. As I sat sipping coffee I decided that, with the slim possibility that other such surprise encounters might occur in the future, I should lose some weight around the midriff and look less like a laundry bag on stilts. On second thought, I reasoned, it might be a whole hell of a lot easier just to climb up there and figure out some way to adjust the pilot light. The increased wisdom that comes with age should never be underestimated.

By mid-summer the student painters were saying goodbye and leaving for home. Susan suggested that since we both hoped to return to France the following summer, we should share a *gite*, the French name for a small rural cottage or apartment, and I had invited her to drive in from the auberge where she was staying so we could spend a last evening together and discuss plans. We sat alone at the bar. Madame Bouchet and Chantal were both taking the night off, and young Yvette was holding down the fort all by herself. With rain so relentless, there would be few people out in such weather. Four men sat together at a table, occasionally raising their voices in a discussion of some sort. They were the only other customers in a place which on most nights might well be filled.

"How will you get your paintings back to the States?" I asked.

"Oh, I'm taking them off their stretchers and rolling them up, and then I'll pack them in with all the rest of my luggage," Susan said.

"That's what I intend to do when I leave here in October, I said. I hope to have completed so many canvases by then I'll need to throw out some clothes in order to get such a big roll into the suitcase. As long as they're rolled loosely with painted side out, they'll travel O.K. Ready for another one?" I raised my glass and motioned to Yvette.

"Sure," she said. "Where are we having dinner?"

"At le Cotriade. I've never eaten there, but I hear it's a good place. I've lived here for over a month now, and during all that time I've eaten only one meal out. And it could hardly be counted as a real meal. One night I splurged and visited the creperie down the street. A single crepe with andouille sausage, onions and tomato and a bottle of cider cost as much as a whole bag of groceries at the big market in Quimper. I used to treat money like it grew on trees, but I sure can't do that anymore. Instead, I'm on a self-imposed budget of four hundred francs a week, not counting what I pay for rent. That's all. No frills."

"Four hundred francs a week. That's next to nothing. What is it, about a hundred dollars?"

"Not even that. At the present rate of exchange it' s more like eighty bucks, the price of one fancy meal and some first rate wine in a good restaurant. But don't get me wrong. I'm happy. I'm here in France doing what I like to do, and I'm doing if for four full months. Half the nine-to-fivers in America with money coming out their ears would give their right arm to trade places with me. Anyway, I'm convinced; the skimping will sooner or later pay off. The time will come when my work will be good enough to start selling, and I believe I'm getting closer to that point every day."

"I think you're on the right track," she said. "I really liked the painting you did at Plage de Riz the other day. I was especially impressed by the way you handled the..." But she got no further. I followed her eyes and the sudden outburst of noise in time to turn and see a chair being swung at a sandy-haired man with a beard who rapidly decided to leave all behind and do a reverse entrechat toward the front door, followed in great haste by two others that I took to be his companions, all three followed at last by a bellowing bull of a man chasing them out into the rainy night, their feet pounding like drum beats on the duck boards laid down along the wet pavement of the Rue du Vieux Port.

"My God!" Susan exclaimed as the small horde swept past us, knocking over an empty bar stool in the process. "Let's get the hell out of here! This place is rough."

"Relax," I said. "They have no quarrel with us. Anyway, I believe I recognized the big bruiser doing the chasing. If he's who I think he is, he'll occupy his time by trying to catch those three guys and throw as many as possible into the harbor. I motioned to Yvette who, throughout the scuffle, continued to paint her nails. "Yvette. L'addition, si'l vous plait."

"How do you happen to know him?" Susan asked.

"I don't really know him, but I know who he is. His name is Jacques. I met him once through Bill. He's cock-of-the-walk in these parts. Bill says he's a very nice guy who just happens to find nothing so enjoyable as throwing adversaries into the drink. Speak of the devil, here he comes now. Apparently his prey outran him and got away."

Jacques sat himself down on a stool at the far end of the bar, looking very wet, out of breath and quite pleased with himself.

"Shall we go have some dinner?" I asked.

"Sure. But I'm picking up my share."

"You're doing nothing of the sort. I invited you as my guest," I said.

"I know, but it will play dirty tricks on your budget," she said.

"Yes, it will, I said, but so what. Since I've been in France I've done nothing but show backbone – strength of character, they call it. Well, tonight, it will please me no end to live up to my past record of being a sucker for a pretty face. Just don't order something like humming bird tongues farci avec caviar and truffles a la Dom Perignon flambe and I think I can handle it. I'll pay myself back from the first painting I sell."

As we walked past Jacques he looked up and grinned. I grinned back. Never a bad idea to be on friendly terms with the local tough guy, I figured.

Woodward stayed on for a couple of weeks after all of the students had gone home. During that time I painted alongside him on several occasions. Once we paid a visit to a sunflower field that he had spotted near the sea. He invited two talented and highly successful French painters to join us: a jolly man named Pierre whose work resembled that of the great impressionist, Alfred Sisley, and Gaston, his equally gifted nephew. Painting in the field with others was, for me, far more pleasant than working solo, but the time finally arrived when, as in Mexico, I was again spending my days painting alone.

Each month when the rent was due I would enter the bar with francs in hand waiting, if necessary, for a time when Madame Bouchet was at liberty to receive the money. The routine was always the same. We would go to a table in a far corner and, after a few pleasantries, I would count the bank notes as I laid them, one at a time, in a pile in front of her. She would then pick them up and give them a fast riffle, satisfying herself that the amount was correct. Once that had been established, she would summon Chantal or Yvette to bring me a small draft beer on the house. We would sit together as I drank it, trying to converse. She spoke not a word of English and her French was next to impossible for me to understand. This was primarily due to my own poor grasp of the language. But she made it even more difficult because of her rapid way of speaking and her Breton accent. Nevertheless, we both went through the motions of polite small talk interspersed with awkward silences as I quaffed my free small glass of foamy beer. Finally, two-way *mercis* and *au revoirs* followed and the rent was paid for another month.

On the day when it was time to pay the last month's rent in advance I walked into Le Colombier and, in due course, sat at the table with Madame Bouchet, prepared to do business as usual. After the customary pleasantries, I reached in my jacket for the rent money I had carefully pre-counted and put by itself in its own special pocket. But before I could get the bills on the table Chantal, as if by prior instruction, came over and placed the small draft beer freebie in front of me. This was certainly a break with tradition, for the rent money had not as yet changed hands. Then, before I even had a chance to thank her for the free beer, Madame Bouchet took the floor and there followed an avalanche of Breton accented French words, most of which I could not understand. But I had long before learned that in the matter of foreign languages, since I seem to be retarded when it comes to a clear understanding of any of them, I should try, as much as possible, to pick up the gist. And the gist of what she was saying to me, I gathered, was that she didn't want me to give her any money for the forthcoming month. Well, that was, without doubt, the most welcome gist I had deciphered in quite some time. What she did want, I slowly deduced, was one of my paintings instead of rent money. A souvenir. Would I be interested?

Once her suggestion sank in, I wasted no time in responding full throttle, doing my best to think fast and come up with the right words, for the saving of hundreds of dollars was at stake. *Certainment, et avec plaisir, Madame*, I found myself saying. *Je suis d'accord. Vous avez une tres bonne idee, Madame. Une idee exceptionnelle!* I hastened to add.

But the words were scarcely spoken until second thoughts began to creep in. Maybe there was a hooker. Maybe she expected me to do a mural the length of the wall in the back room in exchange for a month's rent. I'd better ask some questions, and with that in mind I stumbled along in my pigeon-French as best I could. What did she want the subject to be? It didn't matter. That was for me to decide. What size should I make the painting? It didn't matter. She would leave those details up to me. Once we finished discussing the ground rules, or rather the fact that there weren't any, Madame Bouchet and I sealed the bargain by solemnly shaking hands and, after several times voicing one or another of my own limited versions of *Merci beaucoup, Madame. Je vous donnerai une tres bon tableau,* and one last *Au revoir, Madame,* I walked away flattered and delighted with my good fortune. All that remained was for me to honor my end of the bargain by painting a picture that pleased her, and that shouldn't be at all difficult. For I had a subject in mind that was sure to make her more than happy.

A day or so later I set up my easel at the far end of the jetty closest to the bar-strip section of the Rue du Vieux Port. Yes indeed, I said to myself, here was the perfect vantage point insofar as composition was concerned, with the morning light accentuating the colors of the buildings that I intended to include in the new painting while, at the same time, lending definition to some of the details I would need to emphasize. The shadows, I decided, were good; not too deep in value and, because of the time of day, not overly elongated. I liked what I saw. There, on the top floor of that three-story light-gray plastered house with the forest-green shutters, were my own living and bedroom windows, opening out from the apartment where I had lived, painted, and harbor-watched throughout most of the past summer. It was an easy house to identify, for it was the smallest of the structures stretching along the waterfront heartland that extended several hundred action-packed meters from la place de la Vielle Cote to rue du Bord de la Mer.

But what the venerable little building lacked in height, it more than made up for at street level. For Madame Bouchet had adorned its entrance with a pretty blue-and-white-striped canvas canopy with solid-blue scalloped borders trimmed with navy-blue piping. On the front and side panels, the name Le Colombier was lettered in white. Under the canopy and extending well out toward the water were white metal tables equipped to hold big orange-red parasols bearing the trade name and logo of an aperitif maker. Tubs of red geraniums enclosed the outdoor table area. All in all, the place was pleasing to the eye, colorful and inviting.

On the day I started her painting, a fresh breeze was blowing, and since I was standing near the jetty's edge and some fifteen or twenty feet above the low tide surface of the water, I secured the legs of the easel to the concrete jetty's mooring rings with nylon cords, at the same time reminding myself not to step back too far to examine my work as the painting progressed.

There are various ways to start an oil painting. The approach I chose for that particular scene amounted to drawing with a brush, using a mixture of burnt sienna and burnt umber thinned down with turpentine to almost watercolor consistency. The brush I selected for roughing-in was reasonably small, a number two hog-bristle filbert, and so worn down from previous usage that it was somewhat stiff and stubby, with very little of the normally desirable springiness remaining. With it, I sketched in the general outline and shapes of what would later become solidly painted. After a while, I had the basis for a picture showing the waterfront stretch of buildings, more or less as they actually existed, with the foreground starting at the water's edge and the middle distance including all of the rooftops with their chimney-pots and a segment of the sky above.

I stepped back to take a look. The composition was good, I decided, and the drawing was O.K. Once I started applying color, working out values and concentrating on brushwork, it held every promise of ending up as a good painting, maybe even one of my better ones. The work was going well and I was pleased. But then it hit me like a ton of bricks: the way I was painting it, it would be the wrong painting to give to Madame Bouchet. For the adjoining buildings with their high, multi-gabled and elaborate chimney-pot roof-lines flanking her small house dwarfed it by comparison. No, it would not do to give her such a painting. Her skinny old lady friend and fellow churchgoer, the ever-present pipe smoking ex-seaman with the lame leg, the men who played the pinball machine for hours on end, her cousin from the country that I had met briefly one day, Madame Chauvel, who purportedly lived down the street but was a permanent fixture at the bar; Jacques, of course; all of them, every last one of the regulars, would be shown the painting. And each of them would either say, or think, as they were being shown it by Madame Bouchet, "Yes, there it is. That's your place all right. The smallest of them all."

No, it wouldn't do. So I took the paint rag, soaked it in turps, and in a matter of seconds there was once again a blank canvas before me on the easel. The answers soon began to come, and the solution was simple enough. With a completely new concept in mind, I again picked up the brush and began roughing-in. Make the focal point of the painting Madame Bouchet's proudest possession: Le Colombier. That was my new objective. Without moving the easel, move the viewpoint of the painting up much closer. In so doing, accentuate the striped canopy, the sidewalk tables, the brightly colored parasols, the human interest of customers being waited on; let all this be the center of interest. To establish le Colombier's dominance within the setting, I would show a portion of the tables and outer facade of le Vieux Moulin on the left and, similarly, show the façade and tables of la Belle Etoile on the right, with just a suggestion of its adjacent neighbor, Au Bon Accueil. But, I would cheat a little, or, that is, use artistic license, and minimize their significance by slightly scaling down their proportionate sizes and by subduing the colors and tonal values that represented them as entities within the painting. Now, because of the closer vantage point, I could show a little patch of sky above the red tiled roof of Madame Bouchet's building, but let the structures on either side simply be cut off by the top of the painting, not giving the viewer a clue as to how very much higher they were in actuality.

Pleased with the new scheme, I went to work again, frequently stepping back to look at the work as part of the ongoing series of assessing, changing, amplifying, correcting and trial-and-error brushwork that takes place as a painting progresses. Soon, the canvas was covered, with all the elements in their place and colors and values basically accounted for. But the light was changing and soon the subject would be in shadow. Just as well. Too much wet on wet and the result could well be mud, instead of the fresh look of clean pigment. I had added some siccative to the medium I was using, so the surface would dry faster and be just right for painting the next day or so.

The next time out to my spot at the end of the jetty the air was calm, perfect for the work that lay ahead, for I needed to add detail here and there to what had already been done. But, most importantly, I was at the stage at which I could begin to add life to the painting: figures at the tables, folks being waited on, people strolling by and, tipping my hat to the great French post impressionist, Pierre Bonnard, I painted in a small dog trotting along in the foreground. Next, I heightened the colors of the passages I wanted to emphasize. A little more brushwork here, soften the edges there, try using some of that parasol red-orange as an accent spot. Sure, that works. Finally, did I dare? Well, why not? I painted me looking out of the third floor living room window. Tiny, of course. Just the suggestion of the head and shoulders. I was about to let it go at that and sign my name, but I took one more critical look to see if anything else needed to be done. It was a good painting, I thought, but since it was for Madame Bouchet I should try to examine it through her eyes, insofar as that was possible. Well, again, why not? Why not add still more figures, more customers crowding the tables of her establishment and eliminate some of the people at the tables belonging to competitors. Perhaps I overdid it. But, in the end, one was left with the impression that Madame Bouchet was giving away free beer and the bars on either side were charging double. For their waiters were standing idly by with empty tables, while all of hers were jam-packed and being served by my imaginary new staff of extra help.

A few days later when the painting was sufficiently dry, I walked into le Colombier with it under my arm. Madame Bouchet was talking to a customer but, with the end of the conversation, looked up and saw me. I held the canvas in such a way that she could tell that I had a something I wanted her to see. She came over. I showed her the painting. She looked at it, transfixed, not a word. Suddenly she let out a whoop. Before I realized what was happening, she was kissing me on both cheeks and yelling at Chantal to bring me a beer. "No, no! A large beer for monsieur! Madame Chauval! Come. Take a look. See my Le Colombier! Monsieur Duval, Come. See my picture!"

And so, the celebration continued throughout the rest of the afternoon, with me, who normally couldn't afford the price of even a small beer, being fed all the large beers my stomach would hold. It would be appropriate to say, as the old cliché goes, that a good time was had by all. But I left while the festivities were still in progress, before they had a chance to carry me about like a football hero or before Jacques showed up and decided it would add to the fun if he threw me in the harbor. I had better things in mind.

Day after day I had walked past a small restaurant halfway up the street leading to the big market, and there was no question in my mind but that the smells filling the air were not from the kitchen, as one would suppose but, instead, came straight from heaven. Several times, temptation had almost gotten the better of me, and I had briefly paused and wistfully looked in through the leaded glass windows. I decided that, for the moment, I would go to my rooms and enjoy the luxury of an afternoon nap. Later, I would take a shower, put on a clean shirt, walk to the little restaurant with the smells from heaven, sit at a checkered-cloth, candle lit table, and treat myself to a long overdue gourmet meal and a decent bottle of vintage Bordeaux, a good Paulliac perhaps. Yes, it was time to be good to myself, for in this heartland of painting country I had just enjoyed a miniscule, yet immensly rewarding, acceptance as a painter.

CHAPTER SEVEN
Snake Pit Farm

It was time to think about going back to the States. Most of what I had hoped to accomplish during the time spent on foreign soil had, to one degree or another, been accounted for.

From the very start, my primary objective had been to learn to paint well enough to have a saleable product before my little dab of money ran out. My second goal was to produce a fairly sizable body of work before devoting attention to the all important matter of marketing. Without any sales effort, public exposure or feedback from those in the business of selling paintings, it was hard to know whether or not I had succeeded in painting canvases with customer appeal. My past experience as a collector and part-time dealer gave me the advantage of being able to look at a piece of work objectively. By imposing the same impersonal criteria on my own works that I had previously used in judging the works of others, I felt that I had reason to be optimistic. And, as insignificant as it may have been, I was encouraged by Madame Bouchet preferring one of my paintings to hard cash.

There was another sale I could have made. A total stranger, a well dressed middle aged French woman, stopped her car and watched as I painted a landscape that included her house in the background. She asked if she could buy the painting. At the time I said no because it was one of my better pictures and I felt it would add luster to the inventory I eventually would be presenting back in the States. Other than minor approval of this sort and some favorable comment thrown my way from time to time, there was no meaningful input other than my own assessment. I knew full well that the matter of the acceptance or rejection of my works would need to wait until I returned to America, made the right kind of contacts and knocked on a few doors. The acid test lay some three thousand miles away across the Atlantic,. With my ever diminishing bank account there were frightening moments when I wondered what I would do if, upon presentation, my work was consistently rejected. I tried to throw such thoughts out of my mind.

Throughout the summer I had been so focused on day to day painting activity that I had neglected the matter of making arrangements for a roof over my head once back on my own native soil. As departure time drew near, it began to slowly sink in that unless something was done rather quickly, I might soon give the statistical department of some federal bureau reason to add my name to the list of homeless Americans. So the paint brushes were laid aside and letters hastily sent out to Lisa, Bill Woodward who had been back home for over a month, and Mary Coker, my new friend in Rectortown, Virginia who, the previous year, bought my rendition of William Merritt Chase's "By The Seaside".

With only a few days remaining before it was time to pack up and leave France, a letter came from Lisa announcing that she had located a two-bedroom cottage in the Virginia countryside about fifty miles from Washington, D.C. It was nothing very grand, the letter went on to say, but, on the plus side, it was semi-furnished with ratty old cast-offs. I could have it on a monthly basis and, best of all, the rent was cheap, only $600 a month. Did I want her to reserve it for me? I walked up the hill to the post office where there was a public phone and was soon talking to Lisa. "It sounds ideal for my needs," I said. "Yes, by all means, take it. With that kind of monthly rent I'll start conditioning myself to learn to love ratty old cast-off furniture."

In a matter of hours after the plane landed in New York I was in Fogelsville, Pennsylvania, sitting with Charlie Dent at his kitchen table enjoying a beer. He and I had been close friends the greater part of our lives. Many years before, he and I had together owned a 63 foot gaff-rigged yawl in the days when all flight attendants were lovely youug single females, and since he just happened to be an airline captain we had, as one might imagine, enjoyed many happy sails. Over the years, Charlie had put his eyes, brains and pocket book to work and had acquired what I estimated to be millions of dollars worth of fine art, consisting mostly of Old Masters, Barbizon and Impressionist paintings and Renaissance bronzes. Much of his collection was housed in a huge dome which he had built on the property for the purpose of reconstructing the enormous bronze horse started by Leonardo da Vinci five hundred years earlier but never completed. Ever the art enthusiast, Charlie insisted on seeing the work I had done while away in France, so I unpacked the roll and laid what amounted to a rather sizable stack of canvases face up on the table.

Throughout the years, the two of us had together trudged many a mile up and down the aisles of flea markets and the display rooms of antique shops and art galleries, looking for the rare find, the treasure that had gone unnoticed by the hundreds or thousands of others who had walked right past it. I knew Charlie well enough to know that, although normally gregarious and talkative, when it came to forming an opinion about a piece of art, he typically took on the mode of silent concentration with the intensity of a bird dog on scent. Best to leave him alone and let him take his own time in viewing the paintings. Also, if I was standing there looking on over his shoulder he might be forced to make polite comments whether he felt like it or not.

"Well, here they are," I said. "While you're looking at them I think I'll go out and see if I can start the Rabbi Roadster. Four months is a long time for an old jalopy like that to set idle. We may need to use jumper cables. Wish me luck."

There are people who profess to believe that mechanical things have personalities. This notion is especially prevalent when it comes to cars. I had never thought much about it one way or the other until I began driving the Rabbi Roadster. It seems to me that most any vehicle has good reason not to start right up after having sat untouched for four months in an open field. Certainly, for an aging clunker which, even at best, hits on only about three out of four cylinders and has the permanent symptoms of a car badly out of timing, there would be every excuse in the world for it not starting. But weak and crippled and banged-up and ugly as it was, it apparently possessed an inner goodness and was determined, insofar as its limitations permitted, to faithfully serve its master. With much apprehension I put the key in the ignition, pumped the gas pedal vigorously and pushed the key down to the start position. Suddenly there was sputtering and chugging, a few loud backfires, the screeching of belts and huge enveloping clouds of blue-black smoke, with the little engine all the while going through a faltering I-think-I-can, I-think-I-can, I-think-I-can phase until it at last settled down to performing in its normally erratic and jerky fashion. A custom built Masarati could have done no better. Once the shreds of paper left there by a homesteading family of mice were cleaned out, the sputtering engine would be ready to turn the wheels that could carry me back to ole Virginia.

When I returned to the house Charlie was right where I had left him, studiously examining my canvases. He had spread them out from one end of the kitchen to the other.

"Can you believe it! It started right up." I said.

"Good. It made so much noise I thought for a while we were being attacked by an invading army. Say, Bill, where did you buy these paintings?"

"Buy them my foot. In a way I wish I had. Nope, my own blood, sweat and tears went into painting each and every one of them. Tell me, do you think there's a decent dart board in the bunch?"

Charlie gave me one of his slow, penetrating looks before speaking. "Some of these are damned good, Bill. A couple are surprisingly good. Maybe you don't realize it, but you've come a long way since you started painting in earnest. Let's go in the living room; I want to show you something."

Inside the living room, hanging on the wall next to a sofa was one of my own paintings. It was a small painting, a landscape showing an expanse of meadows and pastureland surrounding a village, some clumps of trees, and a small stream cutting through the middle distance. The sky was one of my better ones, I noted. I had painted it quickly and rather loosely one afternoon just before leaving Mexico.

"I was in the storeroom several weeks ago and happened to see this painting," Charlie said. "I decided to borrow it until you came back. It was here on the wall when my friend Martha dropped by last Friday. You remember her, the curator and art historian who has written several books on nineteenth century American art. While we were talking, she noticed your picture."

"Oh, I see you have a new painting," she said.

"Yes," I said. "What do you think of it?'

"I like it very much," she said. "Who did it?"

"When I told her it was painted by an old friend of mine who only recently started painting full time, she seemed a little embarrassed and we changed the subject. But the point is, Bill, you had one of America's acknowledged experts briefly fooled." It was a good story and Charlie was laughing as he told it.

"Well, that's all very encouraging, Charlie, but I'm the first to admit that I still have a long way to go. I'm really just getting started and have yet to prove myself when it comes to the all important matter of public acceptance. That's the scary part."

"Don't worry, Bill, don't worry. You'll do it. Your work right now is plenty good enough to sell. Your biggest job from here on out is finding the right way to market it. But, believe me, you're on the right track. You'll do it."

As I drove from Fogelsville down route fifteen toward Virginia I thought about what Charlie had said. His positive words of encouragement meant a great deal to me, for I knew they were spoken by a man supremely qualified to pass judgment on matters pertaining to fine art. I knew he was right. Now I had to find a way to successfully market my work. That, I thought, might prove to be an even tougher assignment than learning to paint. Time would tell.

Lisa and I had agreed to rendezvous outside the country store a few miles east of Middleburg in the little village of Aldie. From there she would take me out to my new home. I followed her car past fine estates, attractive horse farms and on and on through countryside expressive of the good life, made all the more pleasing to the eye by foliage here and there that was already starting to change into fall colors. Eventually, she turned off onto a gravel road and I followed her cloud of dust a short distance until, at last, we arrived at a lane that lead us to a clearing of knee high grass and there it sat, a small dingy frame house tucked away in a grove of tall cedars, my new home, off and on, for the next few months. As I brought the Rabbi Roadster to a stop I thought, "Too bad I'm not hiding out for some reason or other for, if I were, they'd never find me here."

"What do you think of it?" Lisa asked.

"Well, it's not exactly Carter Hall," I replied, "but at least it won't break my back to pay the rent each month. What's it like inside? Let's have a look."

Like many another small unpretentious country house, it had the original version of nature's air conditioning, a front porch. From it one entered into the living room and came face to face with a fairly sizable fireplace, a pleasant surprise. The kitchen area had been expanded into one large room with oversized windows and I immediately decided that this would be my studio/ workroom. A bath and two small bedrooms completed the layout.

"It'll do fine, Lisabella," I said. "Thanks for finding it for me. It's so secluded I should be able to get plenty of work done, unless such a quiet environment causes me to start spending all my time baking bread and making wine like a Trappist monk."

"Something smells funny," Lisa said, and with that she walked over and opened the cabinet doors beneath the sink. "I thought maybe some garbage had been left here but there isn't any, so that's not what's causing it."

"The place probably just needs airing," I said, opening the back door. "Maybe it will go away."

While out buying supplies and groceries I found a public phone and began making arrangements for the various utilities to be activated in my name. The weather was still quite warm, but that could suddenly change, so I called the heating company responsible for servicing the furnace and asked them to send someone over to check it out and put it in its operating mode. "We can have someone there tomorrow morning," I was told by the man on the phone. But when I gave him the address, he said: "Wait a minute, isn't that the place with all the snakes in the cellar?"

"Darned if I know." I said. "I've never been down in the cellar. I sure hope there aren't snakes down there. I don't like snakes."

After asking me to repeat the address, he said: "Yeah, well we'll need to re-schedule sending someone over there. Clancy's the only man I've got who's willing to go down your cellar steps and he's busy working on an installation and won't be free until about Thursday afternoon. You can either wait for him or I can tell you over the phone what you need to do to get the furnace working. It's not all that difficult."

"Thanks but no thanks," I said. "I'll wait for Clancy."

During the next few days I became increasingly aware of the fact that I had moved into what amounted to a snake preserve. I saw a big one sunning itself on the dirt driveway and another one slithering through the grass in the side yard. When Clancy showed up to start the furnace he pulled up the floor hatch covering the cellar stairway and there lay a large one coiled up on the first step.

"If you want to come with me I'll show you how the furnace operates," he said. "It may be a handy thing to know if there's a power failure and the furnace has to be re-started."

"No thanks," I said. "If that happens I'll just wait here in the cold for you to show up."

I decided to broach the subject with my new landlady. When I politely confronted her with the suggestion that she hire an exterminator to get rid of the snakes and then have the chinks in the stone foundation plugged so they couldn't get back in she responded by saying: "You're lucky to have black snakes on the property. They keep the copperheads away."

It wasn't long before I discovered that the snakes were the cause of the occasional foul odor that both Lisa and I noticed the day I moved in. I wished very much that the snakes would just plain pack up and move on but, of course, that was not about to happen. While trying to think of some way to get rid of them I remembered hearing about a man who had a somewhat similar snake problem. It seems that he owned a fairly large piece of property that was so snake infested he decided that his only solution lay in employing the help of the snakes' mortal enemy: the mongoose. He therefore inquired around and discovered that there was a mongoose breeder in India who sold these ferret-like critters for snake extermination purposes. After some careful calculations based on what he had read about the effective territorial range of these little animals he reckoned he would need about twelve in order to get the job done properly. With this in mind he got out paper and pen and wrote to the company in India:

Dear Sirs: Please send me twelve mongooses. Mongooses, he thought? No, that doesn't sound right. So he started again, this time saying: Dear Sirs: Please send me twelve mongeese. Mongeese? No that can't be right either. Finally he wrote: Dear Sirs: Please send me a mongoose. Very truly yours, Joe Blow. P.S.: What the hell, make it twelve.

In my own case the postscript might very well be: What the hell, make it two. One for the cellar and one for the yard. I finally decided that I had way too much work to do to waste time fretting over snakes. Better to just joke about them, hold my nose and step carefully.

Now that I was back in America, and since dealers aren't interested in being shown rolled-up canvases, my primary focus had to be to get the more than thirty paintings I had brought back from France in frames and ready to show along with the framed ones painted in Mexico. As soon as that was accomplished, I needed to find dealers who both approved of my work and who were well qualified to market what I turned over to them. I soon realized that I had a major problem on my hands, for decent looking frames are not inexpensive. All of my canvases were purposefully painted in the standard frame sizes, ranging from 11"x14" to 24"x30", with the majority of them near the larger end of the scale, so it would be possible to buy ready-made frames in those sizes. Even so, to get the quality and style I wanted, I figured I would need to pay, on the average, at least $100 each even if I found a cut-rate source. For the past several months I had been so busy concentrating on turning out paintings that I had completely neglected to include in my projected financial planning the money needed for buying frames. The cost of thirty some-odd frames at even a bargain price of $100 each was, in relation to what remained in the kitty, a major expenditure that I could ill-afford. I needed to figure out some way around the problem, if possible.

It had been nearly fourteen months since the liquidation of my household assets and the sale of the Jaguar. Together, I had netted a little over $51,000. I had lived frugally in both Mexico and France, yet with food and shelter, travel expenses, paint supplies, buying the Rabbi Roadster and half interest in the Houlotmobile, plus all the incidentals one doesn't expect, there was only a little over $25,000 left. I was in no position to spend $3,000, or more, on framing, if I could help it. I began to wonder if I could make the frames myself and save a big chunk of the cost. Well, yes I could, I reasoned, if I had a power saw, an electric drill, some framing clamps, and a source of inexpensive molding. With that in mind, I looked in the local paper, saw a house-sale ad that listed, among other things, power tools. I was soon the new owner of a power miter saw and a 3/8" electric drill for a total cost of $43, a good start in the right direction, I told myself. From my art dealing days I knew that there were places that sold lengths of picture molding but, as I recalled, even uncut lengths of the styles and sizes that I wanted for my paintings would cost a lot. It was then I remembered that many years before during the remodeling process of a house I owned, I had gone to a mill-supply house and bought what I believed was called mantle molding. I thought at the time it had the grace and curvature of early American picture-frame molding. So, off I headed to the local dealer in architectural moldings. There I found, for a fraction of the cost per foot, the style of molding that I felt was perfect for my paintings.

Next, I needed a big, sturdy work table. Stacks of old lumber were in a shed near the house, so I called Hazel, my new landlady, and asked what she wanted for five planks and a couple of 2"x4"s. She said I could have all the lumber in the shed, if I wanted it, and save her the cost of having it hauled away. So, first I built a work table, one that was long, wide and solid. Then, with my newly acquired power saw mounted on it, I began cutting molding and making frames. As frames were finished I would fine sand each one, then add a coat of Venetian red paint as an undercoating and, finally, apply the finished gilding with composite gold leaf.

When not working on frames, I added finishing touches here and there to some of the paintings. I wanted to put my best foot forward in my initial presentation to dealers. During it all, there were occasional respites when Lisa would come out for the weekend and set up headquarters in the extra bedroom. Sometimes I would take a break and have dinner with Mary Coker, Bill Woodward or other horse-country friends. But, for the most part, I put in such long hours standing at the worktable, usually starting soon after sun-up and working straight through until near midnight, that I would tumble into bed exhausted.

At last, with the framing job completed, I started giving my full attention to the matter of finding dealers. Fifty-six paintings were far too many for any one dealer to want. Somewhere between eight and twelve paintings per dealer seemed a likely number, so that meant I would need to set up at least four or five dealers that were not too close to each other geographically. One thought led to another until, at the end of some scotch-sipping brainstorming, I came up with a plan that seemed to make some sense.

First of all, I would find a dealer in Washington. Since I already had contacts in the local art world, I figured that shouldn't be too difficult. Then, by mid-November, I would head south, setting up galleries as I went, ending up in Mexico where I would pick up the things I had left there. On my way back I would paint along the Gulf until springtime hit Virginia. Then I would return to Snake Pit Farm, providing I could work out a deal with Hazel whereby I would pay half the monthly rent if she would hold the place for me while I was away. I soon had her on the phone. She wasn't too pleased with my half-rent-while-away proposition. I invited her to come by for drinks and talk further. The second martini did the trick and she, reluctantly, agreed.

The next morning I was on the phone with Frank, a Connecticut Avenue dealer I had known for a number of years who dealt in both early and contemporary works. Even though I was optimistic about getting the representation of a good local gallery, such as the one Frank owned, I was, nevertheless, just a little apprehensive about the possibility of being turned down. I sure didn't want that to happen. When I told Frank what I had in mind he seemed surprised.

"You mean that these are your own paintings? Ones that you, yourself painted? I knew, of course, that you dealt in art, but I didn't know you painted."

"That's all I have been doing for quite a while now, Frank. I'll appreciate it if you'll let me show you some of my work."

"Well, Bill, I'll be glad to take a look. But quite frankly, business hasn't been too good lately, and I'm already overstocked with inventory. But sure. I'll at least be glad to look at what you've got. Maybe I can recommend some other dealer. Come by on Monday. The gallery's closed, but I'll be here doing paperwork."

I hung up feeling a little let-down, and the quotation about a prophet never being without honor except in his own country came to mind. It might not be so easy after all, getting accepted by a good local gallery. But my doubts were short-lived. On Monday, after some complimentary remarks, Frank, to my great relief, took eight of my paintings. So far so good. Only forty-eight more paintings to find homes for. But first, there was a problem in logistics that needed to be solved.

In wanting to give Frank a respectable number of paintings from which to choose, I had loaded twenty-four into the Rabbi Roadster and it was so crammed full that there was hardly room to breathe. I now planned to take twice that many, forty-eight paintings altogether, with me on the trip south, and there was no way on earth I could do that with the Rabbi Roadster, which was little more than a passenger car with some extra room behind the back seat. Upon my return from Mexico I had sold the small trailer, but even if I still owned it, it would not do for transporting paintings. It was becoming more and more obvious, I needed to sell the Rabbi roadster and buy a much larger vehicle.

From asking around I learned that there was a man named Harless who owned a country store several miles from where I was living and who, along with everything else, sold used cars. I drove over to see him, and found him to be a garrulous character in a Norman Rockwell setting, his store and gas pumps looking like something that should be disassembled piece by piece and reconstructed at the Smithsonian as an example of early Americana. There were four older model, ratty looking cars with for-sale signs on them parked in the lot beside the store. When I arrived I found Harless outside wearing a black felt hat and proprietary apron, as focused as a bird-dog on point, and in the process of selling a customer a car. From the way he was extolling the many virtues of the old jalopy, one would have thought it had just come off the assembly line. There was no doubt in my mind; this was the man who could sell the Rabbi Roadster.

When the customer had left, promising to come back with his checkbook, I introduced myself and, pointing to my own dingy blue jalopy, said, "I'd like to sell my car. I'm willing to take $1,500 for it. You can tack on whatever you like above that."

After asking all the expected questions that were apparently answered to his satisfaction, we shook hands. "Just bring it by when you're ready to let go of it, any day but Sunday, we're closed on Sunday. I'm the preacher of that there church on Sunday," he said, pointing to a small, sad looking white frame structure a little farther down the road.

As I drove away, I hoped his Sunday sermons were a bit closer to the truth than what came out of his mouth on his used-car lot. Yes indeed, he was the man for the Rabbi Roadster. Sure enough, he sold it in less than a week after I turned it over to him.

The next day I walked into my friend Gerry's office and told him I wanted to buy a used van.

"How much are you willing to pay?" he asked. When I told him I could only pay $3,500, he shook his head and said with firm finality, "You can't begin to get anything decent for that kind of money. If you think you can you're just kidding yourself, Bill."

"I know I can't, Gerry, but you can. That's why I'm here talking to you instead of some stranger down the street. Anyway, I'm almost out of money and that's all I can afford. Help me on this, Gerry. You've got all kinds of connections when it comes to cars: wholesalers, rental and leasing people, trade-ins. This is important to me. With a van I can head south or southwest in cold weather and paint right through the winter. It's tough trying to break into a new field at a late age, and I need all the help I can get. All I ask is that you call around and find me a brother-in-law deal like you did on the Plymouth. You're the boss of this outfit. You can do it." I shouldn't have mentioned the station wagon, for that gave him a nice bit of negative ammunition.

"Yeah, you see, that's what I mean. Sure, I'm the boss, but I have business partners. They're still giving me hell for letting you have that car for a bag of peanuts. I can't keep making deals like that, Bill."

"Come on, Gerry. Be Mr. Niceguy one more time and I won't bother you again."

"I don't know, Bill. You're getting to be a pain in the ass. I'd like to help you, but..."

"Was I a pain in the ass a few years back when I bought a brand new Jaguar from you at full retail price and two other cars before that? Was I a pain in the ass when I used my connections to help you with that real estate deal?" I lifted the phone on his desk off its cradle and handed it to him. "Here, Gerry. You're a good guy and we've been friends for a long time. Help me now and I won't bug you anymore. I promise."

Several hours later a three-year old Dodge Ram stretch van with only forty-one thousand miles on the odometer had been located. The auto-pro at the other end of the phone assured Gerry that it was in good condition except for some superficial dents here and there and the need of a tune-up. The minute I saw it I knew it would be absolutely perfect for my needs, and before the day was over I owned the van I'd been hoping for at a cost of less than half its Blue Book value. The best part was, the full fifteen feet of length gave me even more room than I needed for transporting paintings. There was plenty of extra space. Why not put that extra space to good use? Why not a studio on wheels, I wondered.

I soon began to visualize the van having a hatch opening in the roof, as this would provide several important advantages when painting on location. Standing on the floor of the van would add elevation, and at times the additional height could make all the difference in the world and permit painting a scene that otherwise could not be viewed from ground level. I remembered how in France I had spotted a field of sunflowers, leaves and petals pristine and ready to be painted, but because the land was flat and stalks as high as six feet, all I was able to see was the front row, so I passed up choice subject matter for lack of vantage point. I thought at the time that if I could somehow raise my eye level by only a few feet the entire field would suddenly become visible and offer me the chance to take back to the States a painting with a subject that would be well received.

Another priceless benefit, I decided, would be that of rendering myself less accessible to kibitzers. Being not only elevated but, for the most part, shielded from onlookers and would-be conversationalists gave promise of greater concentration and fewer interruptions. This in itself, I felt, was enough of an inducement to make the entire project worth pursuing. As in days of yore, I reasoned, an armor-clad man on horseback was unlikely to be overly pestered by those on foot. And the people on foot, well, they would simply remain people on foot, going about their business and leaving me alone, I hoped. Yet, for all my enthusiasm, I hesitated to start ripping through the steel of a perfectly good van roof. It might be a good idea to get some advice from Albert.

He and I had become friends years before when I lived in Georgetown. Both of us enjoyed sharing a bottle of good wine which we each bought by the case, he specializing more in the best of the California reds and me sticking with the classified red wines of Bordeaux. Soon after we met, Albert had his heart set on talking me out of an eighteenth century long case clock and a nineteenth century American painting I owned and, in due course, he succeeded in trading me a sporty English left-hand drive 1952 A.C.Bristol Cabriolet convertible for the pair, plus a little cash from my side.

Albert personified the successful businessman, with enough money and energy left over to intensely pursue a hobby. In his case it was collecting and restoring antique cars. Step by step he had enlarged the underground space below the family home to accommodate as many as eight cars at a time, mostly Rolls Royces, Bentleys and Damliers of limited issue and rare vintage. As an aid to restoration and maintenance he had installed a full-size hydraulic lift and had otherwise stocked the place with a wide variety of tools and equipment. So, I called Albert.

"What do you mean you bought a cargo van? What do you need a van for? You told me you were spending all your time painting pictures," he said with a slight trace of European accent.

"Well, I thought it might come in handy, helping you carry all your money to the bank," I joked. "Listen, Albert. I need your advice. You see, I want to cut a big hole in the roof of the van."

"You crazy guy. Sounds to me like you've got holes in your head. Why don't you bring it over in the morning. We'll have some coffee and I'll have a look at it."

The next morning over coffee as he and his wife Diana listened to my somewhat unorthodox proposal of relieving my newly purchased van of fifteen square feet of good steel rooftop, I could see that Albert was pleased that I had brought the project to his attention. Helping a friend tinker with anything that had four wheels and an engine was a lot more fun than being the boss and going to the office.

As the big overhead door slowly rose above the threshold of the inner sanctum, Albert called across the opening, "You can park the van inside near that work table, Bill. I'll move the drop head Bentley over so you'll have room."

"What an elegant car!" I said as he maneuvered it into position.

"There are only two like this in the entire world. Only two were ever made," he said.

"Who has the other one?" I asked.

"An English lady. You may have heard of her. She goes by the name of 'Your Majesty.' I'll phone the office to let them know that I'll be a little late. This shouldn't take long."

The day wore on. Hour after hour we cut, drilled, sawed, fitted, welded, bolted and glued, interrupted only by Diane calling us to lunch, then to dinner until, at last, a little before eleven o'clock at night the job was finished and the new hatch cover fastened down tighter than the bark on a tree.

"Let's wash up and I'll open up a bottle of wine," Albert said.

"At this time of night? But , well sure, Albert. You have such a persuasive way with words you talked me into it."

As I got close to Middleburg the thunderstorm that had been brewing suddenly gave way to such a blinding downpour it was difficult to see the road in front of me. When I finally pulled up in front of Snake Pit Farm I turned on the dome light to see how the hatch had behaved through such a drenching. Everything was bone dry.

The next morning I called Albert to thank him again.

"Did it rain out your way?" he asked.

"Like a cow peeing on a flat rock," I said. "But our job held tight. There was not a drop of water inside the van."

During the next couple of weeks I focused my efforts on custom building the van's interior, first giving everything in sight a couple of coats of off-white paint. Next, I bought a piece of green indoor/outdoor carpeting big enough for the floor area and cut it to fit the contours of the body. A camper supply store that sold trade-ins provided me with a small stainless steel sink equipped with a neat little hand pump and two matching plastic containers, one for fresh water and the other to catch the run-off from the sink's drain. At the same store I bought a two-burner propane stove and a small refrigerator to operate as needed off the auxiliary battery I had installed to provide power for both it and the interior lighting system soon to be rigged up. Finally, a sani-pottie completed the list of essentials, all picked up at bargain prices.

With most, if not all, of the major components now in hand, I went to work constructing the cabinet work and built-ins that would make life on the open road as safe, convenient, efficient and comfortable as possible within the space limitations of a fifteen foot long van. One of the key features was the hinged bunk I built, that nested against the wall when not in use but, with its foam mattress, provided a comfortable bed for napping or night time sleeping when in the down position.

Construction at last completed, I turned my attention to the bits and pieces of supplies and equipment that would need to be on board when traveling. The list was extensive. Some of the items would need to be bought, but many were things I already had, yet the list reminded me to make sure they were put inside the van instead of being left behind once I had hit the road. Included on the checklist were: extra bottles of propane gas, a couple of folding director chairs, two small folding TV tables, a card table with folding legs, a Coleman lantern, an old-fashioned oil burning lamp, several small flashlights, emergency road flares, about two dozen classical cassettes, my four-quart pressure cooker and a new teflon skillet and stew pan, a small Milano espresso coffee pot, my small Weber grill and the water pistol I kept with it for dousing hot coals, a full bag of easy-light charcoal, the French field easel for painting outside the van, and the lightweight tubular steel Italian easel for inside the van painting, my old broad brimmed felt hat that I wore when I was on safari in Africa, plenty of extra tubes of paint, plenty of Liquin, turps, mineral spirits, a new roll of canvas, canvas pliers, stapling gun, extra boxes of staples, plenty of stretcher bars, a case of inexpensive but drinkable red wine, some Old McSludge scotch whisksy, sheets, blankets, bedroll, small umbrella, my old sailing oilskin parka, camera, film, and on and on with hardly an hour passing without something else being added. One would have thought I was taking off for an expedition to some remote section of the planet where supplies were unavailable.

As I looked at the results of my labors, I felt pleased that the van's interior was not only functional but attractive as well. The carpeted floor, the navy blue curtains and bunk cover, the stainless steel sink and counter top, the dozen or more prints of impressionist and post-impressionist paintings covering the wall above the bunk were all pleasant to look at. But the van's exterior was nothing short of shabby, its dull white enamel bearing all the scratches and dents of a former cargo rental van. So, I called Joe, the man at the nearby filling station who had checked out the transmission, installed new brake pads and performed other minor maintenance. Did he have a dent removing tool and, if so, could he tell me how to use it and could I borrow it? Yes, to all of my questions. By using the tool, along with a can of dent-filling epoxy and considerable sanding, I was able to improve the surface enough to take it into a cheap car painting place and several hours later drive out in a much more respectable looking van wearing a shiny fresh coat of royal blue.

It was Thursday and all that was missing were the personalized license plates I had applied for some weeks before and I was very much hoping they would arrive before I left on Monday. As luck would have it, they were waiting for me at the post office the very next day. The plates not only paid tribute to a great post-impressionist painter, but also recognized the fact that the vehicle they were meant to adorn was worthy of its intended duty. The letters read, "Z VAN GO." With the mounting of the license plates my job was completed.

I brought out one of the director chairs, opened a cold beer and sat admiring the fruits of my labors. It was then I remembered the words of the mystic seer and prophet, Edgar Cayce who had very wisely said, "Mind is the builder." For the project had actually started in France with the fleeting notion that there might be a better way for a landscape painter to make use of his time, rather than trudging about on foot lugging heavy equipment everywhere he went.

I sat admiring Z VAN GO. During a relatively short period of time I had imagined, then found and purchased a late model, low mileage cargo van at considerably less than its wholesale value and, by cutting an opening in the roof and adding various facilities, converted it into a mobile studio, complete with limited living accommodations. With the hatch cover off and a sky stretching to infinity I could stand up and paint. Inside, I had the luxury of a small refrigerator, sink, stove, sani-pottie, stereo deck with classical tapes and a very comfortable seven-foot long bunk. All the supplies I would need for painting were in place and ready for use. In the cupboard under the sink there was some drinkable scotch and red wine in case of snake bite. I would be elevated enough to have a far better view than from ground level. And, being several feet above kibitzers would effectively prevent them from kibitzing. On top of all that, after several hours of standing at the easel, to be able to withdraw into a shell like a turtle and enjoy the luxury of an afternoon snooze in complete privacy would make Z Van Go worth its weight in gold. In addition, and the primary reason for having bought the van, I could now cart around as many paintings as I could produce.

As I sat admiring my work, during the second beer the thought entered my mind that whereas St. Paul had converted the gentiles, St. Patrick had converted the Irish, and untold numbers of missionaries had converted the heathen, I, Bill Lewis, had converted a van.

CHAPTER EIGHT
On The Go In The Z Van Go

Before leaving Virginia for my trip south I gave a lot of thought as to whether or not I should take along some kind of a weapon for personal protection while on the road. Graying hair, an oversized waist line and traveling alone might well set me up as an easy mark for any two legged varmint with evil intent. And even though I intended staying in motels in relatively safe areas, or for brief periods with family or friends, there might still be times when I would want to sleep overnight in the van.

As I loaded the Van-Go with painting supplies and equipment, articles of clothing, personal paraphernalia, kitchen items, sleeping gear and all the various odds and ends that might be useful during several months on the road, the matter of self defense kept begging to be resolved. But rarely have I had such ambivalent feelings about an issue. As the time for departure drew near, and in spite of weighing all of the pros and cons, I still had not made up my mind. One side of me said yes. The other side just as emphatically said no.

From the age of eight, when my grandfather let me fire his double barreled shot gun and, later, when for my twelvth birthday he gave me a Winchester 22 pump rifle, I have felt comfortable around guns and prided myself on being a fairly decent shot. As I kicked the matter back and forth in my mind, I recalled the first day in the field in Africa, many years before, when there were seven others with empty stomachs depending on my shooting ability to bag an antelope for the pot so we could all eat that night. Late in the day Liam O'Connor, the Irish professional hunter I had hired to lead the safari, and I came upon a herd of Impala. There was one old male, notably larger than any of the others, grazing off to one side.

"He's a raving beauty. Near record horns, I'd guess. We could have more than one good meal off him. But the wind's wrong and we can't get any closer. Too bad. You'll never drop him from here," Liam whispered, handing me the glasses.

"Do you mind if I try?" I asked. "I think I can do it."

From a kneeling position I took a deep breath, held it, squeezed off a shot. I missed. The three hundred magnum bullet kicked up dust just under the big buck's belly. Like a streak of lightning he took off and before Liam could comment I was flat on the ground in the prone position, using my left elbow for a crutch. Once again I found the Impala in the scope, this time running hell for leather but still broadside. Leading him half a length and a little high, I squeezed off another shot. Missed him again, I thought, for there was one last, mighty burst of speed. But his legs began to crumble and then, suddenly, the old buck fell lifeless to the ground. No one was more surprised than I.

"That was one hell of a shot!" Liam said, his voice filled with incredulity. "It's happy I am that we'll not be going hungry on this safari with you pullin' the trigger. Half me clients couldn't hit a bull in the arse with a big bass viol." He motioned for the others to follow us the three hundred and forty eight paces to where the dead buck lay.

So yes, I knew how to use a gun. But so what. Going out into the field to hunt game was one thing, but depending on a gun as a means of ensuring personal safety during the course of normal day-to-day living in a professed civilized society made little sense to me. If things had gotten so out of control that a law-abiding citizen, with intent no more harmful than that of painting a few pictures along the way, needed to arm himself in order to survive while traveling, maybe his proposed trip was in the wrong part of the planet. If I armed myself, everyone else traveling cross country had just as much of an excuse to carry a weapon and, if such were to happen, one might argue that we would soon be a nation of motorized pistol toting hotheads, reverting to savagery and barbarism.

At last, I decided, that when all was said and done, common sense could well offer as much protection as any weapon. I would make sure I took all the usual precautions, keeping windows rolled up and doors locked. If I found myself, by chance, driving through a tough neighborhood, I would be especially alert and cautious. Driving after dark would be pretty much a no-no. Overnights would be only in inexpensive but reputable looking lodgings; no sleazy, dirty linen motels in order to save money. And, except for afternoon naps, I would definitely refrain from sleeping in the van at night unless I was in a well lit and protected area where I felt safe. In addition to everything else, I would make it a point, as much as possible, to keep a low profile, not get too friendly with strangers and purposely be vague in answering any questions. In other words, play it safe and stay out of harm's way. And so, it was settled. No gun.

One of the things I did before starting on the trip was to shoot 4"x5" transparencies of each of the forty-eight paintings with an old Speed Graphic plate camera I had purchased during my art dealing days. My plan, in calling on dealers, was to carry two actual paintings with me into the gallery, plus showing them transparencies of the other paintings in the van and pulling out those they would like to physically see. Last on my list of things-to-do was a trip to the National Gallery Library. There I found a book listing art galleries, both public and private, arranged on a state by state basis. Under each listing there was a description of the type of art involved and the names of the artists represented. The cities I had in mind visiting in hopes of making a gallery connection, were Atlanta, New Orleans and Dallas. While still at the library, I used their copy machine and made print-outs of the pages for all three cities.

Later, I studied each sheet carefully, and high-lighted my first, second and third gallery choices, based primarily on the style of art described and other factors. I decided not to call any of the galleries in advance, for I knew I would only be told to send slides of my work. It was better instead, I felt, to wait until I was in or near each city and then make a phone call, talk to the owner of the gallery and let it be known that I was only in town briefly and could he or she be so kind as to spare a few moments to take a look at some of my work. Years in business had taught me to aim high, go for the jugular, so to speak, so in each city I would make the first call to gallery choice number one. The worst that could happen would be that if my top choice said no. Then, and only then, would I settle for something less. Atlanta was a natural choice right off the bat, not only because of its geographic location and importance as a city, but a gallery connection there would give me a chance to visit my sister Laura more frequently.

It was bedtime but I had no desire to sleep. Too many thoughts of past, present and future were racing through my mind. After a long day of driving I was back in Atlanta where many years before as a very young man I had thought seriously about studying to become an artist. For a brief period I took courses at Atlanta's High Museum School of Art and apprenticed under the German-American sculptor, Steffan Thomas. But the world of business and other influences had diverted me from such an "impractical" pursuit. Now, decades later, in the guest room of my sister Laura's home, I sat pondering my chances of making a gallery connection in the city where I had first picked up a brush and used a sculpting tool. Tomorrow I would go knock on some doors and find out if my recent crash course in landscape and genre painting, mostly self taught, justified acceptance by a good gallery. The fact that eight of my paintings were on display in one of Washington's better galleries was not an altogether fair test, I felt, for since I had known Frank, the gallery owner, for a number of years, he may have agreed to represent me only because of a friendly relationship and a desire not to hurt my feelings by saying no. It was a welcome step in the right direction, but it fell short of supplying the boost in confidence that would result from acceptance by a stranger based purely on merit.

Laura and I had finished dinner when, with all the concern and affection of an older sister, she said, "I wish I could help you honey, but I don't know any of the people personally on your list of Atlanta dealers. If you would like, I'll call my old friend Cynthia Clayton. She paints. I'm sure she would know who to recommend. Let me call her."

"No thanks, Sis," I said. "I'd rather follow my own instincts on this. Very early in the morning I intend driving by before any of the galleries on my list opens its doors. I want to check each one out with a superficial once over. I want to see what kind of paintings they have in their show windows and get a feeling for the areas where they're located. After my little tour of inspection I'll come back here and have a second cup of coffee with you. Then, shortly after opening hours I'll get on the phone and set up the day's appointments.

The plan worked beautifully except for some adjustments imposed because of timing. The gallery owner of my number one selection couldn't see me until four in the afternoon, whereas my tentative number three choice was available at eleven, and a two thirty appointment was made with number two on the list. With a painting under each arm and a hard-to-shake feeling of cold-call trepidation, I arrived for my eleven o'clock appointment. The gallery owner was quite businesslike. Yes, she liked my painting style and seemed pleased when I quoted prices and showed 4"x 5" transparencies of many of the other paintings inside the van parked down the street. She informed me that she owned a second gallery, so if I wanted her to represent me my work would be exhibited and promoted in two galleries instead of only one. But I was not all that enchanted with what was hanging on display and honestly felt that my own work was perhaps a notch higher. The old real estate truism flashed through my mind, that it's better to own the worst house on a good block instead of the best house on a bad block. I knew instinctively that I would much rather be low guy on the totem pole in a gallery filled with works by painters better than myself, so I stalled and said I would let her know.

At two-thirty I made a presentation at tentative choice number two gallery. Here, I was well impressed by the works on display and I also had a positive reaction to the gallery director and his assistant. They, in turn, had good things to say about my paintings and expressed an interest in representing me. But company policy required committee approval. Could I let them keep three paintings until my return from Mexico? I said I would give them an answer before leaving town the next morning.

My third interview of the day produced the results I had been hoping for. The gallery was well located in a fashionable section of Atlanta and was owned and operated by a charming lady, ably assisted by her daughter. I liked them both from the start, and was most impressed by the high caliber of the works on display in their showrooms. I could only hope that they would like my work well enough to want to represent me. My wish was granted. The next morning I pulled the Van-Go into their driveway, and after a private showing of all of the paintings in the van, they selected nine keepers for which they issued the appropriate paperwork and, with that, we officially started our business relationship. A few hours later, exhilarated from having made such a good connection, I said goodbye to Laura, she bubbling with pride that her brother Bill had done so well in her own, and what had once been his, home town.

New Orleans was easier than I had expected. Tired from driving and overcome with drowsiness, I checked into a motel about a hundred miles north of the city. As I examined the list of potential prospects for the next day I decided, for some unknown reason, to abandon my system of checking things out before making appointments. So, on the chance that prospective gallery number one might still be open, I picked up the bedside phone in my room. A few minutes later I had firmed up an appointment for ten-thirty the next morning with the director, who sounded like a very nice lady. I then tried calling numbers two and three, but both were closed for the day.

After a good night's sleep and some wake-up coffee, I was off before dawn and a couple of hours later hoofing it down Royal Street with my gallery list in hand. Most of the art on display inside gallery windows was disappointing: pop art contrived for pop art tastes, corny subject matter, garish colors, ugly colors, abstracts that were poorly done, stuff that looked like Hong Kong factory art, all in all, surprisingly few examples of good painting or drawing. I had walked about two blocks when I came upon tentative choice number two. One quick look at what they were touting and I crossed them off the list. A few doors farther and number three was likewise eliminated. Poor quality, bad taste. Another block or so and a window across the street caught my eye.

I crossed over and stood looking at the fine paintings on display, many in beautifully gilded ornate period frames. Here, I saw at once, was a well-conceived mixture of high quality nineteenth and twentieth century paintings, both European and American. And while most were of an earlier period, some of the paintings were obviously done by contemporary artists. All of the works were representational or, to use a term preferred by some, figurative, but no abstract or pop art or weird stuff was anywhere to be seen. This was by far the best gallery on the street, I decided, as I looked first on the show window and then on the front door for the gallery's name. There it was in small gold letters. I looked at my list. Yes, it was on my list, all right, and in front the name was a penciled-in "number 1", the same number 1 where I was to have a ten-thirty meeting with the nice sounding lady director. "Good Lord!" I said under my breath. "Maybe I should cancel the meeting. They'll never accept me here." But for some reason they did accept me, and several hours later I was headed for Texas with eight less paintings in the Van-Go and a nailed-down super connection in New Orleans.

In Dallas I stayed with a couple who had been friends of mine in Virginia before they moved to Texas. Mike, a lawyer, and Joanne, his wife, were both art addicts, with paintings of good quality hanging throughout the house. Soon after my arrival Joanne set up an appointment for me with a large, well established gallery – her first choice out of several potential candidates.

After saying hello, the gallery director asked me to take all of the paintings out of the van and lean them against the outside wall of the building where the light was perfect for viewing. When I finished he came out, took a cursory look at the thirty-one canvases on display and made some complimentary remarks about the way my paintings were framed. He then stopped before each painting, carefully examining and deliberating before moving on to the next one.

I couldn't decide whether it was best to blab a little as he moved down the line, to fill him in on the location of the subject and the circumstances under which I had done each painting, or would he prefer making the tour in silence. I had the feeling that it was best to shut up and let him look, so I held my tongue.

Finally he turned to me and said, "What are your prices? Give me some examples."

I pulled the price list from my pocket. "Well, for that painting directly in front of you, my price to a dealer is $1,250; the smaller one next to it, the French field of poppies, is $1,100; 1 would like to get $1,600 for the large harbor scene; $1,100 for the Mexican fishermen and their families; $1,300 for the Virginia landscape over to your left."

"That's enough. That gives me an idea of your price range. Our policy is to double the artist's price plus 10% for dickering. I think we can sell your work. However, I need board approval before taking on a new artist, but it's pretty much just a formality since they always go along with my recommendation. We have a meeting scheduled for next Wednesday. Could you leave some of these paintings here until you come back through from Mexico?"

"Sure," I said. "Or better still, since they're closer to your shipping room door than they are to my van, I'd like to leave all of them here with you until I get back. It won't help the frames any to be bouncing around on the Mexican roads."

"Why not," he said. "I'll get Clyde to help you. Call me when you get back in the States."

Mike had asked me to drop by his office after the meeting and now, with four home runs out of four times at bat, I was in high spirits and eager to share the news of my good fortune with a friend. But when I arrived at his office I found him involved in a meeting with two other men in the conference room. After introductions and an exchange of pleasantries Mike said with appropriate tact, "I'm anxious to hear how you made out Bill, but perhaps that could wait until after this meeting. In the meantime you're more than welcome to pour yourself a cup of coffee, pull up a chair and sit in." I had nothing better to do, so I joined them.

Jim, a tall self assured man with a friendly manner, and Simon, his more retiring business partner, were discussing with Mike a plan to put together a big, commercial real estate deal. In essence, they were exploring the possibilities of forming a syndicate to help fund the purchase of an option to buy Kenmore, an existing large apartment complex, and then sell it soon thereafter for a very fat profit. With the air of a man long seasoned in such matters, Jim, who did most of the talking, stressed the point that the owners, for reasons of their own, were willing to sell at a price well below market, whereas he and Simon had a bona fide buyer in their hip pocket, so to speak, willing to pay a price considerably higher than the owners were asking. As I understood it, Jim proposed purchasing a short term option for $250,000 and then delivering the property to their buyer within that period. The resulting leverage, he went on to say, made this a super attractive, quick turnover situation with as much as a ten to one return on investment, all in a matter of months. He and Simon were prepared to come up with $100,000. They were planning on Mike raising the remaining $150,000 from individuals contributing increments of $10,000 or more. In summary, Jim concluded, it was a once in a lifetime opportunity too good to pass up.

Simon took the floor next, and with a thick pile of substantiating papers in front of him, began reciting facts and figures and submitting educated guesses based on reasonable probabilities. No matter how you sliced it, it looked like they had a winner, with expectations of big profits from a relatively small outlay of cash up front. As the three men talked, I sat quietly and listened, all the while suppressing a tendency to be a little envious of them for the financial rewards that were due to come their way because of a few hours spent in some smart and timely wheeling and dealing. I, on the other hand, even with my new found gallery connections, would need to tie myself to the easel and paint night and day in order to accumulate even a fraction of the amount of money they were projecting as a return on just one $10,000 investment. Too bad I had so little money left, I told myself. Otherwise, I would write a check for $10,000 and be one of the syndicators. Then, when the payoff came, I would have enough so I wouldn't need to keep scratching so hard, and the daily penny-pinching at every turn would be a thing of the past.

After the meeting had ended and Jim and Simon had said their goodbyes, I filled Mike in on my morning's session at the art gallery. "Congratulations, Bill," he said. "Now with four galleries promoting your work you should soon see some money starting to come back in instead of it all going out."

"Yeah, I've been thinking the same thing," I said. "Tell me Mike, what's your gut feeling about this Kenmore proposition. Based on what you know about it, how safe an investment do you think it will be for the syndicators? I've had enough business experience to know that no investment is completely risk free. What's the downside for Kenmore?"

Mike looked thoughtful for a moment and then said, "Let me put it this way, Bill. I'm investing $20,000 of my own money. Maybe that doesn't prove much, for I won't miss any meals if I lose it all. But Lucille, my wife's mother, is a different case entirely. She's a widow living off a small pension. She has about thirty thousand in savings that she asked me to invest for her if and when the right deal comes along. I'm suggesting that she put the thirty thousand into the Kenmore syndicate. Does that answer your question?"

"Yes, I suppose so, assuming you don't have a grudge relationship with your mother-in-law as is sometimes the case," I replied.

Mike laughed. "No, Bill, I can assure you we're the best of friends. She's the last person on earth I would want to see lose any money based on my recommendation."

Until well after midnight I had sat on the side of the bed weighing the pros and cons. Should I, or should I not, take even the slightest chance with what little there was left in the kitty after a year and a half of unending expenses and no income? On the plus side, the few things I owned, including the Van-Go, had been paid for with cash at the time of purchase. In addition, in order to reserve the cottage near Philippe's Chateau for the coming summer months, I had already paid the first month's rent, and from times past I had racked up enough frequent-flyer miles on Delta to get me a free flight to France and back. But of course the most important consideration on the positive side was the fact that I had an inventory of some fifty paintings. With luck, that many paintings at the disposal of four galleries should begin to produce enough income to sustain me even if, for some reason, the Kenmore investment went sour.

And I wasn't so naive as not to consider the possibility that it might go sour. After all, I was in my present situation only because a "sure thing" with everything going for it had flopped at the very last minute, so I knew all about "sure things." On the other hand, if the Kenmore project were to pay off as advertised I would kick myself for a long time to come if I passed up the chance to invest. I reconciled the checkbook. To make sure, I reconciled it again. If I invested in the Kenmore project there would be just a little over $7,000 left in the bank. Before turning out the light, I pretty much reached a conclusion: if I continued to live frugally, $7,000 should be enough to see me through until money started coming my way from the sale of paintings. So, what should I do? I decided to go for it!

The next morning, after saying goodbye to Joanne, Mike and I stood beside the Van-Go as he gave me directions for getting on the interstate that would lead me to Laredo, my entry point into Mexico, and from there on to picking up the belongings left in Jose Luis's tool shed the year before.

"Phone me if you run into any trouble, or if I can do anything for you," he said as we shook hands.

"If you can wait just a minute, there is one thing you can do for me," I said, finding the checkbook and scribbling out a check for $10,000. "Here, include me with your other syndicators. With four galleries hawking my wares, I should be able to make ends meet without this," I said as I handed him the piece of paper.

Second thoughts have a way of creeping in after rash actions. As I drove west that morning on Interstate 20 my mind kept going back to what I had just done, all too nonchalantly writing out a check for $10,000, as if there were plenty more where that came from.

As had happened once the year before, Mexican darkness was rapidly approaching and I was still on the road looking for a place to spend the night. A succession of huge trucks without headlights came looming out of the twilight, the only sign of warning being the dim glow from the colored bulbs lighting up their lumbering profiles, giving the effect of Christmas decorated cottages chasing each other down the narrow, bumpy highway. These enormous double-trailer transports insisted on taking up much of the road, even giving the impression that they preferred my side rather than their own half. I was trying to figure out the possible motivation for the man at the wheel driving on whichever side happened to strike his fancy when I remembered a conversation I had had many years before with Enganga, the young man who was my gun-bearer and the driver of one of the vehicles when I hunted in Africa.

"How will your life be different when the British leave and turn over the reigns of government to your people and you then have the freedom to govern yourselves; 'Uhuru' as you call it?" I asked him once during a break in the day's activity.

His face brightened as he enthusiastically rattled off a list of anticipated benefits, capping them all by adding, "Now we must drive on the left side of the road. When the British leave we can drive on whichever side we choose." I couldn't help but wonder if Enganga might have become so disenchanted when the material benefits of political freedom didn't turn out to be quite so bountiful as expected, that he had moved to Mexico and opened up a driving school for truckers.

Suddenly out of the darkness there appeared a Pemex station and alongside it, thank God, was a twelve room motel with a small open air bar and eatery connected to it. I checked in, showered, and was soon seated at an outdoor table ravenously devouring an order of frijoles and polishing off a cold bottle of Negro Modelo beer. "Otra vez, por favor," I said to the young girl barely in her teens who was serving me, pointing to the empty plate and holding up the bottle. It was a comforting feeling after a day of hard driving to sit relaxed and refreshed, safe and secure with food and drink in front of me and the night's lodging accounted for. Then I remembered. It was Thanksgiving night, a time to count blessings and be grateful.

Several flashbacks of Thanksgiving-past came to mind. One, involved an incident which I did witness firsthand but was only told about it by my then business partner. It seems that he and his wife had been invited to have Thanksgiving dinner with friends of theirs. The host and hostess had a four-year-old son named Johnny. The food was on the table and all present were seated with heads bowed, waiting for the blessing. Instead of saying it himself or inviting another adult to do so, the host turned to his son and said, "Johnny, would you like to say grace?" There then followed a period of prolonged silence. Johnny, it seemed, had forgotten his lines. But the father was patient, and everyone sat quietly, holding hands with their dinner mates on either side. Eventually, the stillness was broken by Johnny's shrill and unexpected pronouncement.

"Fret not thy gizzard! Amen." he blurted out.

Was there more? No, that was all he had to say.

"Amen," his father said, and with that started carving the turkey.

It's a story I have always cherished. For one would suppose that Johnny did indeed have a more traditional blessing intended, but with the pressure of being on stage before a group of people, it's fair to assume that since he couldn't remember the right words he finally decided he had better say some words, any old words, just to get himself off the hook. In all probability, he had picked up the expression from his father, who perhaps used it around the house instead of saying "Don't worry about that." Unwittingly, the little kid may have uttered a great profundity. For "Fret not thy gizzard", though in itself an absurd oxymoron, especially so since humans don't have gizzards, sounds quite Biblical, like a serious commandment, directing one to stay on the path of rectitude and forbearance and faith in the future even while surrounded by threatening vicissitudes on all sides. Don't worry, be happy, be grateful; don't give into fear and anxiety, it seems to say. Excellent advice. Thank you, Johnny. You will always be welcome to give the blessing at my table.

I looked at my watch. It was getting close to bedtime and I certainly didn't need another beer. It was time to ask Consuela for "la cuenta, por favor."

While waiting for her to show up, I decided to express my own thanks using simple words and speaking from the heart. Aside from good health, family and friends that I cared about and knew I could count on, a few bucks still left in the bank, there were the special blessings that had come my way within the past couple of weeks: the gift of acceptance by galleries in Washington, Atlanta, New Orleans and, in all probability, Dallas. I was especially thankful that I enjoyed my work so much that much of the time, it seemed more like play than work. And, I was grateful that I was my own boss, that I could come and go and do as I pleased. I gave thanks for being incredibly fortunate in having so many good things going for me all at once.

Consuela, responding to my motion to bring the check, smiled as she came up. "You look very happy, senor," she said in halting English as she laid it on the table.

"I am very happy, Consuela. Very happy indeed." I replied as I wished her goodnight and headed to my room for a good night's sleep.

As I pulled up in front of Pieter's house the next afternoon I expected to find him right where I had left him the year before, lying in the hammock on the veranda with a paperback in one hand and either a bottle of beer or a cigarette in the other. The hammock was empty, however, and as I rang the bell I wondered if he might be sick. But the big smile on his face and hearty hello as he greeted me at the door made it plain that he was in good spirits and suffering no pain.

"I was a little worried about you," I said jokingly after we shook hands. "You were not in your customary supine position doing scholarly research into the substantive nature of trashy literature. I thought perhaps you weren't feeling well and had taken to your bed."

"Well you were half right," he said grinning. "'With Rosie out of town I was doing another type of scholarly research. I was lying on the bed watching the Playboy channel. She won't let me turn it on when she's around. Say, is that your vehicle?" he asked pointing to the Van-Go.

"Yeah, it's my traveling studio. I'd just a soon wait awhile before climbing back up the all those steps, but I'll show it to you when we go out to dinner. As I drove in I noticed a car with Pennsylvania plates parked in my former space. It must belong to the people who moved in after I left. Who's living in the house? Are they good neighbors?"

"Oh, I guess they're all right. We speak when we see each other, but that's about all. They're too damned dull to merit much attention which, as you know, is pretty much par for the course around here. How nice it would be, instead of forever being told all about Debbie and Kevin, everyone's generic grandkids back in Toledo or wherever, to encounter a dashing character like one of those in the cheap paperbacks I'm forever reading who would break our tiresome monotony by coming out with something like 'then, with the morning's first light I looked out and could dimly see only broken pieces of the ship's wreckage still stranded on the reef, all else swept away by the fury of the storm from the night just past. The air was warm and balmy, and upon looking about in the half light of dawn I saw that our lifeboat had washed ashore on a lush desert island. Still asleep under the grove of palm trees where I lay, were the others who had gotten in the boat with me. Not until then did I realize that they were the six beautiful girls heading home from the Miss Universe contest. There we were, the only survivors. But, enough of that, I don't want to bore you with my stories.' at which time I would undoubtedly grab him by the arm and shout, 'Hell man, go on! Go on! Don't stop now. Your's is the first decent story I've heard since Bill, who used to be my next door neighbor, moved away. For God's sake go on. You've got to tell me what happened with you and the six beautiful girls.“

He acted out the impromptu dialog with enthusiasm, giving the imaginary storyteller a voice different from his own, and well before he finished I was laughing so hard I awakened the black dog Capolini from his snooze.

Pieter placed a hand on my shoulder and in a tone of profound solemnity said, "Be of good cheer, my friend. All is not lost. I have diligently carried on the good work in your absence. Even as we speak, the ingredients for concocting the esteemed Hell Fire and Damnation Martini await our presence in the kitchen. Shall we proceed to mix an experimental batch?"

"By all means," I said emphatically as I followed him into the kitchen. "And, to celebrate the occasion of this reunion and to express my gratitude to you for having continued such a worthy tradition, tonight I think I'll indulge myself by following the recommendation of a Russian friend of mine and spike my Hell Fire and Damnation Martini with four drops of scotch."

The next day as I drove through town for the trip back north I passed by the little clinic where I spent so much time the year before. A board was nailed across the front door and what looked like a notice was tacked to it. I stopped the Van-Go and crossed the street to take a look. With my limited understanding of Spanish, I deduced from the handwritten statement that the little building had been condemned and was about to be torn down. It gave the new address for the clinic, and I recognized it as being on one of Chapala's better streets.

As I stood there I remembered the long bout with Enfermedad Indeterminado Serio and, of course, the foot-finger incident. I was glad that the sweeping granny had not fallen through the plaster. Also, it was good to know that the doctor and nurse were not discovered "entwined 'neath rubble." I was a little sorry, however, that my Gringo foot still gave me trouble. On some days it hurt so much I limped; on other days it didn't, and I made out pretty well. The good news, I decided, was that I still walked. With that in mind I hobbled back across the street, flipped on the Van Go's ignition switch and took off for the good ol' U.S. of A.

CHAPTER NINE
Catfish, Moonshine And Magnolias

With winter coming on and since I was already in the South, I couldn't think of a better plan than to spend the next few months painting along the Gulf, known to some as the Redneck Riviera, while working my way eastward from Padre Island near Corpus Christi, Texas to some place on the Florida coast and let early spring take hold before heading back to Virginia. Even though the coastal area is not always warm enough throughout the winter months for swimming, sunbathing or water sports, I was not interested in those kinds of activities, and there should be plenty of days ideal for being outdoors and painting coastal and marine subject matter including all the fishing, oyster and shrimp boats one could hope for. The best way to accomplish the objective, I discovered, was to pull into an area that looked promising, scout around until I found a clean and respectable but otherwise down-at-the-heels, usually off the beaten track, motel where I could rent a room with a kitchenette for no more than my budget price of a hundred and fifty dollars a week, and agree to take the place for two weeks.

The first such place was well situated, with good painting sites in either direction along the coast, and was owned and run by a resident mom and pop combination. The decor inside the unit that served as their office/living quarters was, without question, eligible for top prize in a national corny-folksy-cutesy contest if such a thing existed. She played the piano badly and sang gospel hymns and songs like "God Bless America" and Home On The Range in a voice that sounded like a musical saw with vocal chords. Pop was a retired mail carrier who spoke in transposed syllables, leaving me puzzled as to whether he didn't know any better, was doing it on purpose, or if he suffered from dyslexia. Berserk became beresk; irrelevant became irrevalant; veracity became veraticy. They, and their cheap motel owning counterparts that I encountered later on, seemed to view me as something of an oddity, spending my time painting when I could be engaged in more normal activities, such as sitting around all day doing little or nothing, or something constructive like fishing.

Well I certainly wasn't one to turn up my nose at fishing, having deep-sea fished in years past and fly-fished in both the States and Great Britain. But brushes had become more important to me than fly rods. My immediate gameplan was to take advantage of the combination of coastal scenery and fishing activity taking place along the sandy shores of Padre Island, where surf-casters parked their pick-ups or campers almost at the water's edge and waded well out into the rolling surf to lure their catch. With the Van-Go barely easing forward along a lengthy stretch of beach I came upon a small spread-out assemblage of what appeared to be unrelated vehicles and their owners. Some were cooking breakfast, while kids and dogs were playing, one guy was in a folding chair reading, but most were involved in the main event, surf-casting. Knowing that I would be hard-pressed to find better subject matter I stopped, took off the hatch cover and stood in the open hatch viewing the scene. I knew it was material for a good painting, and I was soon set up and roughing everything in. Aside from the human interest near shore, there was an especially interesting cloud formation I wanted to quickly capture, for it was of a long, twisting, trailing, unbroken shape with dramatic lights and darks of a kind that seems to have a special kinship with the sea.

Closer to me than any of the others was a middle-aged husband and wife couple who were fishing some twenty or so yards out in the water and were busily casting away. They, I decided, would be my center of interest. Their bright red pick-up truck was parked nearby, and occasionally one or the other of them would slosh their way back to it to take a break, change bait, or pour what I assumed was coffee from a thermos. He was clad, head to foot, in matching brilliant yellow waterproof parka and waders and she wore the identical outfit only the color of hers was an intense scarlet. During a break he glanced over and obviously saw that I was looking their way, then doing something with a paintbrush, then looking their way again, then more with the paintbrush. I could tell that his curiosity was about to get the better of him and that I might soon have a visitor. Sure enough, he was soon heading my way.

"Whatcha' paintin'?" he asked in a stern tone of voice that made it sound like he had the right to approve of whatever it was I was painting.

"I'm painting what I see," I replied. "I'm painting the ocean, the beach, the vehicles, the people fishing. Would you like to see?"

He said nothing, but gave a slight nod.

I was not about to invite such a surly person into the van, so I took the painting off the easel and held it over the side so he could look at it. "It's only about half finished," I said. I had purposely painted the truck brown instead of red, for I didn't want it detracting visual focus from the bright red his wife was wearing, for the two of them were the center of interest, not the truck. It was pointless trying to explain any of that to him as he stood staring at it silently as if he wanted to pick a fight.

"That don't look like my truck," he said.

"Sorry," I said. "As I told you, I'm not finished with it yet."

About an hour later I saw her coming my way. The wind was from off the sea, and I had been able to catch enough of their truck-side talk to learn that his name was Homer and hers was Edna. As she approached I noted that in addition to carrying a lot of extra weight, she was so splay-legged that the pedals would need to be extended a few inches in order for her to ride a bicycle. Much to her credit, her facial expression was reasonably pleasant, and I was quite willing to oblige when she looked up and said, "Good Morning. Mind if I see your picture?"

She looked at it intently for a few seconds while I held it over the edge, then said "My, that sure is pretty. But, well, Homer's right. That doesn't look like our truck."

I didn't want to run the risk of offending her by telling her that I didn't want it to look like their truck, and came close to making up a story by saying something such as, "Well, I'm only the advance man. The real artist will be here soon and he'll make it look enough like your truck you'll feel like climbing in and driving it away." Instead, I told her I was still working on it and would try a little harder to make it look like their truck.

As I moved the Van-Go to new positions along the Gulf and became engaged in conversations with various kibitzers, admission of their own artistic ineptitude based on being unable to draw a straight line was by far the most frequent comment directed my way by onlookers. Invariably, the tone of voice and facial expression implied that this inability to connect two points in space by the shortest possible route forever negated any chance they might otherwise have had of being an artist. My response varied, depending on the confessor and my own mood. (1) Sympathy: "Gee, that's too bad. I'm sorry to hear it." (2) Pretended Concern: "Of course I'm interested. Thank you for sharing that with me." (3) Didactic Reassurance: "Well, I certainly wouldn't worry about it. Straight lines have a lot to do with geometry, practically nothing at all to do with art." (4) Fellow Sufferer: "I can't draw one either. Not without using a straight-edged mall stick."

On one such occasion I was being set upon by a lady with a regional accent whose constant use of diphthongs in her pronunciation made words of only one vowel sound as if they had two different vowels in sequence, so that line kept sounding like li-on. On or about the fourth time she informed me that she couldn't draw a straight li-on, I felt like telling her that it was easy to draw a straight lion. Just draw him surrounded by a group of admiring female lions, and that would show that old Leo was straight as an arrow. With considerable restraint, I refrained from such a smart-aleck comment.

After a few hours drive into new territory I found a place well off the beaten track where cottages could be rented by the week. Soon after I moved in it started to rain, and that was the mode of the weather most of the time I was there. Determined not to let the rain stop me, I scouted the area until I found a major highway bridge linking a fairly wide inlet from the gulf. There were work boats and some paintable scenery along an interesting stretch of water. After a few wrong turns, I ended up on the dirt road running along the water's edge and under the bridge. There, sheltered from the rain, I parked the Van-Go and painted for several days. My companions were a handful of fishermen and a small group of outlandish looking herons, who spent their entire time bickering over territorial rights or mating privileges or, perhaps, a combination of both. One day as I was taking a noontime break I was joined by Sheldon, who fished every day in his small run-about and professed to be an out of work intellectual, although he let it slip that from time to time he had done other things such as tending bar.

Sheldon had a good stock of stories, and one I particularly liked was about a prisoner's wife who sent him a letter asking, "What shall I do about planting a garden?"

He, knowing that prison mail was censored, wrote back, "Don't plant the garden. I don't want you digging in it. That's where I hid the money I stole from the bank". Her letter in reply said, "Today there were eight sheriff's deputies here and they dug up every square inch of the garden."

He wrote back, "Now, you can plant the garden."

In New Orleans I wanted to be close to the action, so I prepared myself for having to exceed my budget so far as lodging was concerned. My best bet, I reasoned, was to find an inexpensive bed and breakfast, if such a thing existed. Mardi Gras had come and gone, and since it was still officially winter I perhaps would not be faced with the steep rents of high season. Even so, I was in the dilemma of either skipping New Orleans or paying more than my pocketbook could afford. Martha, the director of the gallery where my paintings hung, was my only contact and she was away on vacation. I looked in the yellow pages of the phone book and after calling a B&B that was well located in the Garden District, I decided to drive by and take a look. Lady Luck was with me. As I sat having coffee with the pleasant and personable couple who owned the place, which was more like an inn than a B&B, they asked what I did. I told them I was a painter. What kind of a painter? they asked.

From having been asked that question several times before, I had learned that the best answer was to show rather than tell, so I showed them the small photo album containing prints of some of my paintings. Minutes later it was agreed that they would give me two weeks free rent if I would paint a portrait of the elegant old mansion they had recently bought and were converting into a second facility. Some quick mental arithmetic told me I could probably do the painting in two or three days, in exchange for which I was promised two weeks in what was described by the owners as the finest bedroom in the old mansion.

With the Van Go parked in front of my new residence, I was soon brushing paint on canvas depicting a grand example of Southern neo-classic homes of a bygone era. Corinthian columns supporting double tiered galleries that rimmed the house on three sides in a setting of magnolias and boxwoods presented me with a charming subject. A couple of days after moving in I finished the painting, but I laid it aside until near the end of my visit, for I wanted to give it a proper vernissage by inviting a few people in for an unveiling reception. Laren and Paul, friends of Lisa's, were in town to have some fun and get away from New York winter, Lisa flew down from Washington and, with the three of them in attendance plus the landlord couple and about a half-dozen other guests who were staying in the mansion, I threw a cocktail party with my painting on display in the handsomely detailed great hall with guests assembled beneath a Venetian chandelier hanging from a twenty-two foot high elaborately embellished ceiling. Lisa graced the occasion with some of her beautifully sung arias. The contrast to my recently accustomed mom-and-pop plastic and polyester kitchenette habitats was nothing short of startling and, two days later, when it was time to move out, I reminded myself with regret of the old adage that all good things must come to an end.

I had promised my friend Anne, who lived on the other side of Mobile Bay, that I would show up in time to take her to dinner, and I was driving east with that in mind. Soon after driving through Biloxi, Mississippi I began to hear radio warnings of tornadoes, but they all seemed to be doing their dirty work well behind me, so I gave no thought to my own personal safety. As I approached Mobile, however, the main force of the storm was described as being in that immediate area and, in effect, right on my tail. I knew that the bridge-causeway combination that traverses the northern end of the bay that would get me over to Anne's side of the water was several miles long, the worst possible place to be if approached by a tornado. I toyed with the idea of going to a phone while still in Mobile, calling Anne and postponing our dinner, but then I remembered and decided to paraphrase the words of Admiral Farragut and mentally said, "Damn the Tornadoes. Full speed ahead!" By holding a steady course toward the other side, accompanied by gusting winds and threatening skies and a play-by-play status report by the radio announcer, I arrived in time to have a pleasant dinner with a pretty lady.

To me, one of the most awesome and fascinating scenes in nature is that of a sunrise or sunset with vivid colors lighting up the sky over an expanse of water. I found myself in an area where the locals claimed their days-end celestial extravaganzas were the best show on earth. I took them at their word and painted several sunset canvases and was glad to be able to generously brush on reds, orange and yellows that generally are used quite sparingly. It is, of course, virtually impossible to record at the time what's going on at the time. The light has its own way, and a cloud that was pink on top one moment is pink on the bottom the next. The answer, I think, lies in developing the ability to skillfully observe, and then put something on canvas representative of that observation. The painting that in 1874 shook the art world and gave name to what later became the most popular of all schools of painting, *Impressionism,* was Claude Monet's "Sunrise Impression," painted from his hotel window overlooking the harbor at Le Harve. Artists of that day constantly debated whether one should paint what he sees or paint what he knows. In my opinion, the correct answer came from the great American artist and teacher, William Merritt Chase. He said, quite simply, "Do both."

At the end of each day's painting along the strip of the Alabama coast where I was staying, I would head straight for "Judge Roy Beam-Law West of The Pecos", a nearby so-called "private club" where one had to pay $1 to be a "member" and get through the front door. Once inside, succulent oysters on the half shell were a mere twenty-five cents each. Typically I would sit at the bar and have two or three dozen raw, washed down with several schooners of beer. This long awaited main repast of the day was frequently interrupted by Billy, the big-horned, long-whiskered billygoat in residence who had complete run of the place. He especially enjoyed chewing on those portions of my old Harris tweed jacket that hung down from the barstool at exactly the right height for him to feed on while I was having my meal of beer and oysters. Billy and I dined together in this manner nightly until I left the area and moved on down the coast.

It had been a pleasant day. I had found a subject that appealed to me and painting had gone well. As a result of studying a local map I had followed a winding road that more or less paralleled the course of a river that emptied into the Gulf farther downstream. After a short distance of poking along at ten miles an hour, looking for a scene too good to pass up, I came to a clearing that bordered the water's edge. There were tire tracks and a feeble excuse for a dirt road sloping down to what amounted to a small backwater, where the flow was idle and land and river came together gently. It appeared that I had stumbled upon a place used by locals as a launching site for their boats. The ground was dry, so I drove the Van-Go down closer to the water to see if the setting held promise of being painter-friendly. The minute I arrived at the river's edge where, for the first time, I could get a clear view upstream, it was obvious that it would be pointless to look any farther, for there was plenty to paint right where I was.

A few hundred yards to my left at a broad bend in the river was a cluster of long, low buildings hugging the bank with piers fingering out into the brackish water that served as home port for a small fleet of shrimp and fishing boats. Next to a gray metal hangar-type shed, the largest of the structures, was a yard with a marine railway and cradles for hauling boats out for maintenance and repair. The dozen or so commercial craft nesting along the wharf and the outstretched wooden docks were, to me, a study in themselves, for they each showed the decorative tastes of their owner. Most met the test of tradition and practicality by being white hulled, yet at the same time having a wide variance in the color chosen for boot stripe or gunwale trim, some of which were unnecessarily bright and garish. Others in the group seemed to demand that individuality be recognized so that onlookers from a distance could confidently assert, "There's ol' Sally May," or "Here comes the Samuel T. Porter," and to facilitate this desire to be different, their boats were apt to be the ones painted a bilious pea green or a nauseous baby blue, or some other "artistic" color.

As the river curved around toward where I had parked the Van-Go, there was a small white frame house that had once served as a dwelling, but the one-time residents apparently sold out to an enterprising proprietor who had attached a sign to the drooping front porch advertising freshly caught fish, shrimp and, of all things, live Maine lobsters, wholesale and retail. Live Maine lobsters? Something fishy here, I figured. Still, I liked the looks of the big amateurishly lettered sign on the shabby little run down house, and thought it would add interest to a painting. Next to the fish house was another small establishment of similar architectural persuasion. It boasted the name of "Shorty's" and proclaimed itself to be the best provider of spiced shrimp, catfish dinners, and southern fried chicken in the entire South.

I took the hatch cover off the Van-Go and stood with my head and shoulders above the roof line, absorbing the view in the tentatively warm air of a mid-winter's day on the Gulf Coast, aimlessly watching the greenish brown waters of the wide and silent river sweep slowly past. The wheels of the van had come to rest beneath the broad and shady branches of a mighty, moss draped oak, so shade was accounted for; no need to move on that account. No need to move for any reason. I took another look at Shorty's. My eyes came to rest on an old and battered metal sign that read "Budweiser". Quite possibly he was exaggerating about the shrimp and the catfish and the fried chicken being the best in the South, but at least I could depend on a bottle of beer being as advertised. When it got to be lunch time I would go over and dine at Shorty's. In the meantime, there was a blank canvas on its stretcher waiting to be painted. This ought to be fun, I thought. A beautiful day ahead and no audience, with the "best fried catfish in the South" and a cold beer only a hundred or so yards away.

Some paintings, usually the ones that turn out to be the best, seem to want to paint themseves. The shrimp boat painting at Calvin's Bend was definitely one of those. The clear, untroubled sky, the low growing, windswept trees across the river, the grouping of riverfront buildings and the assortment of boats that gave them reason for being there, the snaggle-toothed scattering of ramshackle houses and, finally, the dull and lazy river itself; these were the elements that combined to create a composition receptive to a painter's brush. Almost everything, from the very start, worked out well, even though the matter of getting the compound curves of the boat hulls foreshortened and in proper perspective, along with other temporary problems, did slow me down.

But by far the toughest part of the painting, I soon discovered, was getting the water of the river to look the way I wanted it to look, which was unattainable, I decided, if I painted it the way it actually did look. For its local color was too drab, too much a dismal hen house brown to evoke the eye appeal needed to hold the viewer's interest. After a little pondering, I used some painter's license and tried introducing both life and energy to the painting of the water by adding colors that I imagined might feel at home upon the surface of the muddy stream, but colors which, without my help, would slip on past unnoticed to the Gulf. With five clean filbert brushes and five freshly mixed batches of color on the palette, I resorted to a procedure that rather quickly gave me what I wanted. It was a technique I stumbled upon in France as a result of employing some by-guess and by-gosh experimentation. I was attempting, at the time, to make a wide expanse of blue sky look more transparent, more atmospheric, more interesting and more painterly. The procedure amounts to nothing more complicated than purposely painting in a series of undertones before applying the final hue that's visually expected.

From all that I have read and from my own limited experience and observation as a landscape painter, it seems true to say that, except for each of the three pure primary colors, every color that we see, to one degree or another, is composed of other colors as well. But the other colors are subordinate to what we perceive to be the dominant color. So, on that day in France when I decided to try to improve on the blue sky in my painting because it looked flat and lifeless, I began to think about those "other" colors and how to incorporate them while, at the same time, ending up with a blue sky. My solution was to mix up batches of subordinate colors, all of them roughly of the same value, and apply each one sparingly (in dabs), and in an ordered sequence that depended on their position on the color wheel as related to the blue, the dominant color I wanted to end up with.

Since orange is the complimentary color of blue and directly opposite blue on the color wheel, I dabbed it on first, more or less at random and with lots of blank canvas in between the dabs. The other subordinate batches were alizarin crimson (to add brightness and variety and perhaps a little mystery - what's it doing there?) and two analogous colors, one cool and the other somewhat warm: viridian green and blue shade mauve, and I applied all three of them, each with its own separate clean brush, in dabs in the order just given. At this point the sky looked as if I had either gone completely nuts or an H bomb had exploded, and I was glad that there were no onlookers. Finally, while the subordinate dabs were still wet, with the clean brush intended only for the blue, I covered the entire sky, making certain that each dab of blue pigment was "placed" not "stroked" on top of the other dabs in such a way as to mostly, but not entirely, obscure what lay beneath. Upon finishing, I can't recall whether I shouted "Eureka!" or "Voila!" or simply poured myself a beer. But I do remember that I was pleased with the results and have since used the same principle to create a degree of vibrancy and a sensation of something happening in what might otherwise be passages dull enough to cause the viewer to yawn.

By using this system of what I call subordinate undertones I soon had the river accounted for. The dominant color consisted of gradated tones of raw umber, amplified with undertones of ultramarine blue, viridian, mauve and cerulean blue, the latter itself becoming dominant in those areas calling for highlights. The result was a wet-looking river with some sparkling passages. In a couple of key places I introduced a hint of alizaron crimson as an unexplained visitor, just to punch things up a bit. It had been a good morning's work. And the way the sun was transiting there would be light on the subject throughout the rest of the day, so I would be able to continue during the afternoon. I laid aside the brushes. It was time to go visit Shorty's.

As I ascended the rickety steps attached to the front porch, I was gratified to note from the fading letters of the sign beside the entrance that the Southern fried chicken and catfish were pan fried. Good for Shorty, I thought, mentally giving him high marks for recognizing the fact that pan frying is the proper way to cook both of these regional favorites, instead of throwing them in the deep fryer, as is too often the case. My mental picture of being warmly greeted by the Shorty of my imagination, a gregarious and convivial individual with the South in his mouth who took daily pleasure in making folks happy with his good, down home cookin', was dispelled the minute I entered the one and a half room eatery converted shanty. For instead of the welcoming host I had imagined, there stood behind the counter a tall, sallow-faced man whose expression caused me to wonder if he was perhaps a little put out with me for coming into his place.

I sat down at one of the counter stools. He looked over in my direction and, without bothering to move, asked, "What can I do for you?"

"I might be interested in your pan-fried catfish and a bottle of Budweiser," I replied. "What goes with the catfish, coleslaw?"

"Nothin' goes with the catfish. We don't serve it anymore. Not since Shorty left. I can let you have a hamburger or a sandwich with fries," he said, putting the beer on the counter in front of me.

How about the pan fried chicken you talk about on the sign out in front. How long does it take for it to cook?"

"Well, it would take forever to cook if you wanted to get it here. We don't serve that anymore, either. When me and my wife moved down here from up north and bought Shorty out last year we didn't realize that Shorty had got all these people around here accustomed to him pan frying this and pan frying that. Pan frying takes time and attention, see what I mean? Who's got time for it in this day and age, see what I mean? For a while we give the customers just as good catfish and chicken that we cooked in the deep fryer. Every bit as good, see what I mean? But some of these people said they didn't like it as good as the way Shorty cooked it, so we quit serving either chicken or catfish. Nope. No more chicken. No more catfish. Who's got time to stand around watching something slow cook in a skillet, see what I mean? How about a hamburger? We make a good hamburger."

With his last "see what I mean" the wise-guy side of me was tempted to hit him with something like, "Say, would you mind repeating everything you've just told me? I don't quite get it." Another alternative that came to mind would be to simply say to him, "Goodbye. See what I mean?" But I was hungry, so I stayed put and ordered a ham and cheese on rye, switching to whole wheat when told that there was no rye, but finally settling for white because, "We don't get enough calls for those other two, see what I mean?" Come back, Shorty. They need you here!

After a morning of standing in one spot, doing nothing more active than moving a small brush from point A to point B, a little leg stretching seemed to be in order, so 1 walked over toward the boatyard, partly for the exercise and partly to get a closer look at what I had chosen as the subject for a painting. I stood watching for a while as one of the older wooden fishing boats resting in a cradle was having its bilge scraped and sanded in preparation for the coatings of antifouling chemicals and bottom paint that would eventually follow. A man who looked and acted like he might be the foreman gave me a friendly hello, and the two of us were soon discussing some of the characteristics of the boat being overhauled. I guessed him to be a reasonably trustworthy sort of person, and since I had not as yet made any arrangements for the night, I asked him about the advisability of me leaving the big blue van where it was and sleeping in it overnight. He followed my glance and looked across the water to where I was pointing to the Van-Go.

"Well, I'll tell you mister, the folks around here is either too dad-blamed lazy or too busy watchin' TV to be out doing any unnecessary harm after dark. Course, since today's pay day and tomorrow's Saturday there might be a few drunks out looking for trouble, but I'd say you got nothin' to worry about. Anyway, there's Shelby. He's the night watchman for this whole complex: buildings, boats and all. He comes on duty when we leave. This place is lit up like a Christmas tree after dark and he'll be able to see your van plain enough. I'll tell him to keep an eye on you. He'll do a good job of it too, if he don't fall asleep while he's at it. Sure, you'll be safe enough there. Shouldn't no one bother you."

On the way back to the Van-Go I passed the fish house. I stopped and asked the owner if he really did have live Maine lobsters.

"Sure, sometimes, but not now."

"How about catfish," I asked

"Pulled out flappin' fresh just this morning," he told me.

I bought a nice-looking fillet, had it wrapped with some crushed ice, and put the small, cool parcel to rest until dinner time in the van's little micky-mouse refrigerator.

For me, the toughest part of a painting is usually the first half. That's when a lot of the decisions need to be made and most of the problems solved. The process of painting a picture is similar, in my opinion, to the various progressive steps involved in building a house. All the vital support members and the studs, joists and fixtures hidden behind walls and beneath floors must be accounted for, oftentimes by grunt labor. And these parts that don't show are every bit as important as the parts that do. But in the end, the finished surfaces are what everyone sees, and the general effect of all of them combined is what the builder gets praised for. In my view, the same is true with the "building" of a painting. The under-painting that lies beneath the surface and doesn't show is, in a sense, as important as the final brushstrokes. Once this grunt labor part of a painting is concluded, it's more or less down hill from then on. The touching up, the chance to refine, to make improvements and concentrate on accents and brushwork are, for me, the areas of attention that are the most enjoyable, for by then I have begun to feel that I may have a decent painting in the bag. At about five-thirty I started cleaning brushes and scraping down the palette. I took the painting off the easel and put it in the rear section of the Van-Go reserved for wet canvases. It was time to quit, and I felt good about the day's work, for I knew I had painted myself a keeper.

I had long before discovered that the hours between cleaning the brushes and bedtime held the threat of being an unpleasant vacuum unless I purposefully went out of my way to prevent this from happening. Past decisions and personal tastes had left me with fewer options for occupying my time than I would have liked. Years before, when I foolishly thought I would remain young forever with endless chances to choose some as yet un-met soulmate for the perfect wife, I had walked down the aisle numerous times as someone else's best man or usher, with the church bells almost, but never quite, ringing for me. So, when the day's work ended, there was no good woman to keep me company and possibly remind me from time to time that while she had married me for better or for worse, for richer or for poorer, we had recently plunged all too rapidly from better and richer to worse and poorer. She would be quite justified in feeling that way too, I reasoned, for the life I was presently leading was either the pits or utopia, depending on how one felt about it.

Sports might well have been a diversion. But even though I had briefly played football (rather poorly) in high school, had played tennis (somewhat better) most of my life, had hunted, fly fished, ridden horses and raced A class sailboats, I was certainly not addicted to spectator sports

Of course, there was always the national pastime, television. But there again, I ran into a snag. In the late fifties I bought my first T.V., a top-of-the-line portable. After several years I gave the set away to a neighboring married couple who had come to my house for dinner. As they walked away, congratulating themselves on their good fortune in being given a perfectly good T.V., I stood congratulating myself on my own good fortune in having gotten rid of it. Some twenty-five years later, Lisa and I had gone to look at a painting said to be by the early American painter, Charles Wilson Peale. Upon seeing it we both thought it was probably the work of a lesser hand and were about to leave when its owner announced that he was moving to Florida and many of the things in the house were for sale. He pointed to a large console, late model color TV "You can have that, if you'd like, for only a hundred dollars," turning it on and flipping through a series of stations as he spoke.

"No thanks," I said. "I don't need a T.V."

"Boss, you're crazy not to buy it for only a hundred dollars," Lisa had said. "I know you think television's a waste of time, but at least you can watch the news with it." We loaded it in the trunk of the car and I took it home.

A few years later I was having my own house sale before moving to Mexico. One of the people who showed up was a woman who kept looking at the big TV set, which was priced at exactly what I had paid for it, one hundred dollars. "What's the least you would take for it?" she had asked very timidly. She looked pathetically poor, with two small kids clinging to her skirt.

"Take it as a gift. It won't cost you anything," I told her, asking a man I had hired to help out with the sale to see to it that it got loaded onto the back of her pick-up.

I promised myself at the time that I would not own any more TVs, else I might become known as "that goofy man who gives away television sets". Throughout the many years during which I have not owned television, people are forever chiding me for missing out on all the treasures that are offered by the boob tube. In rebuttal, I point out that there are probably many treasures to be found among the trash of any city dump, but going there to search for them doesn't interest me either.

After enduring some very lonely evenings while painting along the Gulf, I decided it was vital that I do something to fill this evening void. The solution was relatively simple. I would start reading again. For many years I had enjoyed owning a library of a couple of thousand books. Almost every subject I cared about was within eyesight and at my fingertips. There were scores of art books, books on classical music; volumes of ancient and modern history; books on sailing, hunting, botany; sections devoted to antique furniture, English china, Georgian silver, oriental rugs, religion, philosophy, metaphysics; several sets of encyclopedia and many volumes of classic fiction, some of which, like Huckleberry Finn, War and Peace and The Brothers Karamazov, I had read through more than once. Because of these diverse and carefully selected volumes that I had collected over the years, my life had been enriched by many a pleasant and fulfilling evening spent in a room filled from floor to ceiling with books, comfortably relaxed in the big leather easy chair with feet stretched out on the ottoman and light from the old-fashioned floor lamp shining down just right on the pages as I read. These were among my list of treasures I felt forced to part with in order to raise the money needed for my new career. Ironically, I had sold my books on painting so that I might have the funds needed to become a painter.

Having determined to make good use of my spare time by getting back into the reading habit, I set about trying to find some worthwhile books at prices I could afford. I would be on the lookout for yard sale signs as I drove through strange towns and stop and take a look if there was likelihood that they might have books. I also kept my eyes peeled for the type of bookstore that will sometimes put tables or bins out in front, displaying used books marked way down. After several fruitless "not fit to read" stops, I eventually spotted a yard-sale sign, with books listed among the household items featured. It was a trim, nice looking neighborhood and there was a decent chance, I hoped, of finding something of a little better quality than the sleazy crop of paperbacks that had made up the major portion of the offerings heretofore encountered. I walked away happy, for inside the brown paper shopping bag the lady had given me, were hard-bound volumes by Hemingway, Twain, Henry James, Steinbeck and a big, thick long out of print and, to me near priceless anthology titled, "Writers of the Western World" that begins with Homer and ends with Eugene O'Neill, and a book containing "The Painted Veil", a complete novel by Somerset Maugham, plus a dozen or more of his short stories. For only fourteen dollars and seventy five cents I had the nucleus of a small traveling library that would provide me with evening reading for weeks.

My work finished for the day, I began to set things up for the long awaited period of rest, thoughtful libation and, eventually, the evening meal, the day's tour de force, featuring freshly caught pan-fried catfish. With the air so unseasonably warm I set about establishing headquarters outdoors, under the big live oak, beside the river. Out came the card table with its red checkered plastic cover, the director's chair, the small radio cassette player with a half dozen tapes including two selected especially because of the riverside setting: Handel's "Water Music Suite" and Bedrich Smetana's river-inspired "The Moldau." Darkness descends quickly and early during the winter, so I brought out all the things I would need for cooking and eating later on. To a low hanging branch of the live oak I tied the wire handle of the Coleman lantern, made heavy by the butane cylinder screwed into its base. The two-burner portable butane stove was about to be transported from its galley mounting when I discovered that the last of the canisters was attached to the lantern, so I carried out the small Weber charcoal grill instead.

At last, seated comfortably and relaxed, a glass of good, bone dry, inexpensive Italian pinot grigio on the ground beside me, the haunting sounds of Antonin Dvorak's "From The New World" symphony adding enchantment to the setting, I began reading the beautifully crafted pages of John Steinbeck's "Cannery Row", all the while filled with profound admiration for his masterful touch as a writer. He was, I decided, among the most skillful of painters, but one whose pictures were painted best with words. I would be indebted to Steinbeck and the other writers I had chosen, if their expertly woven plots and well-spun narratives succeeded in changing the nightly dread of loneliness into the contented solitude that can often best be found between the covers of a book.

The former brightness of the day was dimming, not good light for reading, much more suited to just sitting, waiting patiently while nature changed her dress. As daylight languished, a talent show too good to miss was taking place. I laid aside the book and looked aloft to watch small clusters of pink-orange clouds stretch themselves sideways far across the evening sky, their fluffy underbellies wearing shadowed tones of mauve and umber. The slowly moving river, no longer just a muddy flow, became, instead, as much a mirror as a stream; a broad, illumined crimson path forever heading homeward in its winding journey to the sea. Across the water, clinging closely to the bank, the deep green silhouettes of straggly, windswept trees gave way to subtle reddish hues, then purple, then finally, inky blackness. High above, night swallows darting through the twilight sky in search of insects for their evening meal reminded me that down on earth at Camp Van-Go, it was time to light the lantern and start the charcoal. There was catfish to be cooked.

The night was warm and clear. I had gone to bed with moonlight streaming through the open hatch. Suddenly I was wide awake. Something had bumped against the outside of the van. Best not to move, I told myself. Lie still and wait. Try to figure out what might have caused the disturbance. It had been like a dull thud on the side of the van where I was sleeping, and only inches away from where my head was resting on the pillow. At the time, the van had moved, had rocked slightly. I held my breath and lay listening. It was a person, so close I imagined I could hear him breathing. Again, the van reacted with a movement that was almost imperceptible, but real enough to be disturbing. The moon had set, and pitch black darkness remained in its stead. I wondered about the hour, the time of night, but the hands on my watch were gold and did not fluoresce, so I couldn't tell without a light. There was a small high intensity flashlight on the ledge beside the bunk. The flashlight might very well help in a number of ways if I could get my hands on it. But there was always the danger of knocking something over and making a racket if I was clumsy in finding it.

I lay without moving a muscle, barely breathing, turning over in my mind what little I knew about the situation and, at the same time, pondering the wide gamut of possible unknowns and trying to arrive at some sensible conclusion as to a course of action. It seemed clear to me that whatever choices I might have involved action of one sort or another. I was not about to just pull the covers up over my head and do nothing. Someone, for whatever reason, was deliberately encroaching on my territory, and it was up to me to see to it that he got off and away before doing any damage to either me or the Van-Go. But how? Back in Virginia I had rather piously decided to sally forth, by the grace of God, unarmed. Whether that was wise or stupid could all be sorted out later. But I had never, ever resolved to sally forth without bringing along some brains. Well, I had damned well better start using them fast and think my way out of this one. But, again, how? I had no weapon.

The first order of business was to get the flashlight. I must do it quietly and without any sudden shifting of weight, otherwise, the van would move. With left hand stretching out ever so slowly toward its objective, my fingers eventually came into contact with the ledge, groped cautiously along its surface until, at last, I had the flashlight in my grasp. The beam of light beneath the covers told me it was 5:17 in the morning. Dawn would begin to break in a little over an hour.

The silence was interrupted by a low cough. The moment I heard the cough I knew I could probably assume that the uninvited visitor hanging around outside my van at such an ungodly hour was under the impression that the van was empty; otherwise he would not advertise his presence and give away his position by something so careless as a cough. With this new bit of welcome intelligence, and like one planning a military campaign, I began mentally listing what I perceived as my pros and cons at the time of the forthcoming confrontation. Except for weaponry, it appeared as if it would be mostly in my favor, for no matter how one sliced it, I would enjoy some of the more sought-after advantages attached to ground warfare.

First, the element of surprise: that would be all mine. What about high ground? That would be mine too, by several whole feet. Deciding the time and place for the encounter: well, the chilly night air and my thin pajamas answered that for me, it would be right here and right soon. The matter of home territory was another plus: I had a right to be where I was, he was the invader. I was inside a "fortification;" he was out in the open. I was in defilade, he was in enfilade. I had it all. All, that is, except for one thing. I didn't have a gun and, for all I knew, he did. If it turned out that such was the case, I might be very sorry to make his acquaintance.

Then, it slowly dawned on me. I did, after all, have a pistol. Granted, it was only a water pistol, the one I had used for many years to squirt water on the charcoal and wet things down a bit when I was barbequing and the fire got too hot. In appearance, it was a scaled down version of a German Luger, and on a dark night, if I held it so the tiny diameter of the muzzle didn't give it away, who would know that it wasn't the real thing? Since 1 had used it when cooking the catfish only a few hours before I knew exactly where to find it. With a couple of layers of navy blue sock over the flashlight lens, and moving with the stealth of a cat about to spring, I inched my way down the narrow aisle to where the useful toy had been left on top of the grill at the far end of the galley.

With trigger finger at the ready and left hand holding the small flashlight, I crept back to a spot directly beneath the hatch opening. As a final precaution, I again reminded myself to be sure and keep the gun pointed so he would not be able to see the muzzle; up and to the right should do it, I figured. For a moment I remained crouched within the silent darkness of the van.

Then, after taking a deep breath and with a "this is it" prayer, I extended my body with one quick motion to its full height, an instant later standing with head and shoulders above the surface of the van's roof and a bright beam of light shining down into the surprised and bewildered face of an unexpectedly harmless and respectable looking gentleman whose overall appearance projected no malice of any kind. It might have been understandable if I had merely said something like, "Good evening. Pleasant night, isn't it?" However, just to play it safe, I felt that I should still go through my tough-guy act until I knew for sure what he was up to.

"What the hell are you doing here and who are you?" I bellowed. "No funny stuff. I have a pistol!"

"Yes, I can see that you do," he said in an attempt at a measured voice that, understandably, sounded a bit shaky. "But you have no reason to use it on me. I had no idea that there was anyone inside the van. I assumed that it had been left here by people who had gone fishing, as is oftentimes the case. Anyway, I can assure you I have not the slightest wish to do any harm to either you or your van."

"Well, that's good to know," I said. "Now would you mind telling me who you are and why you're here leaning against my van at an hour of the night when most people are still at home in bed? You've been hanging around for the past fifteen minutes or so. What's on your mind?" As I spoke I quickly sized him up for any signs of potential danger, but I saw none. He was a well-spoken, clean cut man in his early thirties, giving the impression that he 'just happened' to be where he was, and it was no big deal.

"My name is David Jarrett," he said, a hand shading his eyes as he spoke. "Would you mind pointing the light a little off to one side. It's hurting my eyes. Thanks, that's much better. As I was about to say, I just competed a night of emergency duty at the hospital. I'm waiting here for my friend, James Higgins and his father, Matthew Higgins, to pick me up in Dr. Matt's boat, the Frances E. Willard. The two of them and all three of our wives slept aboard last night and were to have left the harbor heading for here about a half hour ago. They should be showing up shortly, if they didn't over sleep. All three of us, James, his father and I are doctors on the staff at the hospital. I'm sorry about waking you up and regret having caused you any concern for your safety. I hope I've answered your questions."

"Yes, you have indeed. Sorry if I sounded a bit testy. Welcome to Camp Van-Go. Did I hear you say that your friend's boat is called the 'Frances E. Willard?' That name is familiar, but I can't quite remember who the lady was. Wait a minute. Didn't she lead the movement that was largely responsible for bringing about prohibition back in the first quarter of this century? Putting a name like that on his boat must mean that Dr. Matt, as you call him, is still something of a crusader against alcoholic beverages.

"Well, you'd be wrong," Jarrett said with a smile. Dr. Matt isn't the one who came up with the name. The original Frances E. Willard, boat number one from which the present-day boat number four is descended, was named by Dr. Matt's father, old Amos Higgins, a legendary bootlegger in these parts who got rich during the fourteen years of prohibition. Old Amos did more good for the people of this area than all the local politicians and philanthropists put together."

Wow! This had all the makings of a good story. He conveyed the impression that he would enjoy telling it and I was more than willing to listen. "I want to hear all about it," I said, "but first let me put on some warm clothes and rid myself of this deadly weapon" (which I belatedly realized had been leaking water, wetting the right sleeve of my pajamas from wrist to elbow). "It will take me only a few minutes to make us a pot of coffee. If you'll come around to the other side I'll open the sliding door and hand you out the card table and a couple of folding chairs and a fluorescent lantern so you can see well enough to get things set up. I hope you like your coffee black, for I don't have any cream or sugar."

We sat at the table sipping our coffee. I waited for Jarrett to speak. "This is good; just the way I like it; strong, but not bitter. Is it espresso?"

"Yes it is and I'm glad you like it," I replied. "I skimp on most other things, but I'm willing to pay more when it comes to coffee. You were telling me about Amos Higgins. It sounds like he was an interesting character. Did you know him? What was he like? I'd enjoy hearing more."

David's facial expression was one of pleasant concentration, as if he might be organizing his thoughts in order to express himself in the best possible manner. I waited quietly as he readjusted himself in the chair, wiped his glasses with a pocket handkerchief, crossed his legs, settled back and began: "He died while I was still just a little kid, so although I do barely remember him, I can't say that I actually knew him in any meaningful sense. Everything I know is from what I've been told by Dr. Matt and his contemporaries. I'll do my best to tell you the story as I have heard it from their point of view.

"Prior to the passing of the eighteenth amendment, Amos Higgins eked out his living as a fisherman. He owned a leaky old dry-rot infested tub of a trawler, with an ancient burnt-out engine barely strong enough to pull an empty net through the water. He had only a few years of grammar school, but he managed to know how to read and write and do simple arithmetic. It seems he professed to be a God-fearing man and was accepted as one of the pillars of his church, so to speak. But his personal and family life was going from bad to worse. With rent coming due each month and hardly enough money to feed his family, the situation was chronically nothing short of desperate. Well, according to his own story, in the midst of all this misery and despair, he was sitting one night reading the Bible. That's when, again according to him, he came across two verses of scripture, and eventually a third verse, that changed his whole life and set him on the high road of becoming, as he termed it, a 'Beverage Distributing Missionary'. He claimed that he was 'called', and he never once wavered from that stand. The amazing thing is, until the very end, he got by with it. Can you believe it!"

"What on earth does it say in the Bible that could possibly be interpreted as 'calling' a person to be a bootlegger?" I asked.

"Well, it seems that even the preacher had to admit that the verses of scripture old Amos used to justify his new 'calling' were fairly explicit. So much so, in fact, it was hard to win by arguing against him. Eventually, everyone gave up trying."

"Do you remember specifically the verses and references?"

"Sure I know. But only because Amos Higgins quoted the verses night and day to anyone who cared to listen and more especially to those who in any way questioned him about the moral aspects of his 'Beverage Distributing Missionary' activities. Subsequently, the story has been repeated so many times by older people that all of us around here of my generation now know the scripture by heart. According to him, he was doing 'the Lord's work,' because in chapter thirty-one, verses six and seven of the Book of Proverbs it says: 'Give strong drink to him who is perishing, and wine to those in bitter distress; let them drink and forget their poverty, and remember their misery no more.'"

"I'm pleasantly surprised," I said. "For years I've been more righteous than I realized. Please go on."

David Jarrett sat silently for a moment, as if he was once again collecting his thoughts. He then continued, "Those were the verses that prompted Amos Higgins to put on his thinking cap and start nosing around with the objective of developing trust and friendships with the various moonshiners that were cropping up in this area as a result of prohibition. He tackled his self-appointed mission with a zeal appropriate for one who has been inspired by scripture to take action. Day after day, he would head his old trawler into the backwaters of this area where Amos began making what he called his business contacts."

"Well, it wasn't too long before his financial situation began to improve considerably. That's when, out of gratitude, he changed the name of his boat from the "Swamp Rat" to the 'Frances E. Willard', saying at the time that Mrs. Willard didn't know it but she was by far the best friend he ever had. He soon replaced the trawler with a high-powered modern boat, the second boat keeping the same name as the first. In the course of time, no longer actively doing 'the Lord's work', he spent his later years aboard his sleek new cruiser, Frances E. Willard the Third." David suddenly glanced at his watch, then looked down the estuary toward the gulf. "I can't imagine what's happened. They should have been here by now. Say, if I'm boring you with this long-winded story or you want to go back to sleep, just say so and …"

I broke in before he had a chance to finish. "No, David, please don't stop. I want to know what the message was that he received from the second bit of scripture; and, did they kick him out of the church; did the revenuers ever catch him; what did he do that was so great for the community; in short, how did it all end. Hell, man, don't stop now. You're just getting warmed up. Keep going!"

Fortified by my vote of confidence and, with Dr. Matt's boat not yet in sight, the young doctor again took up where he had left off. "Well, it seems that it wasn't too long after his original gift of enlightenment that, either on his own or because of somebody else's help, a second useful bit of Holy Writ surfaced. First Timothy, chapter five, verse twenty-three said quite plainly: 'Drink no longer water, but use a little wine for thy stomach's sake and for thy frequent ailments.' After much cogitation he concluded that his new job description should thereafter be 'Beverage Distributing <u>Medical</u> Missionary'. To his credit, perhaps, he did stop short of calling himself 'doctor.'"

"What about the revenuers?" I asked. "He must have had plenty of brushes with the law."

"Yes he did, and no he didn't," David answered. "He was always too smart for them."

The sound of engines, and the running lights of a luxury yacht emerged from the darkness and drew closer.

"Good. Here she comes." David said. "I was beginning to think they had gotten lost. Well, Bill, I enjoyed talking with you. Thanks for the coffee."

"It was a pleasure talking with you, David. And I especially thank you for telling me about Amos Higgins. What a fascinating character! I would have liked knowing him."

"I feel sure he would have liked knowing you." he replied.

"Yeah; What makes you think so," I asked.

"Because, I suspect he would have admired your willingness to face the unknown armed only with a water pistol. It sounds like something he might have done."

"A water pistol!" I repeated. "What makes you think that the weapon I was using was a water pistol?"

"Well it wasn't too difficult to figure out," he said looking pleased with himself as he said it. "When I asked you to point the flashlight beam away from my eyes, you shined it more sideways and, from that time on, there was enough light on your right hand for me to see water dripping down and wetting your arm. Next time, before you confront a nighttime intruder, perhaps you would do well to drain all the water out of what you earlier referred to as a 'deadly weapon'. But, I must admit, for a while, it did have me fooled."

I walked with him toward the big yacht, now riding motionless at a dock alongside the grassy bank with boarding ladder extended. As he climbed on deck he turned and waved. "So long, Bill."

I waved back. "So long, David. Thanks for your comments about the leaky stopper in my Little Squirt Special. I'll make sure to drain its crankcase before I challenge anymore dangerous criminals."

Sunrise and sunset are both suggestive of a quiet time for reverie and reflection. I sat alone and watched the early light chase out the darkness of the night before. A misty veil, ethereal and haunting, displayed itself from bank to bank along the surface of the river. Events encountered in a tiny increment of universe called Calvin's Bend paraded slowly through my mind. Less than a score of hours had transpired since the Van-Go was brought to rest beneath the spreading oak beside the river. Pure chance had brought me to a peaceful setting that had briefly served as home and offered subject matter for a nearly finished painting. During my short visit I had dined on freshly caught catfish, read two chapters of Steinbeck's Cannery Row with Dvorak, Rachmaninoff and Grieg adding beauty to the background. I had experienced some adrenaline raising moments with a water pistol. Best of all, and the feature attraction of the evening, was the time spent listening to a friendly Mr. Niceguy tell a fascinating story about the eventful life of a local character, a homespun philanthropist of years past: a Bible-toting bootlegger intent on carrying out his own strange version of "doing the Lord's work."

The sun was rising. I might as well have one more cup of coffee and then pack up and move out. Where to? I didn't know. Pure chance had brought me to Calvin's Bend. Pure chance would help me find the next place. Fifty, a hundred miles down the coast there would be another back road, another live oak beside the water, another scene to paint, another bend in the river, and I would paint more pictures until, in a few weeks, I would point the nose of the Van-Go north, regroup at Snake Pit Farm, and then, in June, head back to France for four more months of painting in Brittany.

CHAPTER TEN
Fosse Septique Sur Mer

Philippe greeted me with a friendly smile as I came in off the early morning flight from Paris, and as we shook hands said, "Welcome back to Brittany, my friend."

Driving along the road leading to his chateau I was glad to once again be in France during the month of June, a time of the year when spring flowers hug the roadsides and splotches of blood-red poppies display themselves in fields and meadows. Before leaving France the year before I had arranged with Michel that I would once again have four months of driving rights to his car, and upon our arrival at the chateau it was comforting to see that the dowdy and somewhat embarrassed looking, spray-can painted, 24-year-old Peugeot was waiting for me in the courtyard. I quickly let it know I was back on duty and in charge of its comings and goings by loading some of the art supplies left in William Woodward's studio from the year before into its trunk. After phoning Monsieur Boudreau, my new landlord, transferring luggage from one car to the other, and saying goodbye to Philippe with promise of getting together soon, I climbed into the old car and was off and away to the place I would call home for the next four months.

The summer before, at the very last minute, I had found and reserved a newly built three-bedroom rental cottage, called a *gite* in France, in a tiny village within a mile of the sea. Along with about a dozen or so houses, the cluster of buildings was site of a still much used ancient and historic church and, in addition, boasted a two-star *auberge* that, among other choice dishes, served a superb dinner of roast duck with orange sauce, but because it was a French duck it was better known in those parts as *canard à l'orange*.

My new landlords, Monsieur and Madame Boudreau were standing in front as I brought my noisy old rattletrap of a Peugeot to a halt and shut off the engine, both of them wearing such pleasant expressions I wondered whether it was because they were glad to see me or if they were amused by the ludicrous appearance of the car I was driving. Other summer visitors typically were in and out of rental houses in a matter of weeks, for they had to pack up and leave to go back to the daily grind, whereas I had rented their house for four full months, every summer-*gite* landlord's dream, and that, no doubt, gave me most favored status in their eyes. As to the car, they perhaps thought I was such a rich and eccentric American I just plain didn't give a damn. I soon learned that the cottage had been bought by the Boudreaus as an investment, and that I was their very first tenant. In any event, as the walk-through progressed, they couldn't have been more obliging in every respect, or at least so I thought, for neither of them spoke a word of English and I understood only part of what they said, and that may have been why we all kept smiling so agreeably and everything went so smoothly.

Of the three bedrooms, I quite naturally took the largest one for myself, it being on the front side of the house and situated in such a manner that a fully grown giraffe, by sticking its head out the window and twisting its neck only slightly, could get a segmented view of the ocean. Next, by pushing the bed over against the wall and entirely removing the fabric draperies from the windows, I turned the smaller of the two front bedrooms into what would serve as studio space, with the Italian tubular steel easel that I had left in France the previous year being permanently set up near the windows. The third bedroom, on the side of the house next to the garden, would be used as a guest chamber when family members Betsy and Jack Lewis, my niece Laura, and later my good friend Lisa came for a visit.

Typically, on days when the weather was suitable for painting *en plein air* I would load up the old Peugeot and strike out for location unknown, driving until I saw an appealing subject. If, because of the light it was a morning painting, I would try to get it either all, or mostly, finished by mid-day. Lunch almost always took place inside the car or else sitting on the little folding camper seat I carried with me, or on a bench, if one was handy. Day after day, the menu was basically the same onion and tomato sandwich I had become accustomed to while painting in France the year before. That, along with a glass or so of red wine and a few bites of cheese, was my painter's lunch. Some days after lunch I would doze on location but, if not, I would try to work in a nap after I got home. If in the morning it was raining or for some other reason I didn't get started until noon or later, I would merely reverse the procedure by driving until I found what I wanted to paint, have lunch if I hadn't eaten, take a nap if I felt like it, and then paint until it was time to quit, whenever that occurred.

The weather can change quite rapidly in Brittany, for it relates directly to whatever is, or has been, happening within the long expanse of ocean separating the east coast of North America with this most westerly portion of the French mainland. Thick, low flying clouds with indigo, mauve and umber underbellies drip and tumble as they chase each other eastward over coastal land until suddenly they tire, the game is over, and once again the sun shines forth. It was nearly noon, and because the weather had been uninviting I had spent the morning painting in the studio and was standing near the open window when Monsieur Boudreau's maroon Renault pulled up in front of the *gite*. I waved a greeting as he looked my way and a few moments later as he stood beneath the window we went through the customary French exchanges of:

"Good day, Monsieur."

"Good day, Monsieur, how's it going?"

"Very well, thank you, and you?"

"Very well, thank you."

After that, I waited for him to announce the purpose of his visit, but instead he was craning his neck to get a better view of the painting that was on the easel. I did some mental fumbling in trying to think of the French equivalent for "What's up?" and decided to try, *"Qu'est-ce qui se passe?"* which seemed to work all right, for it prompted a lengthy response with me frequently interjecting some old standbys like, "I don't understand, please speak more slowly, and please repeat." In the end, I deduced that he and Madame Boudreau had come up with the idea that I needed a tour guide, someone to show me the points of interest that would be best for me to paint and, since he had lived within a few miles of the village his entire life, he was the ideal one for the job. So come on, get in, we would start at once.

It was not at all what I had planned for the rest of the day, but he seemed so eager to carry out his assignment I couldn't bring myself to say no. I had already learned during the short time spent as a landscape painter that the layman's notion of what's paintable is often far different from what the painter sees as a good subject, so I was prepared for his so-called points of interest which, as it turned out, were better suited to the folks in a tour bus. A well-traveled road led us to our first stop, which had been the home of the most illustrious man in those parts. As we stood peering through the iron fence I braced myself for more of the same. After driving me to see the ruins of an ancient church, and then off in another direction to look at a *calvaire* that I had seen several times before, I felt it was time to put him straight as to where my interest lay insofar as subject matter was concerned.

For some reason, water mills popped into my mind and, after pausing long enough to think of the right French words, I asked him if he might happen to know of any old water mill we might look at. Ah, but of course he did! He knew the location of every abandoned water mill in that part of Brittany. Please forgive him, he said, for not realizing that I specialized in painting water mills. Yes, there was one, a fine one, less than a mile from the *gite*. He would take me there at once. And so it was that for the rest of the summer I enjoyed the services of a dedicated volunteer water-mill scout who introduced me to some very choice sites in out-of-the-way settings, several of which were unfamiliar even to William Woodward, who had spent the past twenty-five summers painting in that part of Brittany.

For the most part, I found the subjects that I wanted to paint while just poking about on my own. On one occasion I came across a broad serpentine estuary that narrowed to a chocolate colored ditch when the tide was at its nadir. I drove out to the end of a jetty and was soon painting the stranded boats that lined the channel. It wasn't long before I noticed that an occupant on board the old and battered oyster barge tied up near me was one of the most beautiful women I had ever seen. She and two burly companions were hard at work dislodging oysters from the long metal poles they had retrieved from the oyster beds. Her delicate features, soft golden hair and pale blue eyes seemed oddly out keeping with the heavy overalls and thick work gloves she was wearing. She looked my way and smiled.

It was a smile that prompted within me a Walter Mitty fantasy... an oyster would fall gently at my feet. Inside a note would read: "Please to help me Monsieur. I am held zee preezinair by zeez two ruffians. Tak me weez you in zat fonny leetle car and I be for you zee parfact modelle. Gabrielle." The daydream was soon brought to a close, however, by the three of them laughing gaily as they closed down the barge, piled into a shiny black Citroen and drove away. "Oh well," I said to myself, "There are still these damned boats in the mud that need to be painted. I'd better finish painting them before it gets dark." And so I did.

A few days later I was driving down a back road looking for a scene to paint when up ahead on my right I saw, from the waist up, a very ancient peasant woman, the rest of whom appeared to be standing in a ditch. As the car drew nearer she began waving her arms at me and, thinking at first that it was only her strange way of being friendly, I waved back and would have kept on going had I not heard her shout "A*u secours! M'aidez!* as I drove past. *M'aidez* sounds enough like May Day that even a linguistic moron can recognize that it's a cry for help, so I slammed on the brakes and backed up. She was a short, heavy, toothless old lady who apparently had walked across the field and had gotten as far as the roadside ditch but couldn't make it up the steep bank to the level of the road. For whatever reason, she was barefooted and had placed her slippers side by side along the edge of the road. It was obvious that she was in pain, for there were tears in her eyes and with her hand on her back she kept repeating, "*J'ai mal ici, j'ai mal ici*" – It hurts me here.

She extended both hands toward me and in a frail voice begged me to pull her out, but it was not quite that simple. First of all, the poor old thing was built like a fire hydrant and I doubted my ability to pull her up and out of the ditch without her nearly two hundred pounds of dead weight pulling me down into it. My second concern was the matter of her back causing her so much pain, and I feared that moving her might do it serious damage. But I had to do something and do it fast, for her suffering was pathetic, and so far as help was concerned I seemed to be the only game in town. I looked up and down the road, and about a quarter of a mile ahead on the left was a small building. Perhaps there was a telephone there and I could call for assistance, but when I suggested that to her she shook her head and said no, there was no one in the place and no phone. The best plan, I knew, was to go get some help, but I didn't have the heart to drive off and leave her there. Where were the people? Where were the cars when you needed them, damn it!"

Suddenly, I thought of a possible solution. It involved a certain amount of risk so far as her back was concerned, but it at least would enable me to get her up out of the ditch. From the trunk of the car I found a length of nylon line that I occasionally used for bracing the easel on windy days. With the car near the middle of the road and one end of the rope lashed around the seat frame and the other tied around my waist with just enough slack so that by stretching I could barely reach her hands I was ready, as the British say, to give it a go. I was about to simply take hold of her hands and start pulling when it occurred to me that a little bit of timing might be helpful, so that we were both exerting maximum effort at the same instant. I wondered if the French used 'one, two, three, go' similar to the way we do.

"*Comprenez-vous 'un, deux, trois, commencer?'*" I asked. "*Oui,*" she answered. Good. With that, I grabbed her outstretched hands, took a deep breath and said, "O.K. old girl, give it all you've got. *Un, deux, trois, commencez!*" And with feet braced and a mighty heave I pulled her up the steep bank with her eyes bulging and her suddenly miraculously strengthened vocal chords belting out a prolonged and hearty "Eeeeeeeeeeh…!" followed at once by a broad toothless grin that told me more than all her words of thanks that she was all right and out of pain. As I watched her, shoes in hand, shuffle along through the field on the other side of the road, continuing her journey as if nothing had happened, I wondered if the back problem might have been a slipped disc, and the act of pulling her out of the ditch its cure. "Hell, maybe I'm a chiropractor and don't know it," I said to myself as I drove away.

As I finished each landscape I cut a piece of stiff cardboard to the same size as the painting, removed the painting from its stretchers and wrapped the excess canvas around the back side of the cardboard with the edges held in place with strips of duct tape. It was very much a jury-rigged arrangement, but it gave me a way to keep re-using my limited number of stretcher bars for new paintings while, at the same time, making it possible to view the work already completed. Whether the Boudreaus, or the previous owners, had run out of outlandish wallpaper options by the time they got to it, or for some other reason, the walls of the front hall offered the least offensive background for displaying my steady output of nearby scenes, so the hall, with a long bench on one side and a shelf-topped radiator on the other, became the official art gallery. I didn't want to upset the Boudreaus by asking permission to drive nails in the wall, and I was able to get around the need for doing so by stretching string on each side of the hall, and with still more string and tape, hang the lightweight paintings down from it. As wall hanging space got filled up, paintings were placed on the radiator shelf, the bench, and lined up along the floor. The result was that upon entering the cottage, one got the impression of being in a pint size, claustrophobic, poor man's local travelogue in which the sound system was on the blink.

Monsieur Boudreau appeared to be overjoyed with the arrangement. On days when he showed up for self-appointed tour guide duty he would stand as if spell-bound, gazing at the various paintings while talking mostly to the room in general but occasionally directing his remarks to me. "Yes, that's the lighthouse at Point de Raz." Next it was, "Ah, the harbor at Duarnenez. I like it very much, yes, yes, very nice." "Well, here's one of my favorites, the mill beyond the old schoolhouse I took us to two weeks ago. And this one, Monsieur, I don't think I've seen this one. Now, where did you paint this one?"

On each visit, without fail, he would first focus his attention and then comment on every single painting in the hall, regardless of whether he had seen it numerous times before or not at all. "I shall bring Madame with me the next time, Monsieur Lewis. She must see your work," he said enthusiastically, and then added what sounded to me like: "We are pleased to have a famous painter staying in the *gite*." Famous. What on earth gave him the idea that I was famous? Should I put him straight, I wondered, or say nothing and let him think it? I decided that since I didn't qualify as one who really knew or understood much of the language but, instead, typically confined himself to speaking it as little as possible, I should keep it that way. And, at the very least, it was somewhat flattering to know that there was at least one person on earth, possibly two including his wife, who, even if misguided, thought I was famous.

Anyway, a better need for a French vocabulary had presented itself. It concerned the *fosse septique*, the French counterpart of a septic tank but, from what my nose was experiencing, a far less efficient variety. Not being an expert in such matters, I could only guess that the fault had to lie in either improper venting of the plumbing inside the house or else something was wrong in the drain field department outside. Whatever the source of the problem, it was undoubtedly made even worse by the summer-long parade of short term tenants, usually couples with young children, renting the two-bedroom apartment in the basement. Soon after the situation started to become offensive I told Monsieur Boudreau about it and he assured me he would call in the man in charge of inspecting *fosse septics*, and whatever was wrong would be corrected immediately. A week transpired without me seeing the good landlord. When I did see him again I asked how much longer it would be before the inspector got around to doing his inspecting for, with the warmer weather, the situation was at times quite unpleasant.

"Oh, he's already been here, Monsieur. He came the very next day while you were out. I was with him the entire time and he reports that there is nothing at all wrong," Boudreau said, looking quite pleased with himself. I refrained from telling him, partly because he was such a nice guy, but mainly because I didn't know how to say it in French, that the two of them should go at once and see a doctor, for he and the inspector each damn well had something drastically wrong with his nose. Instead, I rationalized that it wasn't all that bad when there was a sea breeze, and a good part of the time there was one. In conformance with my custom of giving names to places where I lived, the cottage, being not far from the sea, soon became known as Fosse Septique Sur Mer. Sea breeze or no sea breeze, on my next trip to the store I stocked up on aerosol cans of jasmine, gardenia, honeysuckle and lilac, all in time for freshening the air a bit and practicing up on spray-gun technique before the arrival of Betsy and Jack Lewis who would visit me for several days while driving through Brittany, and then my niece Laura and, of course, Lisa who would stay, I hoped, for about a month.

There was no shower in the bathroom, only a bathtub which was designed, I'm certain, with the intent of saving water by reducing its volume capacity, for although it had a normal size opening at the top, the sides slanted in so much that one would need an extremely well tapered butt in order to sit down in it without getting hopelessly stuck. The possibility of this happening was further advanced by the fact that there was no hand grip anywhere that might offer some assistance when the time came to climb out. Nope, apparently that would be against the rules. Instead, only the slippery sides of the tub itself were all one could hope to hang onto in making the potentially perilous exit. Before any of my guests arrived I posted a notice of disclaimer near this imbecilically designed piece of equipment.

ATTENTION ALL HOUSE GUESTS
(Disclaimer of Host's Bathtub Responsibility)
House guests without the advantage of wedge-shaped bottoms may experience considerable difficulty in extricating themselves from this sadistically designed hydrous entrapment. For assistance, one should shout "Au secours", pronounced "Oh scoors". If, however, "Oh <u>something else</u>" is screamed out instead, the guest will not be criticized for doing so.

After a day of painting, the sound of someone knocking at the front door woke me up from a nap. *"Un moment,"* I yelled out through the window as I groped for the khakis I had taken off. Without a telephone, people just showed up whenever they damn well felt like it, I thought as I got ready to go greet whoever it was. After quickly brushing my hair and tucking in my shirttail, I opened the door and there stood Madame and Monsieur Boudreau with a gentleman I had not seen before. He was a corpulent, round-faced, balding man with an affable expression, and was introduced by the Boudreaus as his honor the mayor, Monsieur le Goff.

The tiny village where the cottage was located was too small to have its own civic officials, but it was part of a larger town that did indeed have a mayor, and that was the gentleman now giving me a warm smile, extending his hand and saying *"Enchanté Monsieur,"* followed by what sounded like a pretty little speech, the gist of which, I deduced, was how glad he was to have a famous painter spending the summer in their community and, if I could spare the time, how much he would enjoy seeing my work. Four people do not fit well inside a sardine can, so in the company of Madame Boudreau, who had been shown my work the week before, I remained outside on the veranda and yielded to Monsieur Boudreau's enthusiasm as newly appointed art guide who, by now, knew more about my paintings than I did. Even if I tried, I could not have followed all that Boudreau was dishing out, but I felt sure he was identifying the exact locale of each painting and then giving it his own big build up, to which hizzoner would respond with something such as, *"Oui, oui, c'est superbe."* I got the feeling that if those two guys had anything to do with it, I would be a famous painter whether the rest of the world liked it or not.

Soon after Lisa arrived, she and I began painting together on days when the weather was nice. Her interesting landscapes were proof of a solid foundation in academic art training, and her art history background was perhaps partly responsible for paintings that showed the influence of the symbolism of painters like A.B. Davies, Puvis de Chavannes, Odilon Redon and Gustav Moreau.

The first day in the field together, we painted on the banks of an estuary with green and gentle hills rising up beyond the water. At break time I walked over to see how she was doing. The estuary had been transformed into a mythical Hellespont, with sibyls and nymphs playing lyres while resting beside overturned amphoras, their angelic faces as timeless as those in a painting by Botticelli.

I stood beside her looking at the work on the easel. 'Hi, Boss. I've added a few things," she said almost apologetically. Then, "I'm having problems."

"No you're not, Lisa," I said with conviction. "It's good. Your style is uniquely sophisticated. Keep doing more of the same. Don't argue with beauty."

We arrived back at the cottage to find a note on the door left there by Philippe. "Hey, good news," I called out to Lisa who was still unloading things from the trunk. "Woodward flew in yesterday and will be here for several weeks. Let's throw a dinner party. I'll pick up a leg of lamb, if it's not too late in the season to find one, and we'll invite Philippe and Bill and Carol Farmer if she's in Brittany and maybe Claudette, whom you haven't met. I'll even stretch my skimpy budget and buy a few bottles of good classified wine instead of the cheap stuff I usually keep around here. Maybe you'll sing some opera for us."

A few nights later we sat at table dining on what may have been the last spring lamb left in Brittany, washing it down with some very drinkable cru bourgeois Bordeaux, laughing our heads off at Bill Woodward's well-told raunchy jokes, with Philippe goading him on. For a finale, we sat quietly as Lisa sang Verdi and Puccini arias. I felt lucky to be part of this happy group with all of us enjoying such a pleasant evening. As there was a steady breeze from off the land that night, it was, without question, made all the more pleasant by me occasionally excusing myself, and a few seconds later pointing a spray can out the bathroom window toward the open windows of the room where we were all sitting. After all, what can be more delightful on a lovely summer evening than the soft, scented night air wafting in through open windows, carrying with it the fragrance of jasmine, gardenia, honeysuckle and lilac.

Lisa and I were in the very act of driving off on one of our painting missions when I heard the insistent honking of a car horn, and in my rearview mirror saw Monsieur Boudreau in the car behind us, wildly waving his arm and, with his head stuck out the window, shouting *"Attendez! Attendez!"* After both cars had stopped, and as he came running toward us looking as excited as if he had just won the lottery, I figured that in such a condition his intended message was certain to involve a great outpouring of French words in rapid succession, a combination always lost on me, so before he could open his mouth I gestured toward Lisa and said, *"Ma interprete, Monsieur. Parle vous avec Mademoiselle Johnson, s'il vous plait"*. With Boudreau on my side of the car and Lisa in the passenger seat, I sat like a dummy in between, frequently turning impatiently to Lisa asking, What's he saying?" to which I would be told to shut up so she could listen to what he was saying.

At long last, with Boudreau having run out of steam, she turned to me and said, "Well, Boss, they all think you're famous and I didn't tell him any different. It seems that after Monsieur Boudreau brought the mayor by to see your work, the mayor – I think his name is Monsieur le Goff – called Paris and spoke with the Member of the Chamber of Deputies who represents this part of France, something like a U.S. Congressman in our country. Monsieur le Goff told him that a famous American painter was spending the summer painting in the heart of his district, and he recommended, now don't laugh, that you be awarded a medal for contributing to the cultural life of the community. Some years ago they prepared a medal to honor people within this area for outstanding activities or accomplishments. The first of these medals was given away last year to a local citizen who wrote a book, something about a horse. He says you would be the second recipient."

"Well it sounds like my part of Virginia where horses take precedence," I said. "Lisa, this is downright silly; in fact, it's become an absolute farce. They think I'm famous, and of course I don't even come close to that. It's a case of mistaken identity, like in a comic opera. So please tell Monsieur Boudreau thanks but no thanks. I don't deserve any medal and I don't care who knows it. What the hell, I've only been painting for a couple of years. Just tell him that."

With that off my chest, I paid no attention to what she then said to Boudreau, but was somewhat surprised by what appeared to be his pleased response even though only a few words passed between them, which piqued my curiosity.

"What did you say to him?" I asked. "I thought I understood him to say something about a presentation this Saturday afternoon."

"All I told him was that you would be honored to receive the medal. 'Famous' is relative. Obviously, they like the way you paint, and if they think you're famous, why not let it go at that? Anyway, it's something they want to do and I think they'll be disappointed if you turn them down. Cheer up, Boss. It could be worse."

In preparation for receiving such a distinguished visitor, I bought several bottles of decent wine, some paté and other snack food and went so far as to put on a freshly laundered shirt, clean khakis and blue blazer. The expected time of the deputy's arrival was a matter of confusion for the planning committee, for Monsieur le Goff's secretary had understood one thing, and the mayor was relying on that, whereas Lisa informed me that Monsieur Boudreau felt certain that because of the schedule for arriving flights from Paris, our illustrious visitor with medal in hand couldn't possibly show up until sometime later. The wives, I gathered, had no notion of what to expect, but were apparently quite happy chattering away with each other. The only thing I could count on, it seemed, was the benign nature of the constant ocean breeze, making spray can employment unnecessary. Without a telephone, there was no way to find out what was what, and as the afternoon drew to a close and the pictures on their flimsy hangings were straightened for the final time and the last bottle of wine emptied and all the goodies eaten, there was repeated grave comment about what a very busy man Monsieur le Deputy was, and how there must be some major government crisis that prevented him from appearing as scheduled. After they all had left I said, "Come on, Lisa. I'm tired of being famous. Let's go have a cheap meal somewhere."

It had been another productive week, with the kind of weather that invites *plein air* painters to hit the open road, and we had done so each day in the aging Peugeot, which increasingly gave the impression that on some mornings it didn't feel well and had rather not go out. Saturday had rolled around again, and Lisa suggested that we should give the brushes a rest and drive a considerable distance to attend the *Grande Pardon* at Saint Anne de Palud, said to be one of the most important of the colorful church festivals that occur with great pageantry each year in Brittany. The important thing was to get out of the house, for the land breeze was not at all friendly. No need for me to look pretty, so I left on the clean but paint-smeared Breton fisherman's shirt I had been wearing. We were about ready to leave and I was in the act of closing the front windows, when a long, shiny black Citroen pulled up in front and stopped.

"Oh my gosh, I think we've got ourselves a French Deputy for a visitor." I yelled at Lisa, who appeared to be in the last stages of cosmetic adornment. "Quick! You spray the hell out of the living room and front hall and I'll go let him in."

He was a tall, thin man perhaps in his late forties, with black eyes deeply set within a face of prominent bone structure, a countenance at once both solemn and friendly. As we shook hands I apologized for my poor French; he laughed and said the only reason he knew a little English was from having to read Shakespeare in college. I invited him in.

"It smells good in here," I understood him to say. "Yes, the garden," I lied, gesturing toward the still-open windows of the living room.

Lisa appeared, looking fresh and pretty and saying all the right things in his own language. Everything was going well, and I excused myself to bring out some wine. Damn. We had polished off all the good stuff the week before and all I had to serve now was the cheap local jug wine. Well, it would have to do.

As curator of my own exhibit in the space of an oversized phone booth, I was soon describing to him the exact setting of each painting, with Lisa interpreting what I was unable to say in French. His positive response, as we went along, seemed genuine, and I doubted his sincerity only briefly when, upon re-filling his wine glass he remarked, "This is very good wine." I attributed that to gentlemanly politeness. As to the matter of him not showing up the week before, that was never on, and ...there must have been a misunderstanding by the folks at this end, he said, smiling.

The presentation of the medal, a small bronze medallion, took place out in the front yard, so Lisa could take pictures. The inscription on the back indicated that I had somehow added to the cultural life of the community, although to this day I am still trying to figure out how I did that.

After a few more weeks of exalted status as a famous painter, I closed the front door of *la Fosse Septique Sur Mer* for the last time and returned to the States and the who-the-hell-is-he ranking I actually deserved.

But, I must say, it was fun while it lasted.

CHAPTER ELEVEN
No Time To Smell The Flowers

As I stuffed yet another log into the belly of the cast iron stove that heated both kitchen and living room, I remembered an early W.C. Fields comedy that took place in a hammed-up movie set version of the Yukon in which Fields repeatedly sticks his head out of the cabin door and declares, "T'aint a fit night out for man nor beast." According to the radio weather man, the bone-chilling February winds now racing down off the mountain and howling past the clapboards of my lonely cottage would bring a foot or so of snow by daybreak. I wondered if the anticipated cold weather would be enough to keep things quiet up on the roof above my bedroom.

Frequently, since I had moved into the place several months before, I had been awakened from a deep sleep by the sound of pounding footsteps racing across the roof. The first time it happened I thought maybe a bobcat or black bear had come down off the mountain and was doing something bizarre like try-outs for a circus. But, a few weeks later, after being jolted awake for the second time by the sound of running feet, I mentioned it to Paul, my landlord, who told me rather matter-of-factly that the property we occupied was the site of the last Indian massacre in northern Virginia. From then on, whenever it became too disturbing, I would go open the front door and yell toward the roof something like, "Hey up there. I had nothing to do with it. Now cut that out!" Whether I was addressing the chasees or the chasors I'll never know, but the result was always the same: peace and quiet for the rest of the night. And, even though I was able to control things to some extent, overall it was still a weird and bizarre situation, causing the house I was living in to thereafter be referred to by me as Creepy Cottage.

With the weather being what it was, it was the kind of night that invited staying home and paying the monthly bills, or would have been except for the fact that my financial condition, as I soon learned, was even more bleak than the winter night closing in around me. After arranging the accounts payable, each with its return envelope, into little piles on the kitchen table, I reluctantly set about reconciling the checkbook. There must be a mistake somewhere, I told myself as I looked at the depressingly low balance. Slowly and deliberately I went through the process again. But it was a needless exercise. The hoped for mistake in my favor didn't exist. As they say, figures don't lie. It finally sank in that after the last check was written I would be left with only two hundred and forty-three dollars and seventy-eight cents in my bank account. I counted what was in my pocket. Eight dollars and some change was the bad news there. There was no escaping the hard fact that, no matter how I sliced it, I was broke.

With the last of the envelopes stamped and ready for mailing I sat lost in thought, staring vacantly at the kitchen window that was now being pelted by blinding sheets of snow. What a hell of a time and what a hell of a place to run out of money, smack in the middle of the boonies in the dead of winter with a nasty snow storm brewing. "How had I managed to let such a dismal situation creep into this late stage of my life?" I kept asking myself. The year before when my work had been accepted by four major galleries I naively thought I had it made, that I was over the hump financially. Rather stupidly, I had failed to consider the possibility that from time to time gallery sales might be so slow and far between as to not equal or exceed expenses.

Also, the four original galleries representing my work had been reduced to only three when I withdrew all of the paintings from one establishment when I learned from a reliable source that they violated our fifty-fifty sales agreement. The word got back to me that a small canvas painted near Middleburg and consigned at a price to me of $750 was sold by them for $5,000, yet I received only $750. At the time, rejecting the bad vibes and expense of a lawsuit, I just wrote it off as a good news-bad news situation. Good news that a fancy gallery sold an eleven by fourteen inch painting of mine for five thousand dollars. Bad news that I had gotten the short end of the money stick.

Of course, I myself was the cause of having run out of money so soon. It was completely my own decision to invest $10,000 in the Kenmore Option project. The "sure thing" buyer that was part of the equation, saw things differently than the promoters and investors and the deal fell through. But I didn't blame Mike or the promoters or myself. I took a chance and lost. That was all. I had long ago made up my mind to treat the matter with "bigboyism." in line with having been taught as a kid that big boys don't cry, whimper or complain.

The back door was nearly rattling off its hinges, and cold drafts that seemed to come straight through the kitchen's north wall called for more heat from the stove that again needed feeding. I pulled my chair closer to the fire, grateful that I had bought another half cord of seasoned firewood from Mr. Porter the week before when the weather was unseasonably warm and he had offered me a special price. Bargain prices, I reflected, had been consistent with my lifestyle throughout the time I had been painting. Whether in Mexico, France, along the Gulf or back home in Virginia I had repeatedly paid bottom dollar for rent and had lived frugally in other respects, driving either an old car that barely made it up hills or a used van that had been bought for half price, cooking my own inexpensive and mostly vegetarian meals, drinking cheap sludge instead of the good scotch and superb red wine I once enjoyed and, in general, pinching pennies and cutting corners. Most days I considered the need for skimping to be no great hardship, for I realized that I was fortunate to have the freedom and reward of doing what I wanted to do and, best of all, my work was showing steady improvement.

In some areas, however, I hadn't been able to cheap out. Paints could be expensive. A quality brand tube of certain hues, such as cobalt blue and the cadmium warm colors can leave little if any change from two twenty dollar bills, while a color such as rose madder can cost as much as $80 a tube. Impasto technique done with a palette knife or laid on heavily with a brush can consume paint rapidly. Brushes are expendable, and even the best of them lose their bounce after several paintings and need replacing with a new set of the various sizes. There is both cotton and linen canvas and, unfortunately, much of the time my preference had been to use linen, the more expensive of the two. Then, there was the matter of having to invest in easels: The big sturdy wooden one that Bill Woodward had given me was great for at-home studio painting, but I had needed to buy a French combination easel-paintbox for *en plein air* painting in the field and a half-size version of the same thing for cross-country back packing. In addition, I found I needed a different type of easel when painting aboard the Van-Go, so for that purpose I bought a tubular steel Italian model.

If I hadn't pursued the do-it-yourself mode, framing would have been an on-going expense that would have certainly eaten a big hole in my pocket. From the start I had absolutely refused to encase my paintings in strip frames or those made out of skinny stamped-out molding with the cheap gilt spray-paint look offered by many frame shops or mail-order frame catalogs. In my view, impressionist-style paintings required impressionist-style frames. In Mexico I had hired Xavier, with partial success, to make frames for me, but I soon found out that having similar frames custom made in the States was prohibitive for paintings in my price range. By constructing and gilding my own frames I was able to save a bundle and pass the savings on to the buyer. Even so, there were drawbacks due to the lack of design variety that could be produced by using only the moldings available from mill-supply houses. So, for some time, I had toyed with the idea of making latex molds of frames of the styles used by the French impressionists and turning out my own plaster-on-wood replicas. With that in mind and before realizing how near broke I was, I had placed a prepaid order and was awaiting delivery on nearly a thousand dollars worth of plastic ingredients that would make the project possible.

I got up from the chair and heated a bowl of soup. Through the increasingly obscure view through the window I could see what looked like ridges of snow building up on the rails of the horse paddock fence only a few yards away. Unless plow trucks did their work during the night there would be no way to get to either Leesburg or Middleburg in the morning. In the meantime, I told myself, you'd better focus whatever brains you've got on figuring a way out of this present mess.

In a searching moment I remembered that my sister Laura had said on several occasions that she stood ready to help tide me over if I ran into financial difficulties. Jack, my nephew, had made a similarly caring and generous offer. But borrowing money from family members threatened to create problems rather than solve them, for without knowing how or when such a loan could be repaid I ran the risk of damaging otherwise good relationships. In addition, my pride just plain wouldn't let me do it. I felt that anybody with good sense would have every reason to point out that for me even to have tried making a living as a painter was a crazy idea to begin with and should not be further encouraged by additional funding. No, I must find the answer within myself.

The morning brought bright sunshine and glistening snow with drifts piled high against the outbuildings where the horses lived, while fresh windswept patterns had carved themselves upon the frozen surface of the rail-fenced pastures. The storm was over, the wind had spent itself and there was promise of a calm and sunny day, far different from the howling tempest of the night before. Nature once again was making a fresh new start. With it there seemed to come a subtle message aimed at me: the need to rethink and possibly come up with a new approach, a turnaround, a change of focus while, at the same time reaffirming my resolve that come hell or high water I would not throw in the towel and give up painting. No, I had come too far for that. The encouraging, yet at the same time frustrating, thing was that each of the highly professional galleries had sold a number of my paintings, and while they all had good things to say about my work, the combined income from total sales still fell short of what was needed for a bare-bones lifestyle. Obviously, I could paint and spend money faster than three or four galleries could sell. My immediate objective, I felt, was to try to goose each of them into speeding things up, to sell some paintings sooner rather than later and get a little money in the kitty before things got even worse.

The first order of business, once they opened their doors, was to call each of the galleries and ask some questions. Has anything sold since we last spoke? If so, is the proverbial check in the mail? Would it help if I lowered the price on the painting that some nice person has expressed an interest in buying but hasn't done so as yet? Within seconds after ten o'clock I was on the phone with Dorothy who owned one of the galleries in the eastern time zone. She had found customers for five of my paintings within the past year and was generally very supportive. No, business had been unseasonably slow, she told me, and there were no new sales to report. She then added that my work was attracting favorable interest and she felt sure sales would pick up soon.

"I thought I had your 'Sailboats At Low Tide' sold the other day," she said. A woman came in the gallery who must have spent thirty minutes staring at it. She finally left without buying it but came back in on Saturday with her husband. He seemed to like it too, but all I could get out of them was, 'We'll think it over.' They've been in here before and I have their name and phone number but you know how it is, I don't want to be pushy."

"Maybe we should come up with such a good reason to call them that you would appear helpful rather than pushy," I replied. "How about telling them that I run the risk of facing the modern day equivalent of debtors' prison, or something even worse if I don't sell a painting soon, and am therefore willing to reduce my price on 'Sailboats At Low Tide.' According to the consignment sheet my price has been thirteen hundred, so I assume you've priced it to sell at about twenty-six hundred. If I came down to eleven hundred would you want to call and offer them the painting for twenty-two hundred?"

"Well, it's O.K. with me, Bill, but are you sure you want to go that low? I think the painting's under-priced as it is. Why don't we wait a couple of weeks and see if it won't sell and, if it doesn't, then maybe we should talk about lowering the price." The way she said it let me know she hadn't taken the imagery of my financial plight the least bit seriously, so before I knew it I found myself saying, "Sure, Dorothy, that makes sense. Let's hope things pick up soon. I'm sure you'll let me know the minute any of my paintings sell."

My luck was no better with the other galleries. No, nothing had sold. Yes, they would let me know the minute anything did. After the last call, as I placed the phone back in its cradle, I sat pondering the fact that because of relying only on galleries for the sale of my work, the timing of any future income was entirely in their hands. That might be fine under normal circumstances, but having to depend solely on others was anything but fine now that I was so close to being flat broke that I might soon go belly-up if something wasn't done to prevent it from happening. Ideally, I should figure out some way whereby I could personally take charge and sell my own work. But how? I had no place where my work could be shown, and people don't buy paintings sight unseen. What if I rented a place and had a one-man show? Not a bad idea, except for the fact that renting space, sending out invitations and supplying guests with drinks and finger food would require far more money than I had left in the bank. And, of course there was the possibility that I wouldn't sell all that much and might do little better than break even. Even so, I found myself getting hooked on the concept and decided that if I could ever bulldoze my way into even the skimpiest opportunity along those lines I would take matters in hand and put on my own one-man show.

In the meantime there was the necessity of generating some quick cash, some walking around money. At the time the house sale took place and before moving to Mexico, I had held on to several small, somewhat cherished and easily transportable items that were now far more compatible to my former lifestyle than to the present set of circumstances. One such object was a Whistler etching of an old lady sitting in a doorway. Another was a Hestor Bateman serving spoon bearing a 1784 London hallmark. A third item was an armorial Lowestoft plate displaying the crest of the Lupton family, of which my mother was a descendant, and who was proud to have been christened with Lupton as her middle name. These three remnants of my collecting days were still packed in the same cardboard box that had carried them to Mexico and back. With apprehension I started unwrapping, half expecting to see damage as I placed each piece on the big work table. To my relief, everything was in good condition in spite of having been bounced along thousands of miles of Mexican roads. As I sat looking at the three pieces I did my best to think of some other way in which I could raise some quick cash, some way in which I could avoid the feeling of disappointment with myself for being reduced to having to part with what amounted to almost the last vestiges of a once relatively prosperous life. But, try as I might, no other solution came to mind. Finally, after the third cup of coffee, I addressed my remarks to the wall I had been silently staring at for the past few minutes, "Well, damn it, they're only trappings and, in terms of dollars and cents, not all that valuable. Anyway, there's nothing here that's irreplaceable. When things get better I can always buy another Hestor Bateman spoon, another armorial Lowestoft plate without this one's special significance, another Whistler etching. So take 'em to a dealer and raise some cash. And, do it today, if the roads are clear."

A few minutes later I was on the phone with Peter Columbo. He owned a Connecticut Avenue gallery that offered a wide range of paintings, oriental rugs, fine antiques and *objets d'art*. Peter was a dealer I had known and dealt with off and on for years. I knew that the pieces I had for sale fit right into his gallery's format, but whether or not he would have any interest in buying them or the ready cash with which to do so remained to be seen. He told me on the phone that because of the heavy snow the night before he had canceled some outside appointments and would be in the gallery all day and happy to see me provided, of course, I could make it into the city.

I looked out through the kitchen window at the series of drifts and furrows covering the path between the cottage and the now half buried Van-Go, frozen reminders left there by the raw, screaming gusts of wind from the night before. Reluctantly, I found some work gloves, high-stepped my way to the tool shed, removed the snow shovel and set about doing what to me is one of the most unpleasant chores known to man – shoveling snow. Mr. Wagner, who came by earlier on his tractor, plowing the long driveway that encircled the main house, my cottage and all the outbuildings, had shouted to me over the sound of the motor that the five miles of winding country road leading out to Route 50 was clear but a little slippery – so be careful, he warned, or I might end up in a ditch.

All the way into the city I wondered what I would do if Peter, for whatever reason, said no. The more I thought about it the more convinced I became that I didn't have a lot of choice in the matter other than to accept any reasonable offer he might make, for I desperately needed to raise some money and he was by far my best hope for doing so. Repeatedly, I went over in my mind what might be the expected price from a dealer for the contents of the shopping bag that contained spoon, plate and etching. Several years before when I had hired Peter to give me an appraisal of my household belongings for insurance purposes and he had come up with an itemized total of just over $250,000, he had set a value on numerous items that were closely akin to the ones I would soon be showing him. Without a copy of the list and relying only on my memory along with an educated guess suggested that the combined retail value of all three items would be about $2,300. Cutting that in half and then knocking off another $150 would bring the price down to an even $1,000. Well, I'd go for that, I decided. It would be less than I had hoped, but I was in no position to hold out for top dollar. Even if Peter made a rock-bottom offer I would probably do well to accept his price, for if he turned me down I knew I would dread the embarrassment of going up and down the street to other dealers, flogging a small collection of items, out of sheer necessity, to raise a few bucks. "Please, God, let Peter say yes," I found myself saying as I pulled up at a parking space on Connecticut Avenue only a block from his gallery.

There's a saying, which I soon verified as being true, that trouble comes in bunches – like bananas. Snow plows and salt trucks had done their work along the center of the street, but there was almost more snow and slush than the Van-Go was equipped to handle as I maneuvered into position and parked as far off the traffic lane as possible. After cutting off the engine, I had second thoughts about whether I was close enough to the curb. I opened the door to step out and take a look when, a split second later, my feet flew out from under me and I found myself flat on my back perilously close to being hit by oncoming motorists. Scrambling to my feet undamaged, except for a bruised hip, I stood beside the car regaining my composure, brushing dirty snow off my light tan gabardine storm coat, straightening my tie and, in general, trying to make myself look as presentable as possible for the forthcoming all important fund-raising mission. And, oh yes, better lock the car. With that I pressed down on the lock button and closed the door.

At the very instant the door slammed shut I realized, to my dismay, that the keys were still in the ignition switch with all four windows and back hatch securely locked. I stood staring helplessly at the shopping bag containing my mini-treasures, still resting where I had placed it on the passenger side floor, my only hope for some urgently needed ready cash now suddenly removed from my grasp. I reached in my pocket and counted my cash: a little over eight dollars, nowhere near enough for a locksmith. If I walked a few blocks I could no doubt find an ATM and get enough money to pay a locksmith, but it would be a cold two-way trip and, in the end, I would be spending more of what little I had left in the bank instead of adding to it, which was the reason for driving into the city in the first place. Maybe I could ask Peter to advance me enough cash to pay a locksmith. No, that would not only be embarrassing but it would put me in a bad bargaining position. What about... I looked down the street and saw a police car coming toward me. I stepped out from the van and hailed it.

"Good morning, officer. I've just done a very stupid thing: I locked the keys inside the car. Do you have anything I could use to break the little vent window on the drivers' side? Or maybe you have a better idea?"

"Yeah, I've got a better idea. Why don't you call a locksmith?"

"Because I don't have enough money to pay for one," I answered lamely.

The scowl on the ebony face of a beefy, tough-looking cop suddenly softened into an expression of concern. "That's too bad," he said. "If we break the window it'll probably cost you more in the long run to replace it than it would to call a locksmith. Patrol cars used to carry lock jimmys, but not anymore. But let me see what I can do. Maybe I can find a car that still has one. I'll give it a try, but the odds are pretty slim, so don't get your hopes up."

I thanked him and stood shivering while he went to his car and started working the radio. He had hardly been gone before he came back and announced, "You must be doing something right, Mister. I just got an answer from one of the few men who can help you. He's only a couple of blocks away and will be here in nothin' flat." Sure enough, within minutes a tall policeman with a poker face expertly slid a long, slim sliver of steel between the door frame and the window glass and, viola! the button popped up and the door unlocked.

Peter removed the jeweler's loupe from his eye, laid the spoon back on the table and again looked in the reference book of British hallmarks. "You're right, Bill. For the years 1784 through '86 the leopard head hall-mark for London sterling was incised instead of standing proud as in all the other years. I think I knew that, but if I did I must have forgotten it," he chuckled.

"That makes the spoon all the more valuable because of its rarity," I said. "I think you'll agree, Peter, one would need to look a long time to find a more beautiful Hestor Bateman serving spoon in such perfect condition," I added. The other two items had already passed muster. Peter had taken the etching out from under the glass and satisfied himself that it was genuine and he had examined the plate for hairline cracks or chips, but there were none.

Finally Peter said, "I like all three pieces, Bill. What are you asking for them?"

I would have liked it better if he had been the first to name a price but I knew that he knew that I had enough knowledge about the value of such things to have an amount in mind.

"Well," I said, "I think a fair retail price for the etching would be about $2,000, but let's make it easy and cut it down to $1,750; I'd say the plate is easily worth $400, at least $350; as we both know, the spoon is a beauty and should sell fast at a price of, let's say, $250. The total low-ball customer price for all three comes to $2,350. I guess I'd be willing to take half of that, $1,175. How does that sound to you?"

Peter looked thoughtful for a moment, scribbled some figures on a notepad, and then said, "Normally, it would sound O.K. but, unfortunately, business has been the slowest we've seen in several years and we recently over-extended by buying some great pieces from a Middleburg estate that cleaned out our bank account. I'd offer to write you a postdated check but, under the circumstances, Marie would kill me if I did. There was a guy just in here who bought an unsigned British watercolor for $675 and paid me in cash. I could let you have that, but that's the best I can offer. I'm sorry, Bill. I'd like to do better but, right now, I can't."

Six hundred and seventy-five dollars. That was a just fraction of the true value of the three objects and barely two-thirds of what I had earlier decided, that if I had to, I would accept as a disappointingly rock-bottom amount. I stood up, took one last look at the spoon, plate and etching and, trying to control my voice, said, "Thanks, Peter. I understand. I'll take it."

During the days that followed I stood at the big work table from early morning until late at night in preparation for working with the plastic components that had arrived, hoping to eventually produce a latex mold from the master model of a picture frame I constructed especially for that purpose. The frame was of a modified foliate design with center and corner medallions that I fabricated by using the compo bits and pieces I had bought and which, by heating over my homemade steam table, became flexible enough to fit the curvature of the frame. I then connected the space between the compo ornamentation with molding plaster which, after it dried, I modeled with sculpting tools. In the end I was satisfied that the design and workmanship of my master frame would have pleased even the most critical of the French impressionists. So far so good, I decided, and with that started reading, for the first time, the how-to literature inside the shipping carton containing the large drum of slurry-like plastic and the heavy glass bottles of chemical additives.

Shouldn't be too difficult, I remember thinking after reading the somewhat ambiguously written instructions, only slightly disturbed by the fact that all the examples given in the manual were for small objects with relatively uncomplicated shapes, whereas the outside dimensions of my intricately patterned frame with deep undercuts measured a full thirty-four by forty inches. Common sense suggested that since my project was bigger in scale than normal, I should beef things up considerably to accommodate the larger size and, as I went along, come up with some decisions of my own making to fit the situation.

It was time, I said to myself, to put on my academically earned but never worn engineering hat. Filled with confidence, I spent hour after hour in the careful step-by-step preparation that needed to take place before the latex mixture could be applied. First, I took all the numerous steps that needed to be accounted for before starting the construction of the mother mold that I intended to produce from a beautiful Barbizon frame I had found in an antique store. Once the mother mold was completed, it was disassembled and laid aside while I meticulously removed all traces of the modeling clay from the frame. After that, I brushed the entire frame with a releasing agent so the latex would flow into all the intricate contours of the frame's design but not stick to it. I then drilled a one inch hole in a section of the mother mold just above the highest surface of the frame, and another hole in the corresponding section at the opposite corner - one for pouring and the other for allowing air to escape. Finally, I reassembled the mother mold within the wooden casings.

I looked at my watch; it was ten-thirty. If I kept going I could measure and mix the ingredients, use a funnel and pour liquid latex into the half inch thick cavity surrounding the picture frame, space once occupied by the modeling clay, clean up the tools and utensils used during the long day's work and be in bed by midnight. While I slept the plastic would set up and I could climb out of bed in the morning with the satisfaction of knowing that with my two hands and a little sweat I had created a rubber mold from which, whenever I chose, I could produce my own picture frames. I must admit, I was downright pleased with myself.

With the first light of dawn I was out of bed and on my way to the kitchen, eager to see the results of my handiwork from the day before. As I approached the big work table I could hardly believe my eyes. A creamy white layer of latex, now solidified, had spread itself across the surface of the table, leaving a border of icicle-like drippings along the edge which, while still liquid, had trickled down onto the hooked rug, creating a peripheral pattern of what looked like deposits of lava left after the eruption of a series of tiny volcanoes, with each little mound anchored solidly to the fabric. Without prior experience in its handling, I had completely failed to allow for the ooze factor of liquid latex. As I stood glaring at the awful mess, I must admit, I was not too happy.

About the only choice I had, it seemed, was to clean it all up and start again, but I did so with good reason to expect that my second attempt would be successful. For it was obvious that the liquid plastic had crept in under the wooden casings. Before the next pouring I would see to it that their bottom edges were well fortified by angle bracing to the plywood and that precaution, plus reinforcing with modeling clay along the seams, would prevent it from happening again. One battle doesn't lose a war, I told myself.

Well, if one battle doesn't, six battles nearly did. Murphy's law took over, and for the next five mornings in a row I arrived at the worktable only to discover to my dismay that the efforts of the day before had resulted in failure due to some new, unexpected and totally different mishap having occurred while the latex was in the process of setting up during the night. Every morning, upon starting over I mentally said to myself, "Well, now that I know not to do that again there can't be many more mistakes left to be made." Even so, I was tempted to throw in the towel and go back to making frames from plain wooden molding. Perhaps I would have if it had not been for the fact that, first of all, it had become a challenge to succeed and, secondly, I couldn't afford to waste the money invested in the plastic materials. There was also another reason for me to keep trying. Years before I read what might be termed an aphorism, or statement of principle, attributed to Calvin Coolidge. I was so impressed by the message I had had it etched onto a small bronze plaque which thereafter remained permanently on my desk.

> "*Press on.*
> *Nothing in the world can take the place of persistence.*
> *Talent will not; nothing is more common than unsuccessful men with talent.*
> *Genius will not; unrewarded genius is almost a proverb.*
> *Education alone will not; the world is full of educated derelicts*
> *Persistence and Determination alone are Omnipotent.*"

Along with this bit of wisdom I remembered, when as a young kid attending a school whose proclaimed mission was to build character, one of the placards prominently displayed in hallways and on bulletin boards which read:

> "*Don't tell us why you couldn't do it. Tell us how you did it.*"

So, with such inspirational truisms goading me forward, I felt I had little choice but to keep trying, whether I liked it or not.

Early on the morning of my seventh day as round-the-clock mold-maker I wearily headed for the kitchen and the coffee pot. The serial disappointments of the past six mornings had taught me the wisdom of coffee first--mold inspection later. After a few warming sips I approached the worktable. No latex had oozed underneath the casing boards. Good. I began lifting sections of mother mold and, instead of sticking, they parted easily from the rubber. Well done. A quick glance told me that the latex had flowed into all of the cavities, as intended. Splendid. A mold of only one long side and a separate mold of one short side, instead of the cumbersome four sided one- piece mold I had tried originally, had made everything much easier. Smart. Obviously, on this pour I had finally gotten the mixture of components just right. No soft, runny spots. Super. So far so good. But the real and final test, I knew, would be the quality of impression the rubber molds had picked up from the master model. With a degree of apprehension I gently pulled each mold away from its model and turned both of the rubber pieces concave side up so I could see all of the minute details. Everything was exactly as it should be, with remarkably good fidelity and clean and crisp indentations, no pinholes from air bubbles, no slurred passages. Absolutely perfect!

And on the seventh day I rested.

A day or so later, as I stood admiring my first ornate plaster-cast frame, I decided to create two more master models and from them make rubber molds so as to have a variety of designs from which to choose, with all three styles adaptable, within limits, to a variance of size. In the field of do-it-yourself frame making I had learned, the hard way, a few things about what works and everything about what doesn't and so, by avoiding the pitfalls of the recent past, I was able within just a few days to turn out 18 elegant-looking, hand gilded, period type frames in three different models ready to fit the several sizes of canvases for which they were intended. I was so pleased with how important the paintings looked in their new frames I wanted others to see the results of my handiwork. For during the past week and a half of round the clock slaving, I had hardly left the house. It was time for a break, a time to invite a few friends from the outside world in for some conversation and a glass of wine. I picked up the phone and started calling, inviting people to drop by for drinks on Thursday evening.

By the late afternoon I had hung twenty-six paintings, so that just about every available inch of eye-level wall space was covered in the living room, kitchen-dining area and the hall leading to the bedrooms. Lisa had agreed to come a little early in case I needed some last minute help. She showed up with her friend Shannon just as I finished opening the wine and checking, once more, to make sure every picture was hanging straight.

"This place looks like an art museum," she said, her gaze going slowly from wall to wall in the picture-packed living room. "And Boss, where did you get all these fancy frames? When we talked on the phone last week you said something about trying a new way of making frames. But you didn't make these, did you?"

"I sure did," I said. "Do you like them?"

"Do I like them? Of course I like them, they're beautiful. But I can't believe it! I know you've been making wooden frames for quite a while, but these new ones look too fancy, too ornate to be homemade. How on earth did you do it?"

"Thanks for the kind words, Lisa. I'm glad you think they're O.K. It means a lot."

Lisa had dependably good taste in such matters and would be the first to let me know if her reaction was anything less than positive, so I was pleased to have her approval, seconded by flattering comments from Shannon, which I especially welcomed for she too was a painter. "Well, there's more of the same to look at in here," I said as we walked past the stove and into the kitchen, stopping near the big all-purpose worktable now cleared of its usual workday clutter and, instead, dressed for the occasion in a red checked gingham cloth on which were plates of cheese, paté, bottles of wine and a vase of daisies.

"Here, let me pour you a glass of wine, Shannon – you too, Lisa. What'll it be, red or white?"

It was a small, pleasant gathering composed entirely of good friends, most of whom, because of fox hunting or other rural interests, had chosen the beauty and lifestyle of the country, with homes in the vicinity of places like Warrenton, The Plains, Middleburg, Rectortown, or as in my own case at that time, Upperville. I had invited Bill Woodward but, unfortunately, he had something else on his schedule and was unable to come. As the evening wore on, my guests were generous with complimentary remarks about the twenty-six paintings, all in their handmade frames and being displayed for the first time. It was nice to have supportive friends saying kind things about my work. After the recent stretch of frugality and miserly living, with long hours at the worktable, a little praise was just what I needed to hear, even though I realized at the time that some of it may have been said out of politeness or maybe the wine was talking. Whatever the motivation, the verbal pats on the back came at a time when my confidence badly needed a long overdue shot in the arm.

It was a week night and, although still fairly early, people were beginning to leave. I was returning from the front door after having said goodnight to Mary Coker along with Jean Bowman and her friend Russ, when Lisa came up to me and, in a low voice said, "I think I should tell you, Boss, that your friends Sheila and Paul seem interested in buying the painting hanging just to the left of the worktable in the kitchen. You know the one I mean. It's one you did in France last summer, 'Coastal Marsh'. They've been looking at it for quite a while. Maybe you should go over and talk to them."

I was taken completely off guard. "Hell, Lisa, I can't do that. I invited friends here to enjoy some wine and to show off my most recent paintings and get some feedback on my new style of frames, but not with the thought of selling anything to anybody. That was not the idea. Talking to Sheila and Paul about buying a painting while they're guests in my house is not my idea of hospitality. No, Lisa, just forget it."

Lisa, in her womanly wisdom, decided not to forget it, for as I turned from saying goodnight to another departing guest she again approached me, accompanied by Paul and Sheila.

"Hi, Boss," she began, as if she hadn't spoken to me in quite some time, "I think these two want to talk to you about one of your paintings."

Paul, grinning broadly, got right to the point. "Sheila and I really like 'Coastal Marsh', Bill. What can you tell us about it?"

It quickly flashed through my mind that since I was not the one who had initiated the conversation, I was in no way guilty of flogging paintings at my own social gathering. Anyway, I was glad to talk about the painting, and responded by saying, "Thanks for liking it, Paul. It happens to be one of my own favorites, possibly because blues and greens used in combination have a way of looking frenchy. In the case of 'Coastal Marsh' there's every reason for it to have that look, for I painted it in Brittany last summer after driving for miles down a country road near the sea that narrowed into a lane which eventually disappeared into two dirt tracks that ended in a field of wildflowers overlooking a beautiful marsh. The scene was indescribably tranquil, and I did my best to capture that feeling when I painted it. That's about all I can tell you."

"Tell us the price, Bill. We're interested in buying it," Paul said with his usual good-natured smile.

It began to sink in. Some desperately needed money might be staring me in the face. I paused for a second before answering, then said: "We're friends, Paul, and were next door country neighbors last year when I lived at Snake Pit Farm. Since I don't have a dealer close by, I'm not ethically obligated to charge a friend retail, so my price to you and Sheila would be half the dealer price. A painting of mine of the size and quality of 'Seaside Marsh' will typically be priced in a galley at $2,200 with a 10% allowance for dickering, so in all probability the painting will sell to a customer for $2,000 with $1,000 coming to me. If you want it for $1,000 it's yours, but if you decide that's more than you want to spend I'll understand and be just as happy. When I invited friends in tonight it was not my intention to sell anything to anyone. Whatever you decide, I'm flattered by the fact that you like the painting-that's a reward in itself."

An assenting look passed between the two of them. "We like it well enough to buy it," Paul said, and with that started writing out a check.

I walked out to the car with Lisa and Shannon. "Well, Boss, that was a fun party," Lisa said as she slid in behind the wheel, "and you're a thousand dollars richer than you were a couple of hours ago. Maybe you should have parties more often."

I stood for a moment thinking about what she had just said, and then replied, "Yeah, you're right, Lisa. You know, you're right. Maybe I should."

CHAPTER TWELVE
Vernissage

Lisa had hit the nail on the head. I would do well to have more parties so my paintings could get some much needed exposure – better still, one large party. Without me even so much as trying, a painting had practically sold itself in a gathering of only twelve friends, and I was of the opinion that the couple who bought it might well have done so even if we had been complete strangers. What if I could expand the group to a hundred or so people and offer them a choice of more paintings, say about 45 altogether? Once again, I was becoming intrigued with the notion of having my own one-man show, not sponsored by a gallery but put together by myself from start to finish, with paintings on view at some suitable place that I could rent especially for the occasion.

Several weeks earlier when the thought first came to mind I had so little money it seemed a waste of time to give the matter any serious consideration. Even now, after combining the recent $1,000 windfall with what was left in the bank and then deducting anticipated out-of-pocket living expenses for the next few weeks, I would still be short of having enough cash to pay all the expenses connected with putting on a show or, at best, it would be borderline. Pretty risky. Better forget it and, instead, sit tight and hope for some gallery sales.

But what if I sat on my butt hoping for gallery sales and none occurred? If that should happen I'd be right back where I was several weeks earlier, only this time it would be far worse, for there was nothing left to sell to Peter, no way for raising even a few bucks, no ace in the hole. The prospect of such a dismal scenario taking place was downright frightening. For whether I liked it or not I would be forced to give up painting as my only means of earning a living and settle for some mundane job just in order to stay alive and pay the bills. Having had a taste of the painter's life, reverting to something less would be like a monarch butterfly going back to being an ugly caterpillar.

As I kept turning it all over in my mind I was sure of one thing: something had to change, for I couldn't go on much longer with things the way they were. And, while it was all well and good to remain calm and keep a stiff upper lip in the face of adversity, that in itself wouldn't solve the problem-the nagging money problem. The Van-Go needed mechanical work, but repairs would need to wait. Insurance premiums on it would soon be due. The same was true of my health supplement policy, which I could neither afford to let lapse, nor afford to keep, adding one more cause for concern to my on-going damned-if-you-do/damned-if-you-don't dilemma.

Without doubt, the most gnawing disappointment emerging as a consequence of my dead-in-the-water financial condition was my inability to come up with the partial prepayment necessary to reserve accommodations for the forthcoming summer in a house in Pont Aven. My heart was set on going there to paint, for it was a very special house in a very special village. The house, presently owned by parents of a French woman with whom I had been put in touch, had been frequented by such renowned painters as Paul Gauguin, Emil Bernard and Paul Serrusier, and the village itself was made famous by painters of this stripe and their followers who, by the hundreds, flocked to this charming little town in Brittany from other parts of France, America and elsewhere. I knew without question that spending the summer in Pont Aven offered a rare opportunity for me to grow as a painter. I had until mid-April to wire-transfer a thousand dollars, or else I would lose the house and forfeit the $500 deposit I had made the previous summer, a misfortune which seemed all too likely to happen.

It's hard to know whether it was guidance coming from the wise inner voice supposedly inherent in each of us or if it was just an ordinary case of an old guy talking to himself but, in any event, I found myself saying, half aloud: "Maybe you should think twice, buster, before you ditch the idea of a one-man show. It may be the only shot you have left. Furthermore, you haven't even begun to poke around and find sources or get cost estimates. Until you do that you're basing everything on the assumption that you can't afford to do anything. But hell, man, who knows, you might get lucky. Maybe you can put together a show for less than you think. Don't be so stupid as to give up before you even start trying. Come on, do something. Get moving!"

I began to think hard and soon realized that I had several connections through friendships that might possibly work to my advantage. One such contact was with Douglass Larson, the director of Airlie, a conference center situated on several thousand acres of rolling Virginia countryside that had once been a private estate near Warrenton. Soon after I started painting I did a fairly ambitious work depicting a Warrenton outdoor summer concert showing a crowd of spectators spread out on the courthouse lawn listening to a group of musicians that were set up on a flat bed trailer on Culpeper Street. Doug bought the painting and hung it in a prominent place on the wall just behind the desk in his office at Airlie.

Over the years the former residence had been enlarged and converted into palatial, Corinthian columned institutional headquarters, and was now surrounded by the cultivated beauty of formal gardens, carefully groomed terraces, a lake where graceful swans resided and, nesting among mature trees and shrubbery, a complex of buildings designed either for meetings or the accommodation of overnight guests. Some months earlier I had attended a showing of watercolors that took place at Airlie in a combination watering-hole and meeting-facility called The Whistling Swan Pub and, at the time, was most favorably impressed by the ambiance of the setting. As I recalled, there were three connecting rooms, the largest of the three housing the pub itself, which consisted of a polished mahogany bar and mirrored back-bar running the entire length of the room at one end, and a large stone fireplace with a grouping of overstuffed leather club chairs and a divan at the other, while clusters of tables and chairs occupied the remaining space. All in all, it was an inviting room. In addition to small sections of wall space on two of the sides, there was one long wall that would be ideal for hanging pictures. At the opposite end of the suite was a conference room of comparable size with three inside walls offering a maximum of display area. The middle room, I remembered, was basically not much more than a passageway between the other two, but I could probably hang several small paintings in that space. The more I thought about it, the more I liked the idea of The Whistling Swan Pub as the place to display my paintings.

I was soon on the phone and made an appointment to see Doug Larson, and a few days later I was sitting across from him in his office. Throughout the time I had known Doug, I had been impressed by his good-natured and seemingly unruffled manner. On each of the previous occasions when he and I had met in his office to discuss having lithographic prints made of my painting which he now owned, he had always managed, in spite of what I'm sure was a busy schedule, to find time to make pleasant small talk before getting down to business. To my way of thinking, it marked him as a man of generous spirit, and I liked that about him. This time was no different. Once the laughter died down from his account of a funny incident in which he had recently been involved, I got right to the point of my visit.

"Doug, I'm thinking about having a one-man show and before looking elsewhere for display space I decided to first come talk with you to see if it might be at all feasible for me to have the exhibit here at Airlie. I was present a couple of months ago when one of Bill Woodward's colleagues, an art professor from George Washington University, had his watercolor exhibit in the Whistling Swan Pub. I was wondering, is that space available for an opening several weeks from now, the first week in April to be exact, and is there such a thing as a starving-artist discount? If there is, you won't find anyone more qualified for it than I am."

Doug laughed, then in a friendly tone said, "First, let me look at the schedule and see if the pub is available at that time. Nope, I'm afraid not. We have a group using the space through Saturday April third and another group coming in on Monday the fifth. There's only one day when it's not booked, Sunday the fourth. As you can see," he said with a chuckle as he swiveled in his chair and gestured toward my painting, "I heartily approve of your work and would enjoy seeing a full scale exhibition of it here at Airlie. If you can settle for a one day show, I'll try to work out a starving-artist rate. What do you think?"

I was silent for a moment and then answered. "I don't know, Doug. One day isn't much time. I had figured on a show being up for a week or two. If I did cut it down to just one day, Sunday might offer some advantages, but also some distinct disadvantages. People like to either go to church or sleep late on Sunday, so I can't imagine even opening the doors until about twelve-thirty in the afternoon and, since Sunday is typically an early night, I wouldn't expect much traffic after about five. That leaves only four and a half short hours. The folks who can't make it during that time frame won't have a second chance to see my work, and the ones who do show up will need to buy paintings damned fast in order for me to make out financially. In fact, a show scheduled for only four and a half hours during a single day in early April could be an absolute disaster if the weather did something stupid, like a nasty rainstorm or a late snow. I'm not at all sure that I can afford to take such a chance. And, while we're on the subject of affording, what would it cost me to rent the space for one day?"

"Before I answer that, Bill, let me say that since your paintings are the sort that are compatible with the Pub's decor, it's no skin off our nose if they're left hanging for a couple of weeks, even though the show itself ends on Sunday evening. The kind of people who come here for meetings typically aren't the sort to steal paintings, so I think your work would be safe, but that's up to you. You could leave a small placard on the bar announcing the fact that the paintings in all three rooms are for sale and, if you want to, it'll be O.K. to leave a price list and a few of your brochures at the front desk here in the main building. The Pub's hours are irregular, so it's locked up most of the time. But, anyone on your invitation list who wants to look at paintings only needs to make arrangements with the people at the reception desk and I'll authorize them sending someone over to unlock the doors and turn on the lights. Who knows, you might get lucky and sell something to people who are here for other reasons. Now, as to cost. Normally the Pub rents for five hundred dollars a day. But," he added with a twinkle in his eye, "since you qualify for the starving-artist, senior-citizen, AARP, triple A, frequent-flyer, early-April contest winner and friend-of-the-establishment special discount rate you'll save quite a lot. Under the circumstances, I can let you have it for three-fifty."

He was going so far out of his way to give me a good deal that it seemed appropriate to justify his having done so by injecting a little more discount banter: "What about the fact that as a kid I was kind to my mother? And, at the age of nine, I was given a pot-metal gold star for not missing a week of Sunday school for an entire year. Will either one of these get me an even better rate?"

"Sorry, Bill," he said laughing. "I would have expected as much from you without having to be told, so that's already been factored into the price." Then, more seriously, "I should add, any food such as dips, cheese trays and the like would need to be supplied by our catering department. If you want to cheap-out and spend as little as possible, instead of paying someone to pass trays we'll set up a table so people can just help themselves. Figure about a dollar, dollar and a half a person for food. Alcoholic drinks, by law, must be served by one of our bartenders. But our prices are reasonable. For example, you'll be billed a buck and a half for each drink, whether it's a soft drink, a five-ounce glass of wine or a bottle of beer. You can't do much better than that if you did it all yourself."

I mentally added up all the probable costs, as outlined. Not only did they seem surprisingly reasonable but, in all probability, the money from the sale of only one painting would be enough to pay for space, food and drink. I figured I certainly couldn't ask for anything better than that. Yet there was still one major issue that needed to be resolved in my favor before going any further. Nothing had been mentioned about the terms of payment. Dreading the possibility of being expected to put money down in advance and before Doug had a chance to inform me of any such unwelcome news, I said, somewhat apprehensively, "The main reason for having a show, Doug, is because my gallery sales have been so slow lately. That's another way of saying that right now I'm seriously short of cash. I'm one of the locals, with no plans for skipping town or taking off for South America anytime soon, so can we put things on the cuff until after the show? Otherwise, I don't think I can handle it."

Doug, good guy that he was, said that because, as a kid, I had been kind to my mother and hadn't flunked Sunday school, he figured we could work things out. Driving home, the title of an old popular forties song, "What A Difference A Day Makes," came to mind. For days on end I had allowed myself to become overwhelmed by feelings of helplessness bordering on self pity, but now, thanks to Doug Larson's starving-artist deal, there was reason to have renewed hope, for the door of opportunity had opened a crack. Opening the door wide enough to take full advantage of the opportunity, however, was the Herculean task that lay ahead of me. The fourth of April was only twenty days away. I had purposely given myself so little lead time because I figured, with luck, I might sell enough in excess of my costs to send the $1,000 to Pont Aven in time to hold the space and fulfill my dream of painting there all summer. The problem was, there was so much to do to get ready for a show I would have needed to work like a Trojan if I had allowed myself two full months. The only solution, I decided, was to count on 20 days of non-stop working 'round the clock and somehow get it all done, for if I didn't pull this one off I'd have egg on my face for the rest of my life.

I started mentally tabulating all that had to be done between that moment and the afternoon of April fourth. My first concern involved the matter of inventory. Immediately after the meeting with Doug I had walked through the Whistling Swan, carefully making notes while estimating wall dimensions and picture placement. As I had guessed earlier, the arithmetic proved that with my typical size mix the space was ideal for hanging between 45 and 50 paintings. To take advantage of the optimum, in less than three weeks I needed to come up with as many as twenty-five more paintings, framed and ready to show. There were eight unfinished canvases on stretchers leaning against the wall in my bedroom. Several were of scenes that had been started locally, other beginnings were of subjects along the Gulf or in Brittany but subsequently laid aside and never completed. Each of those would require time, attention and the varying amounts of finishing touches necessary to turn them into salable paintings. Eight new frames would need to be made, and that in itself would call for many late night man hours at the worktable. But, even after putting forth all that effort, I would still have only 33, 17 short of the maximum number of 50 that would fill the space and give potential buyers more of a choice. Recalling paintings from galleries offered at least a partial solution and I would get cooking on that right away.

Although I had never before put on a one-man show, common sense suggested that there were three components that must be accounted for in order for the show to be a success: good space; a plentiful selection of well executed paintings at reasonable prices; and an audience with enough buying capability to make the whole thing worthwhile. The space problem, I was happy to say, had now been solved, and I knew myself well enough to feel reasonably certain that somehow, by hook or crook, I would end up covering every bit of hanging area in the Whistling Swan Pub with paintings. But getting a sufficient number of people to attend with pockets deep enough to spend money on paintings might be my biggest challenge, especially so considering the fact that, allowing for the usual two weeks advance notice of a forthcoming event such as an art opening, invitations must be printed and in the mail within the next few days. And, without so much as even a single name and address on an intended mailing list, I would need to start from scratch in putting such a list together, in itself a time-consuming task that should have been done yesterday.

As I thought of how so many things all urgently needed to be taken care of almost simultaneously, I remembered having long ago read in a book, whose title and author have long since remained forgotten, a fragment of a sentence which has forever stayed stuck in my memory because of the marvelous comic imagery it produced: "He jumped on his horse and rode off in all directions at once." I had better do something similar, I reckoned, if I hoped to have every gargantuan detail accounted for by show time. Without question, the very first order of business was to create a mailing list while, at the same time, get the wheels rolling on having about 300 invitations printed. To come up with so many names would require help from others. I had mentioned that to Doug, who suggested that I speak with his secretary, Tina, and she supplied me with a list of about 12 people that she felt might have an interest in attending. Then, as a result of some phone calls, Bill Woodward added about another dozen names and Lisa came up with nearly 30 more. But I hit the mother lode, the real bonanza when I called Mary Coker. In addition to being an accomplished equestrienne, an Asian scholar and a talented sculptor, Mary was a woman of much grace and charm with a long list of friends. I had the good fortune to be on the list. It was typical of her supportive nature when, upon being told of my need, she quickly supplied me with a select list of nearly 100 names. After screening the entries in my own address book I eventually was able to put together a combined master list of 282 names and addresses, an ideal number that would still leave me with a few hand-outs from the three hundred invitations I would order from the printer.

As a result of phone calls, each of the three galleries agreed, somewhat grudgingly, to ship back two of the paintings consigned to them with the understanding that I would send two fresh replacements immediately after the show. It was perhaps to my credit that I refrained from pointing out to any one of them that maybe if they had humped a little harder in promoting the sale of my work, my one-man show would be unnecessary, and they would have been spared the trouble of packing and shipping. The paintings being returned plus the eight I intended finishing gave me a total of 39, still 11 short of my target number of 50. It then occurred to me that there were a half-dozen or so works that local clients had bought from me direct, and perhaps several of them, with red dots to show that they had already been sold, could be borrowed for the exhibition. It worked out as I hoped, and three more paintings were soon added to the list: "Trinity Church" (in Upperville), "Fauquier County Courthouse" (in Warrenton), and "Coastal Marsh" recently bought by my friends Sheila and Paul.

Well, 42 is a respectable number, I told myself, and I might have let it go at that had I not suddenly remembered that behind some boxes in the guest room closet was a stack of unframed watercolors ranging in settings from Great Falls, Virginia, to Murchison Falls in Africa with on-the-spot views I had painted in Mexico, Europe and the Caribbean falling somewhere in between. So, eight works on paper were set aside with instructions from me to me that, in addition to all else, they were to be appropriately matted, framed and on view by Sunday afternoon, April fourth.

With designated entries for the show having finally reached the magic number of 50, it was time to crank up the Van-Go and head for Leesburg where there were printers who, if pressed, do simple things in a matter of minutes, and I had kept the invitation simple. Back in my early years in advertising, the format I devised was called a French fold. This type of fold involves printing on only one side of a sheet of paper and, by folding it a certain way, it's possible to end up with a so-called front cover, inside spread, and a back cover, all of it on the cheap compared with having to run the paper through the press a second time and print both sides. From the printers I went to a one-hour photo place and had them run off three hundred glossies of what I considered my talisman painting, "A View Of Pont Croix", for the invitation's center spread called for text on the left and photo pasted down on the right-hand side of the center spread.

Please come to the Opening of a One Man Show
Exhibiting fifty works in oil and watercolor
By American Impressionist Painter
WM. COVEL LEWIS
Sunday afternoon, April 4th, 12:30 until 5:00
AIRLIE HOUSE - Whistling Swan Pub

Finally, after all the components were in hand, my whining paid off, with Lisa reluctantly agreeing to handle the mailing and, with me assuring her that she would be forever blessed for having done so, my most dreaded, time-consuming chore was mercifully eliminated from the long and frightening list of things to do.

Fully aware that there was not a moment to be wasted and with something akin to controlled panic I set about painting away on each of the eight fairly large canvases that needed to be completely finished and in their frames by show time. Not until I started working on the first one did I realize that I desperately needed some new brushes, with all the characteristic springiness that feels just right when fresh bristles touch the canvas. Upon going through the entire assortment in the big earthenware crock that held dozens of brushes, I selected several fairly large ones that qualified as being usable but found, to my dismay, that not a single one of the smaller size hog-hair filberts measured up to expected standards and should be thrown out and replaced. The first part was easy, but stretcher pieces, wood for the skeletons of the plaster frames, gold leaf and other basic supplies were needed and I couldn't spare the money it would take to buy new brushes. I briefly toyed with the idea of calling Woodward to ask if I might borrow some of his small brushes, but that was too embarrassing to even seriously consider.

Instead, I resolved to complete the paintings using larger than usual brushes and, to some extent, palette knives. It turned out to be a blessing in disguise. Impressionistic paintings, by their very nature, are somewhat subjective and tend to be judged on the basis of impact and overall appeal rather than by some inflexible set of exacting criteria. And, although I had no intention of getting sloppy or adopting a lick and a promise attitude just because the clock was ticking away, with each painting the lack of smaller brushes forced me to resort to faster, bolder brushwork with fewer strokes and less detail, all of which had the effect of speeding things up. Best of all, I was rewarded with far better results, with pictures that projected more verve and spontaneity than would have been the case if I had more painstakingly poked along.

Unfortunately, I had far less latitude when it came to building the frames that would encase each painting. Plaster sets up rapidly, and there's a lot to attend to in a matter of minutes or, if everything isn't done just right and on time, the casting's a throw-away. Finally, after getting 32 structurally sound castings with good impressions from their molds, each would have to be sufficiently cured before being screwed down onto its wooden framework, with the spaces between the sections meticulously filled in with spackle, then dried some more, then sanded and, in due course, given successive coatings of shellac, Venetian-red and gold-leaf size over which, at the critical point of just the right degree of tackiness, the small, wispy, hard-to-handle squares of gold leaf could be applied one by one until, at last, the final antiquing would be brushed on and, with tasteful judgment, partially rubbed off.

Whew! With time running out, how on earth could I ever get it all done? Obviously, I had bitten off far more than I could chew. In fact, I felt like a pianist that had given widespread public notice of a forthcoming recital but, before any notes could be played, he had to first build his own piano.

Near the stove and getting drier each day in preparation for a last minute coat of varnish, were the eight finished paintings, and I was not about to throw in the towel and leave even a single one of them out of the exhibition. The option of putting them in anything less than suitable frames was unthinkable, and there was absolutely no way I could afford to buy frames. Having once dealt in fine paintings I knew that a good frame can not only be aesthetically pleasing, but I also well understood how it can add a look of importance to a painting. No one in his right mind applies for a job looking his worst, and I felt that some of my canvases were a little more ho-hum than I would like, so all the more reason to encase them in frames that would give them every possible advantage, in fact, frames so impressive people would think I had stolen them from a museum. As I fretted over the impossibility of completing the task that lay ahead within the short time left before the show, a bit of silly verse I remembered from many years before came to mind and provoked a sardonic smile:

> *"They showed me the job that 'couldn't be done'.*
> *They said that I couldn't do it.*
> *But I tackled the job that 'couldn't be done'.*
> *...I couldn't do it!"*

That basically described my situation, and I was tempted to give up the notion that I had to make eight more frames and, at best, make only three or four, when another verse came to mind that my father had asked me to memorize while I was still just a kid. Years later I had it printed on a card that thereafter remained in a permanent place near my desk:

> *"The heights of great men reached and kept,*
> *Were not attained through sudden flight.*
> *But they, while their companions slept,*
> *Were toiling upward in the night."*

Well, that was more like it. If great men had to burn the midnight oil in order to get anywhere, an ordinary guy like me had better get his tail in gear and toil upward, downward or sideways, morning, noon and night until all eight frames were finished, and then in the best tradition of the old-fashioned show-biz pitchman I would be able to boast, "As advertised, ladies and gentlemen, direct from Upperville, Virginia, fifty beautiful paintings--count 'em-fifty!"

Mine was a bone-weary arm that fumbled its way over to shut off the bedside clock's rude alarm. It was six A.M. and the first rays of the morning sun were beginning to shine through the bedroom windows. Strange, I still had my work clothes on and must have fallen asleep without getting dressed for bed. I looked over and saw the screen of the computer still lit-up and filled with text. It slowly began to sink in. Last night, after loading the Van-Go with all fifty paintings, I decided it would be a good idea to write a short commentary to accompany some of the more important works and, once I got started I kept going until, I guessed, two or two thirty. By then, from notes and memory, I had managed to find at least something either silly or enlightening, or both, to say about every painting in the show, such as: where it was painted, what was happening when it was being painted and any little bit of trivia that might hold the viewers' interest enough to cause him or her to take a second look at each picture before moving on. I flipped on the printer so it could do its duty while I occupied my own time with starting the coffee pot, shaving off a three day growth of beard and treating a very tired body to a much needed shower.

On the way to Airlie I reflected on how lucky I was to be blessed with such a favorable break in the weather. The Sunday before had barely fallen short of what was heralded on radio and TV as the expected blizzard of the century, and all of northern Virginia was confined to quarters for three days. But then, just as rapidly, the snow had melted and now, only one week later, the day held promise of being warm and sunny, a perfect day for people to get out of the house and mess around at something easy like attending a country art opening. The day before I had called Airlie and made arrangements for Alex, a maintenance man, to meet me at eight o'clock and let me in the Pub. Sure enough, he was standing in front waiting for me as I drove up. He was a pleasant young man who seemed willing to be of help.

"What's happening here today, Mr. Lewis?" he asked after we shook hands.

"I'm a painter and I'm having a vernissage," I replied.

He looked puzzled. "What's a verni., a what did you say?"

"A vernissage." I repeated. "It's a French word. It literally means the act of varnishing just before paintings are shown for the first time. But in the more general sense, it means an art opening. That's what's happening here today," I said, flinging open the rear doors of the Van-Go, then adding, "All fifty of these paintings are about to be hung in the Pub and then looked at for the first time by what I hope will be huge crowds of people who simply can't resist the urge to take one of my pictures home and make it their friend for life."

"Gee, I sure wish I knew how to paint. It sounds like an easy way to make a living," he said as he unlocked the door to the Pub. Then, calling back over his shoulder as he walked away, "Good luck, Mr. Lewis!"

"Yeah, good luck." I repeated under my breath. I would need plenty of it.

In trying to mentally prepare for the possibility of four and a half hours of total disaster, I had said to myself on the drive over from Creepy Cottage, "Look, it's just an art opening. You'll survive no matter how it turns out." But deep down inside I knew, all too well, that if I didn't turn things around on this one, single, last-chance Sunday afternoon it was back to the old drawing board so far as the rest of my life was concerned.

Fifty paintings are a lot for one man to unload and hang, but from years of having owned a gallery I knew all the do's, don'ts and short cuts, so that which would have taken a full committee of amateurs a whole day to discuss, argue over and eventually accomplish was completed in a couple of hours with all three rooms looking even better than I had envisioned. After adjusting the track lighting in the conference room, the only remaining major project was the matter of getting the back wall of the lounge lit with flood lights, and it was along this wall that I had hung my most important and expensive paintings. Normally, the room enjoyed the ambiance that results from soft lighting, but the long unbroken space between bar and fireplace, being the fartherest away from whatever natural light might find its way in through the windows on the other side demanded, for my purposes, special illumination.

Several days before I had anticipated this and provided for it by buying the various components needed for putting together a string of photographic type flood lights. I figured five such lights within metal reflectors angled so the light would bounce down from the ceiling would do the job, and I spaced them eight feet apart, with each light to be held in position by the spring-loaded clamp that's attached to the reflector. I did this knowing that there was a built-up ceiling beam about eight feet in from the wall and running the length of the room, and on its underside was a lip of enough dimension that I felt reasonably certain it would provide a suitable clamping surface. With stepladder in position I confidently ascended with the fixture at the dead-end of the line in hand and clamped it onto the beam. As I did so I noticed that the next light along the line was hanging about a foot above the floor and that its weight, in addition to that of the light to which the clamp was attached, was more than the clamp could handle.

With that in mind, I proceeded cautiously to the end, taking up slack as I went from station to station, making sure each clamp was responsible for supporting only the weight of its own fixture. With everything in place and reflectors aimed at the ceiling between the row of paintings, I retraced my steps, screwed a 500 watt color-corrected bulb into each socket, climbed down off the ladder, inserted the plug into the electrical outlet, flipped on the switch, walked to the middle of the room and stood admiring the wall adorned with twelve brilliantly lit paintings. The effect was magnificent. But only for a brief instant. When the first clamp suddenly gave way I looked on helplessly as each of the other four fixtures lost their grip and came crashing down immediately thereafter in a heartbreaking display of noise, exploding glass and electrical smoke.

My first horror-struck reaction was to look at my watch. Oh my God, it was almost twelve. Early birds, if any, might well be arriving in another half hour. How in the hell were they going to see my best paintings. All twelve might as well be on view in a coal bin unless I could figure out a way to get some light on them. Run into Warrenton and buy a dozen or so flashlights to hand out to guests? Come on, get serious. Think hard. Seconds later I was on the phone asking the Airlie operator to connect me with Alex in maintenance. As I half expected, it was, "No, sorry, Mr. Lewis, no daylight photoflood lamps." But they did have plenty of 200 watt regular light bulbs that he would bring over along with the hammer and the few small nails that I requested. As I hung up the phone I caught a glimpse of myself in the back-bar mirror and was not at all amused by what I saw, for I was still in work clothes and looked as if I had not only been hanging paintings but had taken time out to slop the hogs as well.

There would be no better time to make a quick change, so I high-tailed it out to the Van Go and was back dressed like I was ready to attend a boardroom meeting and was sweeping up glass by the time Jason the bartender arrived, then the girl showed up with the economy-class edibles that I had ordered from catering and, moments later, Alex appeared carrying a hammer in one hand and a bag of what I supposed were lightbulbs.

"Are you having problems, Mr. Lewis?" Alex inquired as he walked over to where I was sweeping up the last fragments of glass.

"Have you ever heard of a man in the Bible by the name of Job?" I asked in reply to his question. "Well I'm here to tell you that his troubles were nothing but a bag of peanuts compared to what I'm going through right now. Yeah, I'm having problems. The damned lights fell down. This wall is so dark that without lights shining on the paintings I might as well be exhibiting them inside a cave. My plan now is to use the bulbs you brought, which are featherweights compared to the ones that broke, and drive a small nail on the upper side of that lip along the beam where the clamps fit, so they can't slip down and fall off like they did before. If you can help me for a few minutes I'll get up on the ladder and....."

"Hello. We're a bit early. Hope you don't mind," a female voice was saying.

I turned to see a couple from Middleburg that I barely knew, but I had heard enough about them to know that they were collectors with enough scratch to buy everything in the show many times over if they felt like it. Here they were, the kind of prospects with whom I should be walking the gallery, all the while getting better acquainted and sneaking in appropriate comments about this or that picture, and here I was, hammer in hand perched halfway up a ladder with my best paintings subdued in cellar-like gloom.

"I'm delighted to see you," I lied, stepping down onto the floor and trying my best to look composed. "I apologize for not being ready to properly receive company, but we're having trouble with the lights in this room. Perhaps you would care to have a glass of wine while you're looking at paintings in the other two rooms. Some of my best paintings are along this wall, but since they don't glow in the dark, we'll need to get the lights working in order for you to see them."

"A good painting should look good in any light," she said rather icily. "Thank you for the offer of wine, but no thanks. Perhaps we'll come back later." And with that they walked off into the sunset, so to speak.

As I stood watching them leave I somehow managed to abstain from uttering the crude expletive that came to mind. Of course, she was dead right in saying that a good painting should look good in any light, and I swore that if by some crazy quirk of fate she ever had an after-dark art opening of her own, I would gladly let her prove the point by personally cutting every electrical wire within a mile of her exhibition. Oh well, no time to fret, for there was still work to be done before people began showing up. Soon the lights in the Pub were working, and even though the less powerful regular light bulbs were not color-corrected and had to be shined directly on the paintings, at least the paintings could be seen, and it sure beat passing out flashlights. I was in the process of sticking the last of the commentaries onto the bottom edge of its matching frame and, in the process, wondering what had happened to Lisa who had promised to arrive early, when a writer friend of mine named Wendy showed up with a publisher friend of hers. They were on their way somewhere and could just stay a minute, she said, but didn't want to miss seeing the show. Even though they practically raced from one painting to another, in no time flat she spotted a small painting that she liked and minutes later was writing out a check. As I stuck a red dot on the frame of "In The Tropics", an 11x14 inch oil done from my veranda while living in Mexico, I wondered if Alex knew something I didn't know about painting being an easy way to make a living.

The phone behind the bar rang and Kevin called over to say it was for me.

"Well, good afternoon, Lisa. How nice of you to call. You perhaps didn't receive my invitation, but I'm having an art opening at Airlie for the next few hours, and if you've nothing better to do you may want to drop by and..."

"Look, don't fuss at me. I know I'm late and I can do without the sarcasm," she said in a voice unmistakably brittle. "I worked on a mural in a house in Georgetown until after one o'clock last night and was back there again at nine this morning trying to finish so I could come help you with your show and I'm tired. I tried calling you earlier and got no answer. I guess you had left. I'm calling now from the Virginia Welcome Center on Route 66. Jeff's been trying to reach you. Has he called you there?"

"Jeff? No. He and I haven't talked since he asked me to send him photographs of my paintings, which I mailed to him in California a couple of weeks ago. What's on his mind?"

"He wants to know if you've sold 'At The Paddock','Tristan's House'and 'Breton Chapel?'"

"No, I haven't sold them. I'm looking at two of them and the third is in one of the other rooms. Why do you ask?"

"Because, Jeff said he's been out of town and just got home last night. When he saw your invitation about the show he was afraid you might sell the three paintings that he likes most, and he asked me to let you know that if you still have them he wants to buy all three. He's moving into a big house in Palo Alto and he thinks..."

"Lisa, please. Let me get this straight. Are you saying that Jeff has actually made up his mind to buy all three paintings, that he's not just considering buying them but has actually made a commitment to buy them, all three of them?"

"That's right."

"Then why the hell didn't you tell me that in the beginning?"

"Huh? I just did. What did you think I said?"

"I mean, all this conversation we've been having, like 'Hi, Boss, how's it going ', and mural painting in Georgetown, and being tired, and all of that kind of stuff. Lise, you don't know what this means to me. The show's barely started and with those three paintings sold I'll have enough to pay for whatever I'll owe here at Airlie and maybe the airfare to France and back. Look, a lady just walked in and I've got to play host. Thanks for making my day with the good news. You're only about fifteen or twenty minutes away, so crank her up and I'll see you when you get here."

While sticking red dots on the three paintings I greeted the newly arrived guest whom I didn't know and couldn't place, a stout woman in a tweedy outfit wearing pink-rimmed eyeglasses who, in the process of viewing, planted her feet firmly in front of each painting. After careful scrutiny, she enthusiastically expelled what appeared to be her one, all-purpose adjective, a single word starting off on an explosive high note prolonged for quite some time in ever descending pitch and with decreasing volume as if most of the gas had been used up by the end of the first syllable, so all I kept hearing was "Wunnnnnnderful". I couldn't help but think how nice it would be if she were to inform me that she wished to buy a painting, so it would be my turn to say, "Wunnnnnnderful." Seeing that she had viewed the last of the paintings, I approached and asked if there was anything in particular that had caught her fancy.

"Oh, yes, they were all just wunnnnnnderful," she replied. "But I especially liked the one with the little dog."

"The little dog?" I repeated, thoroughly puzzled, since there was no little dog in any of the paintings. "I'm afraid I don't quite know which one you mean. Perhaps you would care to show me."

"This one over here." she said, leading me to one of the three paintings in the show that had Pont Croix as its setting. Instead of looking at the picture, she motioned, instead, to the commentary attached to its frame, which read:

"A VIEW OF PONT CROIX" (16" x 20" $1,800)
I have now painted Pont Croix four times, each canvas totally different from the others because of viewpoint, lighting and emphasis. The first time I was with Bill Woodward's group on a misty morning. The second time was with Claudette, a pretty French lady, painting alongside. I was all alone when I painted number three. Finally, the painting shown here was done one afternoon during Lisa Johnson's visit last summer, with the two of us painting together. Out of the picture, up the hill and to the left, is the center of the village of Pont Croix. The town is built around a square, rimmed with leafy plane trees that form a boundary for parked cars, vendors of all description, boule-playing loafers and, almost invariably, a small circus with its little group of moldy animals killing time until the night's performance.

On the sunny side of the square there's a bar with sidewalk tables where one can relax with a glass of wine or Pernod and lazily watch this Gallic microcosm unfold. I especially enjoy witnessing the venom with which the proprietor's small rat terrier claims his territorial rights. Quiet and unnoticed, he crouches beneath a table until he spies some itinerant canine unwittingly entering his domain. Then, without so much as a bark or a growl, he shoots like a bullet straight for his target, causing even much larger dogs to be so unnerved by the unexpected ferocity of his attack they don't stick around to argue. Perhaps one can easily see why I keep going back to Pont Croix."

I was tempted to suggest that if she liked my little write-up all that much she could have it for $1,800 and I would throw the painting in for nothing.

A couple, who were friends of mine and six other people I didn't know, all showed up in pairs within seconds of each other, so I excused myself from Ms. Wunnnnnnderful and put on my best welcoming smile. Warm bodies were beginning to cross the threshold and the imagined scent of captive paintings migrating to happy new owners was in the air. Ah, thank God, Lisa had arrived. She knew how to sell paintings as well or better than I, and could brag about my work, which I couldn't. Two people I had never seen before, a tall man with long hair and his very pretty wife came over and said they were interested in "The Sunflower Field", a picture I had painted alongside Bill Woodward and the talented painters Pierre and his nephew Gaston while in France the summer before. They asked if I could do better on the price. When I said no, it had been recalled from a dealer where the price was much higher so it was already wearing a bargain basement tag, they said fine, no harm in asking, and with that they started writing out a check. And so yet another painting was honored by acceptance into the venerable and much-coveted order of the exalted *red dot*.

Suddenly, as if someone had blown a starting whistle, the rooms were beginning to fill. All around me were people looking at paintings, chatting with each other, nibbling food, getting drinks from the bar and, out through the open French doors and beyond the swimming pool I could see that still more were on their way in to see the show.

There was a hand on my shoulder and I turned to see Dr. Johnson, Lisa's father, a man with an important collection of 19th-and early-20th century art. "Congratulations, Bill," he said. "This is a fine show. I like your paintings, but I'm especially impressed by your frames. Lisa tells me you've made them all yourself. I don't know how you did it, but the very ornate ones of gilded plaster would cost an arm and a leg if you tried to buy something similar in a frame shop. I think you could start a business making frames."

"Thanks for the compliment, Everett," I replied, "Figuring out a way to make frames for my own paintings was born of necessity, for I just plain couldn't afford to buy what I wanted. As to making frames for someone else at any price, I wouldn't touch it with a ten-foot pole. Anyway, thanks for the kind words."

Lisa was motioning to me from where she was standing all by herself on the other side of the room, so I excused myself and joined her with, "What's up?"

"I've sold two paintings in the short time I've been here and we still have nearly three hours yet to go. I don't know how many you've sold, but I'm beginning to see more and more red dots. Are you making notes on who's buying what? So far I've just been trusting my memory, but maybe we should start a list showing each buyer's name, address, title of painting, and amount paid or due. Otherwise, once it's all over we may be so confused we won't be able to remember who bought what for how much or where to reach them when it's time to deliver the painting. What do you think?"

"I think it's a brilliant idea, Lisa, and thanks for reminding me. I brought along a clipboard for that very purpose, but forgot to bring it in. It's in the Van-Go and I'll run out and get it."

On my way back to the Pub with clipboard in hand, I first heard dogs barking and then a voice calling, "Bill!" Straining at their leashes and barking excitedly as they got nearer were Daisy and Abner followed by Spencer, their preent owner. The show would just have to be put on hold, I figured, while I took time out to have a short visit with two very dear little friends, and

I was sitting on the curb hugging them when Shannon came out looking for me with the message that Lisa needed me back inside to talk to a man about doing a commission.

"Sorry to put you to the trouble of having to find me, Shannon," I said as we walked back in, "but I had to say hello to two of my former students."

"Was the guy with the two dogs one of them?" she asked.

"No, the two dogs were both of them." I answered.

As the afternoon wore on, I decided I should give up on trying to out-guess public taste. Several canvases that I thought would be the most acclaimed went virtually unnoticed. On the other hand, a palette knife painting of a scene in coastal Alabama that in my opinion wasn't exactly a show-stopper was verbally fought over by two couples who were apparently looking at it side by side when each claimed they were the first to say they wanted to buy it. I didn't know either of the participants and thought it best to keep my mouth shut and let them settle it between themselves, which they did.

Another painting, one that I liked and might well have kept for myself it if I hadn't needed the money, could easily have been sold twice, only seconds apart. It was the only one in the show that was not done en plein air but, instead, was painted from a photograph of Lisa in costume in a Venetian garden while attending the carnival there a few months earlier. Tim Pegler had just handed me a check for it and I was on my way to put a red dot on the frame when I met Lisa with Karin and Stansfield Turner who were on their way to do the same thing. The check in hand won out and all I could say to my good friends, the admiral and his wife, was "I'm sorry."

It was five o'clock and I told Kevin to close down the bar but to leave me a bottle each of red and white wine, a few bottles of beer and some Coke in case latecomers showed up before the doors were locked. With clipboard in hand I walked along counting red dots. There were twenty. Three were on paintings I had sold earlier but borrowed for the show. Three more were on canvases to be sent to Jeff in California. The remaining fourteen had all sold locally, mostly to people I didn't know, and, in addition, I had picked up two commissions, a total of sixteen sales in only four and a half hours. My cup literally runneth over, I thought as I carried a too-full glass of wine to a table near the fireplace. A better idea, I decided, was to bring bottles and glasses to the table. I walked over to invite Lisa, who was saying goodbye to a couple of stragglers, to come join me when beyond her shoulder I caught a glimpse of a familiar profile intensely looking at one of my paintings in the far room. It was Woodward. He had apparently come in unnoticed through the side door.

"Bill!" I practically shouted. "I can't tell you how pleased I am that you've come to my humble vernissage. Lisa and I are about to sit down and have a glass of wine. Come join us."

"Thanks, I will, but first I want to see what you've done. I notice you've sold a few, so I wouldn't say your work is all that humble. You go ahead. I'll join you after I've finished looking."

Lisa had taken off her shoes and sat with feet stretched out on the chair seat in front of her. "Well nice going, Boss. Yuh done good. Aren't you happy? We sold a lot of paintings today."

"We sure did, Lisa, and you had a lot to do with it. You encouraged me to have a show at a time when I believed I couldn't afford it. And I have you to thank for taking care of the invitations. With all I had on my plate no one would have ever known the show was going to happen if that job had been left up to me. I haven't bothered to count who sold which paintings, but I suspect you sold about as many as I did and I'm indebted. In the morning, as soon as the bank opens I'm sending a wire transfer to the Letourneau's in Pont Aven, clinching the place for the summer. Their daughter Suzy tells me that I'll be getting the entire first floor, which amounts to several rooms and a bath, plus use of the garden. She says her father claims Gauguin and some of his chums painted in the attic on several occasions and, if I want, I can paint there on rainy days. So there's plenty of room for you if you want to come paint in France again this summer. I'm good for a free plane ride there and back and it won't cost you anything but pocket money while you're there. How about it?"

Lisa laughed. "You know me, Boss. I'm always ready to go to France or Italy anytime I get half a chance. When do we leave?"

"Did I hear something about going to France? If so, take me with you," Woodward said as he sat down, reaching for the glass of wine I had waiting for him. "Say, Lewis, I haven't seen so many red dots since I was a kid in bed with measles. You didn't sell all those paintings today, did you?"

"No, I sold only fourteen here this afternoon," I said.

"Plus two commissions," Lisa added.

"You're new at this game Bill. You make it sound like selling fourteen paintings plus two commissions in one afternoon is normal. Believe me, it isn't. It's a lot. In fact, it's a hell of a lot," he added with conviction.

"I know it's a lot, and I was incredibly lucky," I said. "In fact, if I had known I was going to sell so many I would have done a better job of painting them," I said, paraphrasing a George Burns wisecrack.

Bill looked at his watch. "Hey, I've got to run. Congratulations, my friend. You've come a long way since you visited my studio several years ago asking if I could help you get started painting in oils. You're now a good painter. Keep at it. I'm proud of you."

As we stood shaking hands I did my best to express the gratitude I felt for all the support, guidance and encouragement he had so generously given me from that day years before when I had asked for his help.

"There goes a good man and a very talented painter who's been a generous friend. Partly because of what I learned from being around him, you're seeing more red dots on paintings than would be the case otherwise," I said to Lisa as I watched him walk away. Then, adding, "I don't know which I'm the most of, tired or hungry. Do you have any plans for dinner?"

"Yes, I'm having dinner with the family and am due in Chevy Chase in half an hour. I'm already running late, so I'd better get going. Sorry to leave you, but as you know they eat early, and I don't want to get yelled at. Again, Boss, congratulations. I'm proud of you too."

The fire logs, except for an occasional flicker, had reduced themselves to a bed of glowing embers that invited reflection of the human type. What better place to sit quietly, collect thoughts and relax, something I had not had a chance to do for a very long time. One of the tapes I had brought, Mussorgsky's "Pictures At An Exhibition" was playing in the background. Up until several years ago as a successful businessman I had looked upon it as just another piece of music with no special significance, but now it represented the very essence of my present lifestyle. A lifestyle I would now be able to continue living.

"What a lucky guy," I quietly said to myself. "And to top it all, in a couple of months I'll be back painting again in France."

CHAPTER THIRTEEN
Take Me Back To Sotto Passaggio

It is truly written, though I'm not prepared at this moment to quote source, chapter and verse, that, insofar as we are able, we should help those in need when called upon to do so. And, of all the needs I can think of that may be brought to our attention, few, if any, are of a more pleasant nature than to be told by a friend that you are needed in Venice to lend a helping hand.

The voice on the phone requesting my helping hand continued, ".... and oh yes, you'll be staying right on the Grande Canale while you're here, so shelter won't cost you a penny, and we can save money and cook most of our meals in. And the project, well, the project's a real challenge, something I know you'll enjoy. What about it, Boss?

With considerable excitement in her voice, Lisa was telling me that she had just been commissioned by an Italian architect to restore the murals in two large rooms on the top floor of an eighteenth century palazzo. She went on to say that in the larger of the two rooms there was a domed ceiling, the center of which had been adorned with paintings of classical figures and various mythical imagery, but about twenty five to thirty percent of this centuries-old mural had been completely destroyed by water damage from a leaky roof which had since been repaired. In those areas where damage had occurred, only new white plaster replaced what had once been original painting. One large area was completely blank, she told me, as if a gluttonous slice had been taken out of a pie some fifteen feet in diameter. The assignment called for restoring all of the decorative painting in this two room portion of the palazzo, but it was especially important that the murals surrounding the middle area of the domed ceiling be restored so that it looked as if no damage had ever taken place, for it, along with the magnificent Venetian glass chandelier that hung from its center, was the focal point in this imposing suite of rooms.

As Lisa was describing the situation my mind was racing with welcome thoughts about me now having a valid reason to go back to Europe, but not just any old place in Europe, but Venice, a city I had previously visited only once and then all too briefly. At the end of the four months spent painting in Pont Aven the year before, I had resigned myself to no more European summers, but with Lisa's phone call I now had a valid reason to spend as long as it took to help her with an exciting and challenging project in Venice and, after that, I could stop off in Paris on the way back and do some painting there.

"This is a big project. I've never done anything like it before and I'm scared and I need your help. You'll come help me, won't you, Boss?" Lisa was pleading.

"Not only yes, but hell yes," was my instant response. "Give me several days to take care of some things and I'll be on the next flight over."

When we had spoken on the phone she had used glowing superlatives in describing her Venetian living accommodations, and although I expected something rather nice, I was not in the least prepared for what greeted me when I arrived in person. Her apartment was downright elegant, furnished in what appeared to me to be the Italian version of Chippendale, accented with a liberal use of satin fabrics, while beautifully muted oriental rugs covered much of the highly polished parquet floors. The most remarkable thing of all, I felt, was that if one was foolish enough to climb through the open living room window, he had better be a good swimmer, for there was nothing on the other side but the water of the *Grande Canale* lapping against the building. The apartment, I soon learned, was a guest suite in a palazzo lived in by a contessa who occupied the upper floors and whose property included the largest walled garden in Venice. The location within the city was perfect. Only a few yards away was a stop for numbers one and eighty-two *vaporetti*, the water buses that traverse the *Grande Canale*, and a few hundred paces from the canal was *Campo Santa Margarita*, next to St. Mark's the largest square in Venice, a lively setting with market stalls selling fresh produce during the day and a good nighttime assortment of restaurants and bars. All in all, hers was the perfect setting in one of the most fascinating cities in the world.

Eventually I asked, "Where do I hang my hat while I'm here as the assistant muralist in residence?"

"Come on, I'll show you," she replied, and with that we walked past the bathroom, on past her own stylish bedroom with fancy gold leaf inlayed cream colored furniture, then a well-appointed kitchen with a large round table and a half dozen chairs, beyond which was my Venetian pad on the *Grande Canale*, a small dark room with a cot, a chair and not much else, obviously, the servant's room. I thereafter referred to it as the "Dungeon".

"I hope it'll be all right, Boss. I'm sorry there's not another bedroom." Lisa said apologetically.

"Don't give it a thought, Lisa," I said. "I'll be as happy here as if I had good sense. I'm lucky to be in Venice. Come on, I want to go see the palace and the murals we'll be restoring."

After a five-minute walk through Campo Santa Margarita and a couple of *pontes* over small *canales,* we were at a large ornate building, its exterior partially obscured by scaffolding. Lisa let us in with a key she had been given by Antonio, the architect who had awarded her the commission.

Inside, standing in the main salon of the suite that had suffered the water damage, I was impressed by what I saw. "This is a major restoration job," I said. "Have you ever worked on repainting anything this complicated?" I asked.

She shook her head. "No, and quite frankly, I'm scared. I didn't dare ask Antonio what kind of paint I should use to match those portions of the mural that have remained intact. I thought he would think I should know that without asking."

"I see your point," I said. "I just hope it doesn't involve using egg yolks as a binder for powdered pigments, as they did when the original was painted. That could be tiresome and messy." Suddenly, I had an idea. "Is there something comparable we could look at?"

"Yes, there is," she said. "There's restoration going on all the time in Venice. In fact, there's a church not far from here where they're doing major restoration, and I vaguely know the man who's doing the work, but I don't want to ask him either."

"Let's go there anyway, I said. "Who knows, maybe we'll learn something."

When God made Italian men he gave them the good sense to focus their undivided attention on attractive young women, so while Mario, the muralist, was busily flirting with Lisa I busily did a bit of snooping around until, in a small alcove in what may well have been the vestry room for the clergy when the church was in use, I spotted the supply of paints being used to restore the church's wall decorations. As far as I was concerned I had hit the mother lode and, having learned from my older brother Dick to never, ever, go anywhere without something to write with and on, I withdrew from my pocket a ball point pen and a scrap of paper on which I scribbled away in great detail the Italian wording on the labels of the gallon buckets of white paint. I then noticed that there were multiple small containers of powdered pigment used for coloring.

Once outside the church I showed my findings to Lisa who, with her knowledge of Italian, soon declared, "All they're using is what seems to be a standard brand of white latex paint and they're toning it with powdered pigments until they match the colors of the paintings being restored." Thankfully, industrial chemists of the modern age had made it possible for us to paint in tempera without having to use egg yolks as a binder. The next morning, attired in work clothes, the two of us walked from store to store purchasing paint and other supplies until by day's end we had collected everything we anticipated needing.

Our plan was to first of all get started on the large central mural in the grand salon, and although Lisa as the master muralist would end up doing the finished paintings with me doing most of the grunt painting of lesser importance in both rooms, much of the preparatory work in the area where Lisa would be working was a two person job, for tracings of existing images had to be made on large sheets of tissue and then transferred by means of underlying graphite paper to places where there was only blank white plaster. It would have been nice and easy if we could have done all this on the floor and then merely flipped everything a hundred and eighty degrees so that, presto chango, it was suddenly on a twenty-two foot high ceiling. But, unfortunately, such was not the case.

As it was, the two of us stood somewhat precariously on the planks of a scaffold some fifteen feet off the floor while carefully and gingerly grasping the ends of wide sheets of tracing paper with the objective of lifting each one over our heads and taping it securely to the ceiling without it getting torn, wrinkled or otherwise damaged. Time after time, one or the other of us would confidently assert, "I've got it, I've got it!" only to have it come loose and flopping down over us like some ghostly shroud, blinding us and causing a degree of panic due to sudden movements taking place way too high above the floor for comfort. In this manner, we eventually succeeded in transferring drawings onto the damaged areas for the painting that would be undertaken by Lisa.

Our next important challenge was the matter of mixing colors so that all the new painting matched perfectly the work that was still undamaged. We were fortunate, I felt, that we were using water soluble rather than oil based paints. First of all, water based tempera of any variety dries faster than oil paints, and I also well knew from my own experience in using both, that water colors dry a tone lighter, whereas oil paints dry somewhat darker. Lisa, of course, knew this as well, and both of us knew how to mix colors. I was also glad to learn that we would be painting *su secco* rather than *su fresco* (on dry plaster rather than on fresh, uncured plaster.) Our next step was to analyze the colors in the paintings in both rooms, and simplify things by assuming that the original muralist didn't mix colors as he went along but, rather, mixed up batches of color before he started, so he had a good supply of each and every color in jugs, or pig bladders, or whatever. We decided we would do the same. With that in mind, Lisa chose certain colors and I did likewise, and as we progressively got to what we thought was the exact tone of the color we were matching we would make little splotches next to the original, wait for it to dry, and then make adjustments. To speed thing up we bought a couple of hair dryers, so that in a matter of minutes we could make valid judgments.

As days went by we made good progress, Lisa spending her time up on the scaffold in the grand salon while I did touch up on walls and the ceiling on another scaffold in the second room. The October weather was warm and pleasant and we painted away with windows open, my only complaint and discomfort being that I had to listen to the constant nervous, off-key whistling of a bantam size workman on an outside scaffold. It got so bad I felt like writing a letter to the Chinese saying "Forget about your water torture – use this little guy instead."

Eventually the day arrived when, after our own careful scrutiny, we decided that the job was finished. Lisa called Antonio with that bit of news, and he appeared at the appointed time. As she and he walked the premises, stopping here and there while yakking away in Italian, I stood apart, silently looking out the window near the little whistler's perch on the scaffold thinking, "Before I leave I should ask God to forgive me for wanting to kill the little bastard." Once the architect had gone, Lisa came over to where I was standing.

"How'd it go?" I asked.

She was smiling. "It went great," she said.

"What did he have to say about the work?" I asked.

"Oh, he liked it fine. His only suggestion was that we rub a little dirt over it to give it some instant aging. Other than that he thought it was perfect."

There was only one more hurdle to cross. Like many of the venerable structures in Venice, the palazzo where we had been working was on the list of national treasures, and a notice stuck to the entrance door so stated. In order for our work to be finalized it must pass inspection and receive the approval of a member of the arts committee. So it was with considerable apprehension that Lisa and I showed up for that appointment, aware of the possibility that she might be told that everything was all wrong and we didn't pass inspection, and that the work would need to done over, and on and on and on were the negative possibilities that paraded through our minds.

At the appointed hour the huge door to the suite slowly opened, and as the two of us stood with the trepidation one might expect if God himself was coming to call, a pleasant looking gentleman wearing thick glasses and a slight smile surrounded by an oversized jaw entered the room. After introducing himself, he walked toward Lisa, extended his hand and in perfect English said, "You must be Miss Johnson," and, turning to me "And you must be Mr. Lewis." Apparently Antonio had done a good job of briefing.

"Now, show me the part you've restored," he said to Lisa while looking up at the ceiling she had been working on for the past few weeks. From then on it was easy. If he had to be told which was new and which was old she had obviously done her job well, me helping of course, and before leaving he signed a paper for Lisa to give to Antonio, saying that the restoration had been officially approved.

"You should have a party!" I said to Lisa after he was gone. "I'm sure Michelangelo did something festive after he climbed down off the Sistine Chapel scaffolding for the last time, and we should celebrate too. We just completed a tough assignment and you recently had a birthday, so you have two good reasons to invite some of your friends in. We'll both be leaving Venice in a few days and it would give you a chance to say goodbye to the friends you've made during the time you've lived here. What do you say? I'll help you. It'll be fun."

During the weeks spent climbing up and down scaffolds and standing with our necks bent out of shape, we had made it a point to end every work day promptly at five o'clock, go back to the apartment, clean up and enjoy just relaxing, have a glass or so of wine and a leisurely dinner, or sometimes enjoy the nightlife of Venice, oftentimes with friends Lisa had met while the university was in session and on other occasions with people she had gotten to know through quite different circumstances. There was the paunchy, talkative, middle-aged count she had met at an art museum who was the perpetual Venetian night owl and who was referred to by an American acquaintance as Count Windbaggio. She had also made friends with Maria Pia, a refined member of the Venetian aristocracy who had grown up in the family palazzo on the *Grande Canale* but now lived in her own special penthouse in the Lido section of the city, and another friend was Flaminia, with a PhD. in botany, and then there was Gianni, a retired Italian air force colonel who owned a huge villa in the foothills of the Dolomite Mountains an hour and a half's drive north of Venice. We had both met Jane and Bob, an American couple living in Venice and, through them, an Englishman who was a painter with a large studio in the Giudeccca section of the city. I had gotten to know all of these people during the time I had been in Venice, so all of these plus perhaps a dozen more that Lisa knew and we had the makings of a good party.

The weather was warm and balmy the night of the party, and with special permission from the contessa, tables were set up among the tubs of exotic plants in the open courtyard that separated the contessa's walled garden from the door to Lisa's apartment. Laughter and lively conversation soon filled the air as bottle after bottle of sparkling prosecco went down the hatch. As a reminder that all this was taking place in Venice, from time to time the tenor voice of a poor man's Luciano Pavarotti graced our gathering with him belting out "O Sole Mia" and other favorites as he sculled his tourista-occupied gondola past Lisa's windows.

It was Lisa's party and she seemed to be having a grand time, so I was more than content to let her devote all of her attention to her guests, while I acted as waiter and made sure the wine was flowing freely, but in spite of my intention of playing a low-key role I soon learned, to my amusement, that my attire was attracting considerable attention. I had come to Italy by way of New York and Connecticut, visiting friends and family for a couple of days in each place and I knew there would be a cocktail party or so, one of which I had been told was to be at a country club, so I had packed a pair of green summer slacks, some brown and white saddle shoes and a white linen jacket, typical warm weather cocktail attire on the East Coast.

When it came time to get dressed for the party I suddenly realized that everything else I owned had gotten either soiled or wrinkled, so as I later walked around among the guests filling glasses, clad in rather bright green slacks and unfamiliar looking brown and white saddle shoes, my American trappings created so much favorable comment I wondered if my stateside duds might be the cause of starting a new Italian fashion trend.

Lisa left for the States a few days later with plans to return for the second year of her master's program and with the word of the contessa that she could have the same apartment. I left Venice for Paris, having already made up my mind that I too would be back in Italy the next summer, devoting my full time to landscape and genre painting and working on writing this book. The friends I had met through Lisa were now my friends as well, and life was good in this part of the world. Everywhere I looked there was something to paint. I had spent three full summers painting in Brittany and would now spend the remainder of the fall painting in Paris. It was time, I decided, to devote an entire summer painting and writing in Italy. "Someone has to do it," I told myself.

■■■

In William Shakespeare's "As You Like It" he uses the phrase, "Time gallops..." and I realized that for me it truly had. Almost a year had transpired since I was acting as wine steward at Lisa's party, wearing pants green enough to look like some happy Irishman leading a parade on St. Patrick's Day. Lisa had arrived ahead of me, and was settled in her jewel-box of an apartment on the *Grande Canale*. The game plan was that I would stay with her for a couple of days and then move into an apartment that had been arranged for me by Geofredo, a doctor friend of Gianni's who had rented the apartment at a time when he was going through a period of marital difficulties, and both he and Gianni had good things to say about it. Without even seeing it, I liked Geofredo's description of the setting. First of all, it was close, but not in, Venice. An easy train ride, I was told. That suited me perfectly. For that meant that during most days I could paint or write with less distraction than would be the case if I spent several summer months in the heart of Venice. Secondly, rent was within the parameters of what my pocketbook could afford, and that consideration was essential.

The apartment, I learned, was in Treviso, a small, picturesque city of ancient linage about thirty kilometers north of Venice. Trains ran frequently between Venice and Treviso, I was informed, so I could easily enjoy the benefits of both localities. My landlord, Geofredo told me, was a Signore Bettini, but since he lived in Padua I would be dealing with his sister, Signorina Cristiana Bettini, who lived in an apartment in the building and she, luckily for me, spoke a little English. He then handed me a piece of paper with her address and phone number and said she had agreed to be at home the next day to meet me at eleven o'clock to give me the key to the apartment. All I needed to do was just ring the Bettini bell on the directory panel at the street entrance and she would come let me in. It couldn't be easier if it tried.

As the train headed north it soon became obvious that it was something of a commuter train, for it made frequent stops, with people getting on and off at every stop. A little over thirty-five minutes after leaving Venice the train stopped at a rather built up urban area, but I saw no sign identifying the name of the community. Not wanting to ride past my stop, and since I spoke only a few words of Italian, I leaned in my seat toward a guy sitting across the aisle and one seat back and, pointing toward the exit said, "Treviso?"

Perhaps he didn't understand, but the fact remained, he said "Si", and I got off.

As the train pulled away without me, I took a quick look around, and seeing that I was practically out in the boonies, I immediately said to myself and the world in general, "Hell, this can't be Treviso."

I looked at my watch. First of all I'd better call Signorina Bettini and let her know that I'd be late. Fortunately, there was a phone booth nearby and from the year before I had learned how to use Italian public telephones. The woman's voice at the other end greeted me with a lyrical, "Buòn giorno."

"Buòn giorno, Signorina Bettini," I responded. "This is Signore Lewis, the friend of Dr. Dominico's and I'm on my way to rent the apartment."

A lengthy pause, then, "Si, Signore, where-you-are?" she asked haltingly with considerable space between words.

From the way she spoke, with screwed up syntax and what appeared to be her need to think hard before saying each word, I realized almost immediately that her English was about as good as my French which, at best, was somewhere between poor and abysmal. The only French speaking person that I had ever understood perfectly was a Monsieur Mouton who had stood and chatted with me as I was painting in Brittany the year before, and the only reason I understood him so well was because he had a speech impediment, and he had said each word very, very slowly, giving me a chance to wrap my mind around the last word before going on to the next one. I had now better use the Monsieur Mouton system with her, I reasoned. And so, speaking very slowly and carefully enunciating every word, I replied, "I-am-very-sorry-Signorina-Bettini-but-I-got-off-the-train-too-soon." Then, looking quickly up and down the platform, I saw the sign that read, "Sotto Passaggio." "So," I continued, "I-am-now-at-Sotto-Passaggio."

Complete silence, then, "Where-you-are-under-the ground, Signore Lewis, for is many Sotto Passaggios in Italy?"

Now just what in the hell did she mean by me being under the ground, I wondered. My immediate wise-guy answer normally might have been something like, "Yeah, yeah, I'm an old guy with hair turning grayer by the minute and more chins than a Chinese phone book, but I'm still very much alive and kicking, and all I'd like from you right now, Signorina, is to have an intelligent conversation so I can continue on my way to Treviso." As far as there being many Sotto Passagios in Italy, well, I could understand that, for I remembered once reading that in America we had some thirty-five towns with the name of Springfield, and, without question, the name Sotto Passaggio was much prettier.

Instead, hiding my exasperation as best I could, I answered her question by saying, "As-I-said-before-Signorina Bettini,-I-am-at-Sotto Passaggio, And-oh-yes, it-is-the-one-near-Treviso-and-I-will-come-on-to-Treviso-on-the-very-next-train-that-stops-at-Sotto Passaggio. O.K?"

Dead silence. Finally, "Si,-Signore Lewis.- O.K. I-wait-for-you."

On my second try, with the help of a young kid who spoke English, I got off the train at Treviso as planned, and joined the other exiting passengers who all seemed to be heading for the same destination along the platform. It was then, upon looking to see where we were all going, that I saw it again. There it was in bold, black and white letters, "Sotto Passaggio." A few feet from the big sign, bodies and heads were disappearing from view as they descended the concrete steps leading down to the pedestrian tunnel running under the tracks to steps on the other side leading back up to ground level. Obviously, Sotto Passaggio was not the name of a town but the Italian words for "Underground Passage," of which there were no doubt hundreds, maybe thousands, throughout Italy.

"Now if I can only find a dunce cap to be wearing when I meet Signorina Bettini, it will have been a perfect morning." I told myself. Instead, I did find some pretty flowers, which I took to her along with my sincere apologies.

It wasn't long before I realized that moving to Treviso was one of my better decisions. I was happy there, and who wouldn't be. My reasonably priced, yet comfortable, apartment with its canopied bed and other extra touches was a third floor walk-up on a busy street lined with prosperous shops. I liked the fact that my place was an easy walk to the center of things. Across the street from my building's entrance was a pedestrian walkway that led directly to the little city's outdoor market, less than a hundred yards from my front door. It was a large open area devoted entirely to farm fresh produce plus stall after stall displaying plentiful cuts of good Italian lamb, pork, beef and, of course, some of the world's best sausage. Near the open market was the Isola della Pescharia, a small island in the river that ran through the center of the town, where tables topped with fresh caught fish on beds of crushed ice offered up the daily catch. Another hundred yards or so past the market was a tree shaded *canale,* with wooden benches spaced along the gravel path on either side, with one or another of the benches frequently serving as my private office on days when I sat writing, clipboard in hand, or else studying the pages of an Italian phrase book and dictionary. All of this was a perfect setting for my purposes.

I had come to Italy to paint and write, and that's what I did, day after day, week after week. I felt myself to be more fortunate than many of the people I knew, for I never ceased to like what I was doing. On days when I painted, that was what I enjoyed the most, and on days when I wrote, that was what gave me the most pleasure. But along with the painting and the writing there was plenty of agreeable diversion, for there were weekends and, in addition to Lisa who had been the catalyst, I now had a fair number of friends either a short distance south of me in Venice, or Gianni in his magnificent *Villa Pasole-Bertone* near Pedavena some thirty kilometers north, and also Maria Pia in her charming weekend country home in Asolo, a picture-book town about the same distance away. Since I had no car, my painting territory was limited, but on one or two occasions Gianni offered to drive me to a location, leave me there to paint while he attended to business, coming back near the end of the day to pick me up and drop me off in Treviso on his way home.

Bassano del Grappa was the destination for one such trip. I had been there with Lisa and Gianni the year before and had said at the time that I would like to do a painting of the covered wooden bridge that spans the Brenta river. The famous architect, Andrea Palladio had designed the bridge in the sixteenth century, now known as the *Ponte Vecchio,* and although the bridge has been damaged by floods and wars it has always been rebuilt, faithfully adhering to Palladio's original design.

I stood with my feet almost in the sparkling emerald green water as I painted the large canvas depicting the bridge, with the summit of Monte Grappa in the background and ancient structures, campaniles and watchtowers in the middle distance adding interest to the composition. The area was the scene of heavy fighting during the First World War, and it is reported that Ernest Hemingway, who saw action against the Austrians, said that if he were killed he wanted to be buried in Bassano. I was not prepared to go quite that far, but I was more than happy to have been able to paint it.

On another occasion, Jane, an American friend living in Venice, let it be known that Humphrey, the Englishman, was hiring a model for a Saturday afternoon of painting in his studio, and that both Lisa and I were welcome to attend. It would be hard to imagine a more pleasant way for an artist to spend several hours than with a group of other serious painters, all painting away without conversation, a grand view of Venice outside the open windows, and the only sound coming from the stereo playing selections by the local boy made good, Antonio Vivaldi, whose work I could never listen to without being reminded of Igor Stravinsky's comment that whereas Bach had written about four hundred concertos, each one different, Vivaldi had written the same concerto about four hundred times.

Lisa and I, along with our English friend Geraldine and several others, were invited to spend the weekend in Maria Pia's country house in Asolo, a charming picturebook hilltown dating back to pre-Roman times, a favorite hideaway for celebrities of the past, including the poet Robert Browning. It was refreshing to find that there was absolutely no game plan, and that the seven or eight of us could each do whatever we damned well pleased, whether it be poking around the fascinating town, reading a book, lounging beneath the outdoor patio's grape arbor with glass of prosecco in hand, or just sitting in the large rambling living room engaged in the lost art of conversation. And the food we were served. Momma mia! The food we were served! Maria Pia's tiny live-in retainer, Anna, had a magic way with food and the large refectory table always had something to feast on at mealtime or to nibble on in between.

Since I had no telephone of my own, I periodically walked to the little park near my apartment and called Lisa on the public phone to check out what was happening in Venice.

"We're invited to spend next weekend at Gianni's villa," she informed me. "He's hosting a concert in the grand hall, a quintet performing works by Bach, Albinoni and Vivaldi. I suggest we meet at the railroad station here in Venice and we'll take the train up to Pedavena. Gianni said to call him from the station and he'll come pick us up."

I had spent a week as Gianni's houseguest earlier in the summer, painting *en plein air* within walking distance from the villa, so I knew the place well and was more than happy to be returning.

The concert was performed in the villa's atrium, which boasted thirty foot high ceilings, was a huge success, especially so because Gianni had included Pamela Hubert on the program, an American opera singer living in Italy who, as one of her selections, sang Cesar Franc's hauntingly beautiful Panis Angelicus. During the after-concert party, with wine and grappa flowing freely, she and Lisa, who also has a beautiful operatic voice, treated the rest of us to generous servings of Puccini and Verdi.

Lisa would soon receive her master's degree from NYU, and we decided it was time for another party to celebrate her graduation and the two of us to at least partially express our thanks to the friends in and around Venice who had been so kind and generous to us both. This time the group was even larger than the year before, and the festivities, if anything, more good-spirited. Like the year before, it seemed as if the night had been especially made for visiting with friends while drinking large quantities of prosecco in a contessa's private courtyard on the *Grande Canale*.

Finally, the crowd was thinning, and I at last had a chance to rest my legs and pull up a chair at a table where the people I cared for the most, Lisa, Maria Pia, Gianni, and Flaminia, were all happily chatting away, a few sentences in Italian, the next few in English, all interspersed with the laughter of people who were enjoying the evening.

Sitting there beside them I reflected on how lucky I was. Some years before at the age of seventy-one I had decided that I wanted to learn to paint and become a professional landscape painter, at the time not having the foggiest notion where such a downright crazy decision would lead me. Well, here I was at the ripe old age of seventy-six having the time of my life.

As a more-or-less successful, sweaty palmed, business man, I had flown the Atlantic aboard the Concorde wearing a London hand-tailored three piece pin striped suit, and, after landing in New York, checking into a private club I belonged to. Such fancy frills were now out of the question. Now, I looked for bargain flights in order to get back to America, and when I got there, instead of driving the beautiful green Jaguar I used to own, I would now climb in behind the wheel of some not very classy looking, but useful, vehicle. It was now a financially uncertain life, for each day I wondered if one of the galleries, including the new one I had opened up in San Fracisco, had sold one of my paintings.

But what a good life I was enjoying. Here I was surrounded by some of the best people I would ever know, and who, in spite of my age, accepted me as one of their own. And whereas the wealthiest of my fellow countrymen paid dearly for a few days spent between fancy hotel and tour guide, I had been living on the cheap for four whole months among the very people and in the very surroundings that tourists come to Italy hoping to encounter, but rarely do. Best of all, I was happy, I was doing what I liked to do, and making some fabulous friendships in the process.

Looking back, what at the time seemed to be the crushing hand of adversity had turned into the helping hand that led me into an entirely new life. I again recalled the old proverb that had come to mind when, back at Cowpie Manor, I was trying to decide what to do with my life. The promise that God never shuts one door without opening another had certainly held true in my case. It definitely was not a door leading to Easy Street, but it had, instead, opened onto an endless path leading to inner fulfillment, and for that I felt extremely grateful.

Reverting to the secure life I once had, in place of the chancy but rewarding one I now led, even if possible, would be unthinkable. At a late age I had established myself in a new and fulfilling career, one that was forever challenging and stimulating. I was now seventy-six, and I had become what I had set out to be, a man who earns his living as a professional painter.

Pouring myself a nightcap of the chilled, bone dry prosecco while savoring the happy sounds of the warm autumn evening, I leaned back in my chair and silently said to myself, "Congratulations, Bill Lewis. You are a very rich man!"

To see examples of his paintings, visit www.williamlewispaintings.com

(*) Letters of the Scattered Brotherhood, Mary Strong